Hunting & Fishing COOKBOOK

PAGE | TABLE OF CONTENTS

MORE OF THESE GREAT RECIPES INSIDE!

19

57

79

There's no better way
to complete a successful hunting or fishing trip than with a delicious meal prepared from your catch.

Whether you are an avid hunter or fisherman or someone who cooks for one, this must-have game and fish cookbook is for you!

You'll find hundreds of mouthwatering recipes to turn venison, pheasant, duck, wild turkey, elk, trout, walleye, salmon and more into meals that will satisfy the whole family and even your dinner guests.

The easy-to-follow recipes in this book will inspire many wild-caught meals to come. Whether you want a special meal like Roast Christmas Goose (page 47) or the classic Campfire Fried Fish (page 128), this beautifully photographed cookbook has you covered.

The fish and game recipes in this handy volume are all favorites shared by avid hunters and fishermen and have been tested in the kitchens of *Taste of Home*, America's #1 cooking magazine. So you're assured that each one is not only easy to follow for delectable results, but also calls for everyday ingredients you most likely already have on hand.

You'll also find recipes for stick-to-your-ribs breakfast fare and hearty, popular camp meals that can be cooked on a campfire or grill. Turn to these chapters whether you're on a hunting

The great outdoors invigorates us, leaving us with a healthy appetite.

trip, camping with the family or just enjoying your own backyard!

We have also included more than 50 sweet and savory recipes for satisfying portable snacks that are ideal for taking with you into the wilderness. These delicious and wholesome snacks will help keep you energized and focused during your outdoor excursions.

A very special treat awaits you in Chapter 7, "Wild Ingredients." Here, you will find unique recipes that use wild vegetables, berries, flowers and more.

Be sure to check out the "Safe Handling & Preparation of Fish & Game Meat" information on page 226 for tips on how to safely prepare wild game. The complete recipe index starts on page 228. Use it to quickly choose the perfect recipe.

Throughout this unique book, you will discover useful tips from readers, cooks and outdoor enthusiasts like you to help make your next trip into the wild a success.

If you frequently find yourself with a bounty of game or fish, or if you just want to cook up some new camp favorites, the *Taste of Home Hunting & Fishing Cookbook* is the perfect addition to your recipe collection!

126

21

130

170

41

Hunting & Fishing COOKBOOK

In culinary terms, "venison" can be meat from deer, elk, moose, caribou, antelope and pronghorn.

Deer live in woodlands all over Europe, Asia, northern Africa and America. There are many deer species of various sizes, and all the males grow antlers. The meat is lean and has a gamey flavor.

Elk meat tastes like mild, almost sweet, beef, with only a very faint venison flavor. Elk are from North America, Europe and Asia.

Moose, the largest member of the venison family, stand about 6½ feet at the shoulder. Moose are native to North America. The meat is similar to elk.

SHREDDED VENISON SANDWICHES, P. 11
VENISON PARMIGIANA, P. 22
VENISON VEGETABLE STEW, P. 24

VENISON ①

COUNTRY-STYLE POT ROAST,
PAGE 16

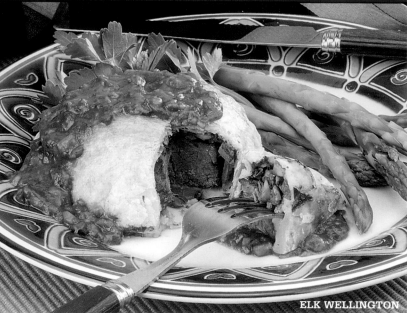

ELK WELLINGTON

**SANDY GREEN
IGNACIO,
COLORADO**

My husband's an avid hunter and fisherman, so we often try new recipes with elk, deer, rabbit, turkey or fish. Our family loves this special game dish. The elk fillets are dressed up in puff pastry and drizzled with a savory onion-mushroom sauce.

elk wellington

    8 elk fillets (about 4 ounces each)
    2 tablespoons olive oil
  1/2 pound fresh mushrooms, chopped
    2 tablespoons minced fresh parsley
    2 tablespoons snipped chives
    1 package (17 1/4 ounces) frozen puff pastry, thawed
    1 egg
    1 tablespoon cold water

MUSHROOM SAUCE:
  1 1/3 cups finely chopped mushrooms
    1 medium onion, finely chopped
    2 tablespoons butter
    3 tablespoons all-purpose flour
    1 can (14 1/2 ounces) beef broth
    1 teaspoon browning sauce, optional
  1/2 teaspoon tomato paste
  1/4 teaspoon pepper

[1] In a large skillet, brown elk fillets in oil on both sides; set aside. In a bowl, combine the mushrooms, parsley and chives; set aside.

[2] On a lightly floured surface, roll out each sheet of pastry into a 16-in. square. Cut each into four 8-in. squares. Top each square with mushroom mixture and one fillet. Fold pastry over fillet; seal seams. Place seam side down

on a rack in a 15-in. x 10-in. x 1-in. baking pan. Beat egg and cold water; brush over pastry. Bake at 350° for 30-35 minutes or until a meat thermometer reads 160°.

[3] Meanwhile, for sauce, saute mushrooms and onion in butter in a saucepan until tender. Sprinkle with flour; stir until blended. Gradually stir in the broth, browning sauce if desired, tomato paste and pepper. Bring to a boil; cook and stir for 2 minutes or until thickened. Spoon over pastry. **Yield:** 8 servings.

italian venison sandwiches

**ANDREW HENSON
MORRISON, ILLINOIS**

The slow cooker makes easy work of these hearty venison sandwiches. The meat always comes out tender and tasty.

    2 cups water
    1 envelope onion soup mix
    1 tablespoon dried basil
    1 tablespoon dried parsley flakes
    1 teaspoon beef bouillon granules
  1/2 teaspoon celery salt
  1/4 teaspoon garlic powder
  1/4 teaspoon cayenne pepper
  1/4 teaspoon pepper
    1 boneless venison roast (3 to 4 pounds), cut into 1-inch cubes
   10 to 12 sandwich rolls, split

Green pepper rings, optional

[1] In a slow cooker, combine the first nine ingredients. Add venison and stir. Cover and cook on low for 8 hours or until the meat is tender.

[2] Using a slotted spoon, carefully spoon into rolls. Top with pepper rings if desired. **Yield:** 10-12 servings.

tip · **HUNTING & FISHING**

Marinate chunks of wild game meat in Italian dressing or any other dressing flavor your family likes.

N. MCCULLOUGH, PENNSYLVANIA

marinated venison steaks

JANELLE INKENS
TIGARD, OREGON

These venison steaks are so good, they're even a hit with my kids. Someone who tried this dish once said, "Wow, if I could make venison taste like this, I'd make it all the time."

- 6 boneless venison steaks (4 to 6 ounces each)
- 1/2 cup white vinegar
- 1/2 cup ketchup
- 1/4 cup vegetable oil
- 1/4 cup Worcestershire sauce
- 4 garlic cloves, minced
- 1 1/2 teaspoons ground mustard
- 1/2 teaspoon salt
- 1/2 teaspoon pepper

[1] Place venison in a large resealable plastic bag. In a bowl, combine the remaining ingredients. Pour half over the venison; seal bag and turn to coat. Refrigerate overnight. Refrigerate remaining marinade.

[2] Drain and discard marinade from steaks. Broil 3-4 in. from the heat for 4 minutes. Turn; baste with reserved marinade. Broil about 4 minutes longer, basting often, or until a meat thermometer reads 160° for medium or 170° for well-done. **Yield:** 6 servings.

elk meat chili

- 2 pounds ground elk or buffalo meat
- 1/2 cup chopped onion
- 3 garlic cloves, minced
- 2 cans (14 1/2 ounces each) diced tomatoes, undrained
- 1 can (28 ounces) pork and beans, undrained
- 3 tablespoons salsa
- 1 tablespoon brown sugar
- 1 tablespoon chili powder
- 1/2 teaspoon garlic salt
- 1/2 teaspoon pepper

In a Dutch oven, cook elk, onion and garlic over medium heat until meat is no longer pink; drain. Stir in the remaining ingredients; bring to a boil. Reduce heat; cover and simmer for 2 hours. **Yield:** 6-8 servings.

JO MAASBERG
FARSON,
WYOMING

The longer this hearty chili simmers, the better it tastes! It's a cold-weather favorite at our ranch.

HUNTING & FISHING COOKBOOK

ELK MEAT CHILI

This stew-like soup is sure to satisfy your hearty hunter's appetite. It's chock-full of tender meat, tomatoes, and chunks of carrot and potato, lightly seasoned with bay leaf and clove.

mountain man soup

- 1 pound buffalo or venison stew meat
- 2 tablespoons vegetable oil
- 2 cups chopped celery
- 2/3 cup chopped onion
- 1/4 cup chopped green pepper
- 2 cans (14 1/2 ounces each) beef broth
- 1 can (28 ounces) diced tomatoes, undrained
- 1 large potato, peeled and cubed
- 1 large carrot, sliced
- 2 teaspoons garlic salt
- 1 whole clove
- 1 bay leaf
- 1/4 cup minced fresh parsley

[1] In a Dutch oven, brown meat in oil; drain. Add the celery, onion and green pepper; saute for 5 minutes or until tender. Stir in the broth, tomatoes, potato, carrot, garlic salt, clove and bay leaf.

[2] Bring to a boil. Reduce heat; simmer, uncovered, for 1 hour or until meat is tender. Discard clove and bay leaf. Stir in parsley. **Yield:** 6 servings.

bachelor chili

**DAN ELLISON
HERMAN, MINNESOTA**

This meaty, zippy chili makes an excellent meal whether you're using venison, elk, moose or beef. Try serving it with slices of crusty bread to soak up the savory sauce.

- 1 boneless venison, elk, moose or beef chuck roast (3 to 3 1/2 pounds)
- 1 tablespoon vegetable oil
- 2 medium onions, chopped

MOUNTAIN MAN SOUP

1 medium green pepper, chopped

2 garlic cloves, minced

¼ to ½ teaspoon crushed red pepper flakes

4 cans (14½ ounces each) diced tomatoes, undrained

1 cup water

1 can (12 ounces) tomato paste

1 tablespoon sugar

½ teaspoon ground cumin

½ teaspoon dried oregano

¼ teaspoon pepper

[1] Cut meat into ¼-in. pieces. In a 4-qt. Dutch oven, brown meat in oil; remove with a slotted spoon and set aside.

[2] In the same pan, saute onions, green pepper, garlic and red pepper flakes until the vegetables are tender. Return meat to the pan. Add the remaining ingredients; bring to a boil. Reduce heat; cover and simmer for 3 hours or until the meat is tender. **Yield:** 10-12 servings (3 quarts).

shredded venison sandwiches

1 boneless venison roast (4 pounds)

1½ cups ketchup

3 tablespoons brown sugar

1 tablespoon ground mustard

1 tablespoon lemon juice

1 tablespoon soy sauce

1 tablespoon Liquid Smoke, optional

2 teaspoons celery salt

2 teaspoons pepper

2 teaspoons Worcestershire sauce

1 teaspoon onion powder

1 teaspoon garlic powder

⅛ teaspoon ground nutmeg

3 drops hot pepper sauce

14 to 18 hamburger buns, split

[1] Cut venison roast in half; place in a 5-qt. slow cooker. In a large bowl, combine the ketchup, brown sugar, mustard, lemon juice, soy sauce, Liquid Smoke if desired and

SHREDDED VENISON SANDWICHES

seasonings. Pour over venison. Cover and cook on high for 4½ to 5 hours or until meat is tender.

[2] Remove the roast; set aside to cool. Strain sauce and return to slow cooker. Shred meat, using two forks; stir into sauce and heat through. Using a slotted spoon, spoon meat mixture onto buns. **Yield:** 14-18 servings.

RUTH SETTERLUND FREYBURG, MAINE

My husband hunts for deer every November, so I'm always looking for new recipes for venison. The whole family loves these slow cooker sandwiches, seasoned with soy sauce, brown sugar, ketchup and hot pepper sauce.

HUNTING & FISHING tip

We are always trying to find new ways to serve venison. This is one of my son's favorites. Put 4 venison cutlets in enough milk to cover. Soak overnight or at least several hours in the fridge to remove the gamey taste. Dust with flour, salt and pepper. Saute in a little butter or oil until golden brown.

Place cutlets in greased baking dish. Pour a can of undiluted cream of tomato soup over cutlets; top with 2 sliced green onions. Bake at 350° for 30 minutes. Spread a cup of sour cream on top and sprinkle with 4 ounces of grated cheddar cheese. Bake another 10-15 minutes.

CAROL, TEXAS

HUNTING & FISHING COOKBOOK

EVA MILLER-VIDETICH CEDAR SPRINGS, MICHIGAN

My husband enjoys hunting, and it's my challenge to find new ways to serve venison. This recipe makes hearty kabobs perfect for grilling. The marinade reduces the wild taste, so guests often don't realize they're eating venison.

GRILLED VENISON AND VEGETABLES

grilled venison and vegetables

1 cup red wine vinegar

$^1/_2$ cup honey

$^1/_2$ cup soy sauce

$^1/_4$ cup ketchup

Dash pepper

Dash garlic powder

1$^1/_2$ pounds boneless venison steak, cut into 1$^1/_4$-inch cubes

8 to 12 cherry tomatoes

8 to 12 fresh mushrooms, optional

$^1/_2$ medium green or sweet red pepper, cut into 1$^1/_2$-inch pieces

1 to 2 small zucchini, cut into 1-inch chunks

1 large onion, cut into wedges

8 to 12 small new potatoes, parboiled

[1] In a large resealable plastic bag, combine vinegar, honey, soy sauce, ketchup, pepper and garlic powder; set aside $^1/_4$ cup for vegetables. Set aside $^3/_4$ cup for basting. Add meat; seal bag and turn to coat. Refrigerate for 4 hours. One hour before grilling, toss vegetables with $^1/_4$ cup reserved marinade. Drain and discard marinade from meat.

[2] Thread meat and vegetables alternately on metal or soaked wooden skewers. Grill over medium-hot heat for 15-20 minutes or until a meat thermometer inserted in the venison reads 160°, turning and basting frequently with reserved $^3/_4$ cup marinade. **Yield:** 4-6 servings.

tip   HUNTING & FISHING

We use a grill basket over the open fire to cook our kabobs. We cut the meat and vegetables into uniform sizes. After cooking, we slide the meat and vegetables into toasted buns and top these sandwiches with a rich, warm cheese sauce.

RENEE, PENNSYLVANIA

bacon-wrapped venison

PHYLLIS ABRAMS
ALTON, NEW YORK

My husband, Ron, and I hunt together and we created this delicious dish that's special enough for company.

- 1½ to 2 pounds venison tenderloin
- 2 tablespoons olive oil, divided
- 1 garlic clove, minced
- ½ cup all-purpose flour
- ¾ teaspoon salt
- ½ teaspoon pepper
- ½ pound fresh mushrooms, sliced
- 4 bacon strips
- 1 tablespoon cornstarch
- 1¼ cups beef broth
- 2 tablespoons minced fresh parsley, optional

[1] Rub tenderloin with 1-2 teaspoons of oil and the garlic. Combine the flour, salt and pepper; sprinkle over tenderloin and shake off excess.

[2] In a skillet, brown tenderloin on all sides in remaining oil. Remove and keep warm. In the same skillet, saute mushrooms until tender; remove and set aside. Wrap bacon around tenderloin, securing the ends with toothpicks. Return to skillet.

[3] Cook over medium heat until bacon is crisp and a thermometer inserted into tenderloin reads 160°, turning frequently. Remove and keep warm.

[4] In a small bowl, combine cornstarch and broth until smooth; add to skillet. Bring to a boil; cook and stir for 2 minutes or until thickened. Add parsley if desired and reserved mushrooms; cook and stir until heated through. Discard toothpicks from tenderloin; serve with mushroom sauce. **Yield:** 6-8 servings.

venison fajitas

- ½ cup orange juice
- ¼ cup white vinegar
- 1 tablespoon seasoned salt
- ¼ teaspoon pepper
- ¼ teaspoon cayenne pepper
- 1½ pounds venison or elk flank steak, cut into thin strips
- 1 medium green pepper, julienned
- 1 medium sweet red pepper, julienned
- 1 medium onion, halved and sliced
- 2 tablespoons vegetable oil, divided
- 8 flour tortillas (8 inches)
- 2 cups (8 ounces) shredded Mexican cheese blend

Sour cream and salsa

[1] In a large resealable plastic bag, combine the first five ingredients. Add meat. Seal bag and turn to coat; refrigerate for 2 hours.

[2] Drain and discard marinade. In a large skillet, saute peppers and onion in 1 tablespoon oil until crisp-tender; remove and set aside. Heat remaining oil; stir-fry meat for 3-5 minutes or until no longer pink. Return vegetables to pan; heat through. Spoon over tortillas; top with cheese, sour cream and salsa. Fold in sides. **Yield:** 4 servings.

DANIELL RISSINGER
DAUPHIN, PENNSYLVANIA

Use either venison or elk in this recipe, and you'll be pleased with the results! My husband asks for these fajitas frequently. He enjoys big-game hunting and usually comes home with an elk. To finish off the meal, we add some Mexican rice and corn bread.

VENISON FAJITAS

**SUSETTE REIF
LIBERTY,
PENNSYLVANIA**

We always seem to have venison in the freezer, so I came up with the recipe for this delicious soup as a different way to use some of that meat. It makes a great lunch or light supper served with garlic bread and a salad.

venison vegetable soup

- ¾ pound venison, cubed
- 1 tablespoon vegetable oil
- 1 cup diced onion
- 1 package (16 ounces) frozen mixed vegetables
- 2 cans (14½ ounces each) diced tomatoes, undrained
- 2 cups cubed peeled potatoes
- 2 cups water
- 1 tablespoon sugar
- 2 teaspoons beef bouillon granules
- 1 teaspoon salt
- ½ teaspoon pepper
- ½ teaspoon garlic powder
- ¼ teaspoon hot pepper sauce

In a Dutch oven or large saucepan, brown venison in oil. Add onion; cover and simmer for 10 minutes or until tender. Add remaining ingredients; cover and simmer 1 hour longer or until meat is tender. **Yield:** 8 servings.

country-fried venison

**SANDRA ROBINSON
FAIR GROVE, MISSOURI**

This is our favorite way to fix venison tenderloin. The marinade and coating eliminate the wild flavor in these mouthwatering steaks.

- 2 pounds venison tenderloin
- ½ cup soy sauce
- ½ cup Worcestershire sauce
- ½ cup butter, melted
- ½ to 2 teaspoons Liquid Smoke, optional
- 1 egg, beaten
- 1 cup buttermilk
- 1 cup all-purpose flour
- 2 teaspoons seasoned salt
- 2 teaspoons vegetable oil

[1] Cut tenderloin into eight steaks. In a large resealable plastic bag, combine the soy sauce, Worcestershire sauce, butter and Liquid Smoke if desired. Add steaks; seal bag and turn to coat. Refrigerate for 2 hours.

VENISON
VEGETABLE
SOUP

VENISON TENDERLOIN
SANDWICHES

[2] In a bowl, combine egg and buttermilk. In another bowl, combine flour and seasoned salt. Drain steaks, discarding marinade. Dip steaks in buttermilk mixture, then roll in flour mixture. In a large skillet over medium-high heat, cook steaks in oil for 12-14 minutes, turning occasionally, or until a meat thermometer reads 160°. **Yield:** 8 servings.

venison tenderloin sandwiches

   2 large onions, sliced

   2 cans (4 ounces each) sliced
     mushrooms, drained

 1/4 cup butter

 1/4 cup Worcestershire sauce

   8 venison tenderloin steaks
     (12 ounces), about 3/4 inch thick

 1/2 teaspoon garlic powder

 1/4 teaspoon pepper

 1/2 teaspoon salt, optional

   4 hard rolls, split

[1] In a skillet, saute the onions and mushrooms in butter and Worcestershire sauce until onions are tender. Flatten steaks to 1/2 in. thick; add to the skillet. Cook over medium heat until meat is done as desired, about 3 minutes on each side.

[2] Sprinkle with garlic powder, pepper and salt if desired. Place two steaks on each roll; top with onions and mushrooms. **Yield:** 4 servings.

PATRICIA EL-ZOGHBI WELLS, NEW YORK

Here in the mountains of upstate New York, venison is a staple food. My son-in-law supplies me with venison for these savory sandwiches. Prepared this way, the meat is very tender and tasty.

HUNTING & FISHING

tip

Any game meat should be cooked as you would a very lean piece of beef.

KELLY, MISSOURI

MOOSE MEATBALLS

**JANIS PLOURDE
SMOOTH ROCK
FALLS, ONTARIO**

Our family has found these meatballs in tangy sauce a great use for moose. I was glad to find a good recipe that incorporates ground moose meat, since we eat a lot of moose steaks and I like to use it differently for a change.

moose meatballs

1 egg, lightly beaten
4 tablespoons cornstarch, divided
1 teaspoon salt
1/4 teaspoon pepper
2 tablespoons chopped onion
1 pound ground moose meat
1 tablespoon vegetable oil
3 tablespoons white vinegar
1 can (8 ounces) pineapple chunks
1/2 cup sugar
1 tablespoon soy sauce
1 medium green pepper, cut into strips

Hot cooked wide egg noodles

[1] In a bowl, combine egg, 1 tablespoon cornstarch, salt, pepper and onion. Crumble ground moose meat over mixture and mix well. Shape into 1 1/2-in. balls. In a large skillet, brown meatballs in oil. Cover and cook over low heat until the meatballs are done, about 10 minutes.

[2] In a saucepan, stir vinegar and remaining cornstarch until smooth. Drain pineapple, reserving juice. Set pineapple aside. Add enough water to juice to equal 1 1/2 cups; stir into vinegar mixture. Add sugar and soy

sauce; cook and stir over medium heat until thickened. Add the meatballs, pineapple and green pepper; cook until heated through and the green pepper is tender. Serve over noodles. **Yield:** 3-4 servings.

country-style pot roast

(PICTURED ON PAGE 7)

**JOAN BEST
GARRISON, MONTANA**

My husband goes deer hunting, so I have quite a few recipes for venison. This is his favorite. Hope you enjoy it, too!

2 cups water
2 cups white vinegar
6 medium onions, thinly sliced
12 whole peppercorns
4 bay leaves
4 whole cloves
2 teaspoons salt
1 teaspoon Worcestershire sauce
1/2 teaspoon pepper
1/2 teaspoon garlic powder
1 boneless venison or beef rump or chuck roast (3 1/2 to 4 pounds)
2 tablespoons vegetable oil
10 medium carrots, cut into 1-inch chunks
5 to 7 tablespoons cornstarch
1/3 cup cold water

[1] In a large resealable plastic bag, combine the first 10 ingredients; add the venison roast. Seal bag and turn to coat; refrigerate for 24 hours.

[2] Remove roast, reserving the marinade. In a Dutch oven, brown roast in oil; drain. Add marinade and carrots; bring to a boil. Reduce

tip ⊕ HUNTING & FISHING

I have found that if you have really gamey venison, adding a little pork helps remove the taste. For example in a dish calling for ground venison, add a little ground pork or cook the venison steaks and a pork chop in the same skillet. MARY, TEXAS

heat; cover and simmer for 3½ to 4 hours or until meat is tender.

[3] Remove roast and keep warm. Strain cooking juices; discard the vegetables and spices. Return juices to pan. Combine cornstarch and cold water until smooth; gradually add to pan juices. Bring to a boil; boil and stir for 2 minutes. Slice roast; serve with the gravy. **Yield:** 6-8 servings.

herbed venison stew

RICK SULLIVAN
HENRYVILLE, INDIANA

When I simmer a pot of this satisfying stew, I stir plenty of garlic and herbs into the hearty meat-and-vegetable mixture. This stew tastes great right off the stove but it's even better if you make it ahead and reheat it.

- 1 pound venison, cubed
- 1 tablespoon olive oil
- 2 cans (14½ ounces each) beef broth
- 2 teaspoons dried thyme
- 2 teaspoons dried marjoram
- 2 teaspoons dried parsley flakes
- 2 garlic cloves, minced
- ½ teaspoon salt
- 6 to 8 whole peppercorns
- 1 bay leaf
- 2 cups cubed peeled potatoes
- 1 large onion, chopped
- 2 medium carrots, sliced
- 2 celery ribs, chopped
- 2 tablespoons all-purpose flour
- 3 tablespoons water
- ⅛ to ¼ teaspoon browning sauce

[1] In a Dutch oven, brown venison in oil over medium-high heat; drain. Stir in the broth, thyme, marjoram, parsley, garlic and salt. Place peppercorns and bay leaf on a double thickness of cheesecloth; bring up corners of cloth and tie with kitchen string to form a bag. Add to pan. Bring to a boil. Reduce heat; cover and simmer for 30 minutes.

[2] Add the potatoes, onion, carrots and celery; return to a boil. Reduce heat; cover and simmer for 30-35 minutes or until meat and vegetables are tender. Discard herb bag. In a

small bowl, combine flour, water and browning sauce until smooth; stir into stew. Bring to a boil; cook and stir for 2 minutes or until thickened. **Yield:** 4 servings.

venison taco pie

- 1 pound ground venison
- 1 can (11 ounces) Mexicorn, drained
- 1 can (8 ounces) tomato sauce
- 1 envelope taco seasoning
- 1 tube (7½ ounces) refrigerated buttermilk biscuits
- 1 cup (4 ounces) shredded cheddar cheese

[1] In a large skillet, cook venison over medium heat until no longer pink; drain. Stir in the corn, tomato sauce and taco seasoning; keep warm.

[2] For crust, press biscuits onto the bottom and up the sides of an ungreased 9-in. pie plate. Bake at 350° for 5 minutes. Spoon venison mixture into crust. Sprinkle with cheese. Bake for 20-25 minutes or until filling is bubbly and biscuits are golden brown. Let stand for 5 minutes before serving. **Yield:** 6 servings.

VENISON TACO PIE

KAREN WITMAN
NORTH IRWIN,
PENNSYLVANIA

The whole family is sure to enjoy this savory Southwestern casserole. A refrigerated biscuit crust and packaged taco seasoning make preparation really easy.

HUNTING & FISHING COOKBOOK

CARMA OCHSE BREMERTON, WASHINGTON

Growing up in Montana, I enjoyed eating elk on a regular basis. You'll find that elk cooks up nice and tender. This tempting dish is elegant enough to serve company.

swiss elk steak

    2 pounds elk steak
All-purpose flour
    2 tablespoons butter
    1 can (15 ounces) tomato sauce
    ½ cup red wine
    2 tablespoons Worcestershire sauce
    ½ cup diced onion
    ½ cup diced green pepper
    1 can (2¼ ounces) sliced ripe olives, drained
    1 cup sliced fresh mushrooms
    ½ teaspoon salt
    ½ teaspoon pepper
    4 slices Swiss cheese, optional
Hot cooked wide egg noodles

[1] Dredge elk steak lightly in flour; shake off excess. Melt butter in a large skillet; brown steak on both sides. Place in a shallow baking pan. Combine the next nine ingredients; pour over steak.

[2] Cover and bake at 350° for 1½ hours or until a meat thermometer reads 160°. If desired, place cheese over steak before serving. Serve over noodles. **Yield:** 4 servings.

venison chili

GARY URNESS KENYON, MINNESOTA

This meaty chili is nicely seasoned and has gotten many "very good" responses from my friends. It's also no trouble to make.

    1 pound boneless venison steak, cubed
    ½ cup chopped onion
    2 tablespoons olive oil
    1 can (15 ounces) chili without beans
    ½ cup water

SWISS ELK STEAK

½ teaspoon garlic powder

½ teaspoon celery salt

In a large saucepan, cook venison and onion in oil until meat is browned. Stir in the remaining ingredients. Bring to a boil. Reduce heat; cover and simmer for 1 hour or until meat is tender. **Yield:** 3-4 servings.

venison cordon bleu

**JANETTE YINGLING
CLEAR, ALASKA**

For this wonderful dish, I roll up venison tenderloin with thin slices of ham and Swiss cheese before baking. I serve the attractive venison rolls with crusty French bread for dipping in the broth.

4 venison tenderloin steaks
 (5 to 6 ounces each)

½ teaspoon salt

¼ teaspoon pepper

4 thin slices Swiss cheese

4 thin slices fully cooked ham

2 tablespoons butter

1 cup beef broth

Sliced French bread, optional

[1] Flatten steaks to ¼-in. thickness; sprinkle with salt and pepper. Top each with a slice of cheese and ham; roll up tightly. Secure with toothpicks.

[2] In a large skillet, brown roll-ups in butter on all sides. Transfer to an ungreased 11-in. x 7-in. x 2-in. baking dish. Pour broth over top. Bake, uncovered, at 350° for 25-30 minutes or until a meat thermometer reads 160° and the meat juices run clear. Serve roll-ups and pan juices with French bread if desired. **Yield:** 4 servings.

venison chili con carne

1 pound bulk hot Italian sausage

1 large onion, diced

1 medium sweet red pepper, diced

2 pounds venison steak, cut into 1½-inch cubes

2 tablespoons olive oil

1 can (28 ounces) crushed tomatoes

1 can (14½ ounces) beef broth

VENISON CHILI CON CARNE

¼ cup tomato paste

1 tablespoon brown sugar

2 teaspoons ground cumin

2 teaspoons chili powder

1 teaspoon dried oregano

½ teaspoon crushed red pepper flakes

Salt and pepper to taste

¼ cup minced fresh parsley

Hot cooked rice, optional

[1] In a Dutch oven, cook the sausage, onion and red pepper over medium heat until meat is no longer pink; drain and set aside.

[2] In the same pan, brown venison in oil; drain. Add the tomatoes, broth, tomato paste, brown sugar, cumin, chili powder, oregano, pepper flakes, salt, pepper and sausage mixture. Simmer, uncovered, for 1-1½ hours or until venison is tender. Stir in parsley. Serve with rice if desired. **Yield:** 6 servings.

**KIM VAUGHN
HAMPTON,
VIRGINIA**

I'm pleased to share the recipe for this thick, spicy chili that we serve over rice. The venison is tender, and the blend of spices, tomatoes and hot Italian sausage gives it plenty of zip.

HUNTING & FISHING COOKBOOK

HUNTING & FISHING tip

Soaking wild game meat in buttermilk in the refrigerator for several hours can help remove some of the gamey taste.

SUZANNE, KENTUCKY

**MARCY CELLA
L'ANSE,
MICHIGAN**

For a good-looking, hearty venison entree without a strong game flavor, I recommend these cabbage rolls. They have a moist, meaty filling and wonderful, old-world flavor.

VENISON CABBAGE ROLLS

venison cabbage rolls

- 8 large cabbage leaves
- 1 pound ground venison
- 1 medium onion, chopped
- 1 teaspoon salt
- 1/4 teaspoon ground nutmeg
- 1 can (15 ounces) tomato sauce, divided
- 2 cups uncooked instant brown rice
- 1 cup (4 ounces) shredded cheddar cheese

[1] In a large pot of boiling water, cook cabbage leaves for 3 minutes; drain and set aside. In a skillet over medium heat, cook venison, onion, salt and nutmeg until meat is no longer pink; drain. Stir in 1 cup tomato sauce.

[2] Place 1/3 cup meat mixture on each cabbage leaf; fold in sides. Starting at an unfolded edge, roll up completely to enclose filling.

[3] Cook rice according to package directions; stir in remaining tomato sauce. Transfer to a large skillet; add the cabbage rolls. Cover and simmer for 20 minutes. Sprinkle with cheddar cheese; heat until the cheese begins to melt. **Yield:** 4 servings.

venison and beans

**JILL KERR
YORK, PENNSYLVANIA**

When I was first married, I had no idea how to cook game. I got this recipe from a friend, and now my husband thinks we should have it every night!

- 1 1/2 pounds ground venison
- 1 medium onion, chopped
- 1 can (16 ounces) pork and beans, undrained

 **HUNTING & FISHING**

tip Since ground venison is very low in fat and calories, you might prefer mixing it with ground beef or pork for a richer texture.

JILL, ILLINO

1 can (16 ounces) kidney beans, rinsed and drained

1 can (15½ ounces) great northern beans, rinsed and drained

1 cup ketchup

⅓ cup packed brown sugar

6 bacon strips, cooked and crumbled

2 tablespoons white vinegar

1 tablespoon Worcestershire sauce

½ teaspoon salt

¼ teaspoon ground mustard

[1] In a large skillet, cook venison and onion over medium heat until the meat is no longer pink; drain. Stir in all of the remaining ingredients and transfer mixture to a 2-qt. baking dish.

[2] Cover and bake at 350° for 35-40 minutes or until heated through. **Yield:** 8 servings.

venison dumpling stew

¼ cup all-purpose flour

1 pound venison stew meat, cut into 1-inch cubes

3 tablespoons butter

4 to 5 cups water

2 bay leaves

2 teaspoons beef bouillon granules

3 tablespoons Worcestershire sauce

1 teaspoon salt

½ to ¾ teaspoon pepper

5 medium potatoes, peeled and cubed

5 medium carrots, peeled and cut into ¾-inch slices

1 medium onion, chopped

DILLED DUMPLINGS:

1 cup all-purpose flour

1 teaspoon baking powder

½ teaspoon salt

½ teaspoon dill weed

1 egg

½ cup milk

[1] In a large resealable plastic bag, combine flour and venison; shake to coat. In a Dutch oven, brown meat in butter. Add water; stir to loosen browned bits from pan. Add bay leaves, bouillon, Worcestershire sauce, salt and pepper.

[2] Bring to a boil. Reduce heat; cover and simmer for 1 hour or until meat is tender. Discard bay leaves. Add potatoes, carrots and onion. Cover and simmer for 25 minutes.

[3] For dumplings, in a bowl, combine the flour, baking powder, salt and dill. Stir in the egg and milk just until moistened. Drop by tablespoonfuls onto simmering stew. Cover and simmer for 15 minutes (do not lift cover) or until dumplings test done. Serve the stew immediately. **Yield:** 4 servings.

ELIZABETH SMITH MIDDLEBURY, VERMONT

Dill-seasoned dumplings top this homey stew featuring tender venison, carrots and potatoes.

VENISON DUMPLING STEW

**PHIL ZIPP
TOMAHAWK,
WISCONSIN**

This Italian classic tastes great prepared with venison. The steaks are breaded and smothered in a tomato sauce and melted mozzarella cheese.

venison parmigiana

2 pounds boneless venison steaks
1 egg
1 tablespoon milk
2/3 cup seasoned bread crumbs
1/3 cup grated Parmesan cheese
5 tablespoons olive oil
1 small onion, finely chopped
2 cups hot water
1 can (6 ounces) tomato paste
1 teaspoon pepper
1/2 teaspoon salt
1/2 teaspoon sugar
1/2 teaspoon dried marjoram
2 cups (8 ounces) shredded part-skim mozzarella cheese

[1] Pound steaks to 1/4-in. thickness; cut into serving-size pieces. In a shallow bowl, beat egg and milk. In another bowl, combine bread crumbs and Parmesan cheese. Dip venison in egg mixture, then coat with crumb mixture.

[2] In a large skillet, brown meat in oil on both sides. Place in a greased 13-in. x 9-in. x 2-in. baking dish. In the drippings, saute onion for 2-3 minutes or until tender. Stir in the water, tomato paste, pepper, salt, sugar and marjoram. Bring to a boil. Reduce heat; simmer, uncovered, for 5 minutes. Pour over venison. Cover and bake at 350° for 50 minutes or until meat is tender.

[3] Uncover; sprinkle with cheese. Bake 10-15 minutes longer or until cheese is melted. **Yield:** 6 servings.

spiedis

**GERTRUDE SKINNER
BINGHAMTON, NEW YORK**

This is our favorite cookout dish. The recipe originated here in my hometown in the 1930s. Our meat preference for spiedis is venison, but we use others when it's not available.

VENISON PARMIGIANA

1 cup vegetable oil

⅔ cup cider vinegar

2 tablespoons Worcestershire sauce

½ medium onion, finely chopped

½ teaspoon salt

½ teaspoon sugar

½ teaspoon dried basil

½ teaspoon dried marjoram

½ teaspoon dried rosemary, crushed

2½ pounds boneless lean venison, pork, beef, lamb, chicken or turkey, cut into 1½ to 2-inch cubes

Italian rolls or hot dog buns

[1] In a large resealable plastic bag, combine first nine ingredients; add meat. Seal bag and turn to coat; refrigerate for 24 hours, stirring occasionally.

[2] Drain and discard marinade. Thread meat on metal or soaked wooden skewers and grill over medium-hot heat until meat reaches desired doneness, abut 10-15 minutes. Remove meat from skewers and serve on long Italian rolls or hot dog buns. **Yield:** 8 servings.

venison tenderloins

BRENDA KOEHMSTEDT
RUGBY, NORTH DAKOTA

Venison is not typically the best meat for grilling, but with this marinade, the steaks come out tender, juicy and delicious. They're so tasty, in fact, that leftovers taste great cold—right from the fridge!

¾ cup soy sauce

½ cup red wine vinegar

½ cup vegetable oil

⅓ cup lemon juice

¼ cup Worcestershire sauce

2 tablespoons ground mustard

1 tablespoon coarsely ground pepper

1½ teaspoons dried parsley flakes

2 garlic cloves, minced

8 venison tenderloin (4 ounces each)

[1] In a large resealable plastic bag, combine the first nine ingredients; add fillets. Seal

VENISON MEATBALLS

bag and turn to coat; refrigerate for 8 hours or overnight.

[2] Drain and discard marinade. Grill fillets, uncovered, over medium-hot heat for 4 minutes on each side or until a meat thermometer reads 160° for medium or 170° for well-done. **Yield:** 8 servings.

venison meatballs

1 medium onion, finely chopped

½ cup uncooked instant rice

1 teaspoon salt

¼ teaspoon pepper

1 pound ground venison

¾ cup water

⅓ cup packed brown sugar

⅓ cup ketchup

⅓ cup condensed tomato soup, undiluted

1 tablespoon ground mustard

2 teaspoons paprika

[1] In a bowl, combine the first four ingredients. Crumble venison over mixture and mix well. Shape into 1½-in. balls. Place in a greased 8-in. square baking dish. Combine the remaining ingredients; pour over the meatballs.

[2] Bake, uncovered, at 375° for 35-45 minutes or until meat is no longer pink. **Yield:** 4 servings.

SHEILA REED
FREDERICTON, NEW BRUNSWICK

I learned to cook game while my husband was a forestry student. We lived off the land as much as possible. I still enjoy these savory meatballs in a slightly sweet barbecue sauce. I make a big batch for an annual pool party and there are never any left.

HUNTING & FISHING COOKBOOK

JENNIFER WHITAKER NORTH CENTRAL, MASSACHUSETTS

My husband and sons see to it that we have a good supply of venison in the freezer each winter, so I've come up with this stew to make good use of it. It smells wonderful as it simmers, and all the hearty appetites that appear around my table enjoy it.

venison vegetable stew

3 bacon strips

2 pounds venison stew meat, cut into 1-inch cubes

2 large onions, chopped

3½ cups water, divided

1 can (8 ounces) tomato sauce

1 envelope onion soup mix

2 teaspoons salt

1 bay leaf

2 teaspoons Italian seasoning

7 medium carrots, cut into 1-inch pieces

5 medium potatoes, peeled and cut into 1-inch cubes

4 celery ribs, sliced

3 tablespoons all-purpose flour

Hot cooked wide egg noodles

[1] In a 4-qt. Dutch oven, cook bacon until crisp. Remove to a paper towel to drain; reserve drippings in pan. Crumble bacon and set aside. Cook venison and onions in drippings until meat is lightly browned. Add 3 cups water, tomato sauce, soup mix, salt, bay leaf and Italian seasoning; bring to a boil. Reduce heat; cover and simmer for 1½ hours or until meat is almost tender.

[2] Add carrots, potatoes and celery; return to a boil. Reduce heat; cover and simmer 30-45 minutes or until meat and vegetables are tender. Combine flour and remaining water until smooth; stir into stew. Cook and stir until boiling and slightly thickened. Stir in bacon. Discard bay leaf before serving. Serve over noodles. **Yield:** 8 servings.

Editor's Note: If desired, beef stew meat or pork can be used in place of the venison.

christmas meat pie

JAN STAHL FLIN FLON, MANITOBA

Because my husband hunts, I'm always trying new ways to use venison. When I incorporated it into my meat pie recipe—a traditional French-Canadian dish—it was a smash hit! We make dozens of these pies as Christmas gifts.

1 pound ground pork

1 pound ground venison

3 cups water

2 medium onions, chopped

1 medium carrot, chopped

2 tablespoons beef gravy mix

2 teaspoons dried thyme

2 teaspoons ground mustard

3 garlic cloves, minced

1 teaspoon rubbed sage

1 teaspoon pepper

½ teaspoon salt

3 cups hot mashed potatoes (prepared without added butter or milk)

Pastry for double-crust pie (9 inches)

Milk

[1] In a large skillet, cook pork and venison over medium heat until no longer pink; drain. Stir in water, onions, carrot, gravy mix, thyme, mustard, garlic, sage, pepper and salt. Bring to a boil. Reduce heat; simmer, uncovered, for 1 hour or until vegetables are tender, stirring occasionally. Drain. Stir in potatoes.

VENISON VEGETABLE STEW

VENISON POT ROAST

[2] Line a 9-in. deep-dish pie plate with bottom pastry; trim even with edge. Add meat mixture. Roll out remaining pastry to fit top of pie. Make decorative cutouts or cut slits in pastry; place over filling. Trim, seal and flute edges.

[3] Brush pastry and cutouts with milk; place cutouts on the pie. Bake at 400° for 15 minutes. Reduce heat to 350°; bake 35-40 minutes longer or until golden brown. **Yield:** 6-8 servings.

venison pot roast

- 3 **tablespoons all-purpose flour**
- ½ **teaspoon salt**
- ½ **teaspoon pepper**
- 1 **boneless shoulder venison roast (3 pounds)**
- 2 **tablespoons vegetable oil**
- 1 **cup apple juice or cider**
- 1 **cup beef broth**
- 1 **medium onion, sliced**
- 1 **teaspoon dried thyme**
- 1 **bay leaf**

- 8 **small potatoes, peeled**
- 6 **medium carrots, cut into 2-inch pieces**
- 4 **celery ribs, cut into 2-inch pieces**

[1] Combine the first three ingredients; rub over roast. In a Dutch oven, brown roast on all sides in oil. Add apple juice, broth, onion, thyme and bay leaf. Bring to a boil; reduce heat. Cover and simmer for 2 hours.

[2] Add potatoes, carrots and celery; cover and simmer for 1 hour or until meat and vegetables are tender. Discard bay leaf. Thicken pan juices if desired. **Yield:** 6-8 servings.

HUNTING & FISHING tip

Italian dressing is a great way to season venison. Cut the venison loin into cubes and marinate several hours in Italian dressing and drain. Coat the cubes in flour and deep fry until cooked. I also pour it over venison steaks before baking.

BECKY, GEORGIA

DEBBIE PHILLIPS PITTSBURG, TEXAS

This hearty dish has tender meat and wonderful seasonings. Game is plentiful around our home, and my family could eat this satisfying meal weekly.

CHRIS MOUNTAIN INNISFAIL, ALBERTA

Our family especially likes this tender moose main dish in the fall and winter, when an oven meal really satisfies. The seasonings cover the game flavor wonderfully, and the tomatoes keep the meat nice and moist.

MOOSE STEAK

moose steak

1 boneless moose or sirloin steak (about 1 inch thick and 1¹/2 pounds)

¹/4 cup cornstarch

1 tablespoon ground mustard

1 teaspoon salt

¹/2 teaspoon pepper

2 tablespoons vegetable oil

1 can (14¹/2 ounces) diced tomatoes, undrained

1 medium onion, thinly sliced

1 medium carrot, diced

Hot cooked wide egg noodles, optional

[1] Cut steak into serving-size pieces. Combine cornstarch, mustard, salt and pepper; rub half over steak. Pound with a meat mallet to tenderize. Rub with remaining cornstarch mixture; pound on both sides with the mallet.

[2] In a skillet, brown steak in oil. Transfer to a greased 2¹/2-qt. baking dish. Top with tomatoes, onion and carrot. Cover and bake at 350° for 1¹/4-1¹/2 hours or until a meat thermometer reads 160° and the meat is tender. Serve over noodles if desired. **Yield:** 4-6 servings.

special venison meatballs

GERALDINE MENNEAR MASTIC, NEW YORK

These meatballs are a savory blend of ground venison and pork sausage, with water chestnuts for crunch.

1 egg, lightly beaten

1 cup soft bread crumbs

1 can (8 ounces) water chestnuts, drained and finely chopped

¹/4 cup soy sauce

2 teaspoons ground ginger

1 garlic clove, minced

1 pound ground venison

1 pound bulk pork sausage

3 to 4 teaspoons vegetable oil, divided

¹/2 pound fresh mushrooms, sliced

1 can (14¹/2 ounces) chicken broth

1¹/4 cups cold water, divided

3 tablespoons cornstarch

Hot cooked noodles

[1] In a bowl, combine the egg, bread crumbs, water chestnuts, soy sauce, ginger and garlic. Crumble the venison and sausage over the mixture and mix well. Shape into 1-in. balls. In a skillet over medium heat, brown meatballs in batches in 2 teaspoons oil, adding 1 teaspoon oil if needed. Transfer meatballs to a slow cooker.

[2] In the same skillet, saute mushrooms in 1 teaspoon oil until tender. Stir in the broth and 1 cup cold water. Pour over the meatballs. Cover and cook on low for 4-5 hours or until a meat thermometer reads 160°.

[3] Remove meatballs and mushrooms with a slotted spoon; keep warm. Strain cooking juices into a saucepan. Combine cornstarch and remaining water until smooth; add to saucepan. Bring to a boil; cook and stir for 2 minutes or until thickened. Serve over the meatballs, mushrooms and noodles. **Yield:** 8-10 servings.

baked venison burgers

TERESA BOWEN
CHOUDRANT, LOUISIANA

Since my husband enjoys hunting, we have an abundance of venison each winter. I adapted a meat loaf recipe to make these baked burgers, and we haven't eaten plain burgers since!

- 3/4 cup quick-cooking oats
- 3/4 cup milk
- 1/4 cup chopped onion
- 1 egg, beaten
- 1/2 to 1 teaspoon seasoned salt
- 1 pound ground venison
- 1 pound ground beef
- 1/3 cup ketchup
- 1 tablespoon brown sugar
- 1 tablespoon Worcestershire sauce
- 1 tablespoon prepared mustard
- 6 sandwich rolls, split

Swiss cheese and tomato slices, optional

[1] In a large bowl, combine the oats, milk, onion, egg and seasoned salt. Crumble venison and beef over mixture; mix well. Shape into eight patties; place in a greased 15-in. x 10-in. x 1-in. baking pan.

[2] In a small bowl, whisk the ketchup, brown sugar, Worcestershire sauce and mustard until blended. Spoon over patties. Bake, uncovered, at 350° for 22-26 minutes or until meat juices run clear. Serve on rolls with cheese and tomato if desired. **Yield:** 8 servings.

pasta pizza venison bake

- 8 ounces uncooked elbow macaroni
- 1 pound ground venison
- 1/2 teaspoon salt
- 1/4 teaspoon pepper
- 1 can (16 ounces) pizza sauce
- 1 can (4 ounces) mushroom stems and pieces, drained
- 2 cups (8 ounces) shredded mozzarella cheese

[1] Cook the macaroni according to package directions.

[2] Meanwhile, in a large skillet, cook the venison, salt and pepper over medium heat until meat is no longer pink; drain if necessary. Drain the macaroni; place half in a greased 2-qt. baking dish. Top with half of the venison, pizza sauce, mushrooms and cheese. Repeat layers. Cover and bake at 350° for 15 minutes.

[3] Uncover; bake 10 minutes longer or until heated through and cheese is melted. **Yield:** 6 servings.

DONNA THOMAS
BARK RIVER, MICHIGAN

Venison gives a pleasant change-of-pace flavor to this easy, delicious pasta casserole. My husband is an avid hunter, so I'm always trying to find new ways to prepare ground venison. Even those who usually don't care for the meat will like this hearty, one-dish meal.

PASTA PIZZA VENISON BAKE

FRANCES
HANSON
MILLS, WYOMING

My sister-in-law, who has cooked for many years at the family ranch, shared this hearty recipe. I make it often during the winter. It sure can warm you up after a hard day working outside in the cold!

wild west chili

2 bacon strips, diced

1 pound ground venison or beef

2 teaspoons chili powder

1½ teaspoons salt

¼ teaspoon garlic salt

¼ teaspoon dried oregano

⅛ teaspoon cayenne pepper

3 to 5 drops hot pepper sauce

1 can (14½ ounces) diced tomatoes, undrained

1 cup each finely chopped celery, onion and carrots

½ cup finely chopped green pepper

1 can (16 ounces) chili beans, undrained

[1] In a large saucepan, cook the bacon and the venison over medium heat until no longer pink; drain. Add the seasonings; cook and stir for 5 minutes.

[2] Stir in the tomatoes, celery, onion, carrots and green pepper; bring to a boil. Reduce heat; cover and simmer for 40 minutes. Stir

in the beans; cook 30 minutes longer. **Yield:** 6 servings.

wild rice venison stew

DARLA HASELTINE
WYOMING, MINNESOTA

With three hunters in the family and plenty of wild rice on hand, this hearty stew is a must at our house.

⅓ cup all-purpose flour

½ teaspoon pepper

1½ pounds venison, cut into 1-inch cubes

2 tablespoons canola oil

2¾ cups water

1 can (14½ ounces) beef broth

½ teaspoon beef bouillon granules

2 medium potatoes, peeled and cubed

1 medium onion, cut into wedges

2 medium carrots, cut into ¾-inch pieces

⅓ cup uncooked wild rice

[1] In a large resealable plastic bag, combine flour and pepper. Add venison; shake to coat. In a Dutch oven, brown meat in oil. Add water, broth and bouillon; bring to a boil. Reduce heat; cover and simmer for 1¼ hours.

[2] Stir in the potatoes, onion, carrots and rice; return to a boil. Reduce heat; cover and simmer for 30-40 minutes or until vegetables and rice are tender. **Yield:** 6 servings.

venison meat loaf

LIZ GILCHRIST
BOLTON, ONTARIO

My mother, who claims she can detect venison in any recipe, didn't have a clue it was in this tender meat loaf until we told her after dinner. She raved about this flavorful main dish the entire time she was eating it!

2 eggs

1 can (8 ounces) tomato sauce

1 medium onion, finely chopped

1 cup dry bread crumbs

1½ teaspoons salt

WILD WEST CHILI

VENISON ROAST

¹/8 teaspoon pepper

1¹/2 pounds ground venison

2 tablespoons brown sugar

2 tablespoons spicy brown mustard

2 tablespoons white vinegar

[1] In a large bowl, lightly beat eggs; add tomato sauce, onion, crumbs, salt and pepper. Crumble ground venison over mixture and mix well.

[2] Press into an ungreased 9-in. x 5-in. loaf pan. Combine the brown sugar, mustard and vinegar; pour over meat loaf. Bake, uncovered, at 350° for 70 minutes or until a meat thermometer reads 160°. **Yield:** 6-8 servings.

venison roast

1 venison roast (3 to 4 pounds)

10 whole garlic cloves, peeled

2 teaspoons dried rosemary, crushed

1¹/2 teaspoons onion powder, divided

1 teaspoon garlic powder

1 teaspoon dried thyme

7 medium carrots, quartered

5 small onions, quartered

1 tablespoon beef bouillon granules

1 teaspoon browning sauce, optional

2 tablespoons cornstarch

3 tablespoons cold water

[1] Cut 10 deep slits in roast; place a garlic clove in each slit. Pierce roast in several places with a meat fork. Combine rosemary, 1 teaspoon onion powder, garlic powder and thyme; rub over entire roast. Cover; refrigerate for 2 hours.

[2] Add ¹/2 in. of water to a roasting pan; place roast, carrots and onions in pan. Cover and bake at 325° for 2¹/2-3 hours or until a meat thermometer reads 160°. Remove meat and vegetables to a serving platter; keep warm.

[3] Strain drippings into a measuring cup. In a saucepan, combine 3 cups drippings, bouillon, browning sauce if desired and remaining onion powder. Combine cornstarch and cold water until smooth; stir into drippings. Bring to a boil; cook and stir for 2 minutes or until thickened. Serve gravy with the roast. **Yield:** 8 servings.

RUTH MCLAREN SHERMANS DALE, PENNSYLVANIA

We've always cooked with venison…and this flavorful roast and gravy have been a favorite at our house for years.

DIANNA
CROSKEY
GIBSONIA,
PENNSYLVANIA

The first time I served this dish to my deer-hunting family, everyone thought I had ordered from an Italian restaurant. My brother-in-law even asked me to make this for his birthday dinner.

venison stromboli

- 2 loaves (1 pound each) frozen bread dough, thawed
- 1 pound ground venison
- 1 medium onion, chopped
- 1/2 medium green pepper, chopped
- 1 can (4 ounces) mushroom stems and pieces, drained
- 2 tablespoons olive oil
- 1 teaspoon Italian seasoning
- 3 tablespoons prepared Italian salad dressing, divided
- 1 cup (4 ounces) shredded cheddar cheese
- 1 cup (4 ounces) shredded mozzarella cheese
- 2 packages (3 ounces each) sliced pepperoni
- 1/4 cup grated Parmesan cheese

Spaghetti sauce, warmed, optional

[1] Let dough rise in a warm place until doubled. Meanwhile, in a skillet over medium heat, cook venison, onion, green pepper and mushrooms in oil until meat is no longer pink. Drain. Stir in Italian seasoning; set aside.

[2] On a lightly floured surface, punch dough down. Roll out each loaf into a 16-in. x 8-in. rectangle; cut in half widthwise. Brush 1/2 tablespoon Italian dressing over each square to within 1 in. of edges. On half of each square, mound a fourth of the venison mixture, cheddar cheese, mozzarella and pepperoni. Fold dough over filling and seal edges well.

[3] Place on a greased baking sheet. Brush with the remaining dressing; sprinkle with Parmesan cheese. Bake at 350° for 30-35 minutes or until golden brown. Slice; serve with spaghetti sauce if desired. **Yield:** 4 loaves (1-2 servings each).

VENISON STROMBOLI

tangy venison stroganoff

ELLEN SPES
CARO, MICHIGAN

I coat tender chunks of venison with horseradish cream sauce in this delicious, flavorul take on a classic recipe. Your family is sure to savor every forkful. Add mushrooms if you like.

- 1½ pounds boneless venison steak, cubed
- 1 medium onion, sliced
- 1 can (10½ ounces) condensed beef broth, undiluted
- 1 tablespoon Worcestershire sauce
- 1 tablespoon ketchup
- 1 teaspoon curry powder
- ½ teaspoon ground ginger
- ½ teaspoon salt
- ¼ teaspoon pepper
- 4½ teaspoons cornstarch
- ½ cup sour cream
- 2 tablespoons prepared horseradish

Hot cooked noodles

[1] Place venison and onion in a slow cooker. Combine the next seven ingredients; pour over venison. Cover and cook on high for 3-3½ hours or until meat is tender.

[2] In a small bowl, combine the cornstarch, sour cream and horseradish; mix well. Gradually stir into venison mixture. Cover and cook 15 minutes longer or until sauce is thickened. Serve over noodles. **Yield:** 4 servings.

venison pot roast with spaetzle

- 1 boneless shoulder venison roast (3 to 4 pounds)
- 3 tablespoons vegetable oil
- 1 can (14½ ounces) chicken broth
- ⅓ cup soy sauce
- 1 large onion, sliced
- 4 garlic cloves, minced
- ½ teaspoon ground ginger

SPAETZLE:
- 2 eggs

VENISON POT ROAST WITH SPAETZLE

- ½ teaspoon salt
- 2¼ cups all-purpose flour
- ⅔ cup milk
- 2 quarts beef broth
- ¼ cup butter, melted
- ⅛ teaspoon pepper

GRAVY
- ⅓ cup water
- ⅓ cup all-purpose flour

[1] In a Dutch oven, brown roast in oil; add the next five ingredients. Cover and simmer for 4 hours or until meat is tender.

[2] For spaetzle, beat eggs and salt in a medium bowl. With a wooden spoon, gradually stir in flour and milk. In a large saucepan, bring broth to a boil. Place dough in a colander or spaetzle maker; place over boiling broth. Press dough with a wooden spoon until bits drop into broth. Cook for 5 minutes or until tender. Drain; toss spaetzle with butter. Sprinkle with pepper and keep warm.

[3] Remove roast to a serving platter and keep warm. Measure 3 cups pan juices; return to pan. Combine water and flour; stir into pan juices. Cook and stir until thickened and bubbly. Cook and stir 1 minute more. Slice roast; serve with spaetzle and gravy. **Yield:** 6-8 servings.

HELEN FEATHERLY
HAMBURG, MICHIGAN

My husband enjoyed deer hunting for many years, so I was challenged to find ways to put that meat to good use. This nicely seasoned roast is a real treat with the homemade spaetzle and flavorful gravy.

HUNTING & FISHING COOKBOOK

ELK PARMESAN

sweet-and-sour elk

SUSAN BOWDLE
EPHRATA, WASHINGTON

Baked elk steaks smothered with a simple, savory sauce is a special dinner we've enjoyed for years. My husband, Ralph, and I used to do quite a bit of hunting, so I accumulated lots of terrific recipes like this one.

  1 envelope onion soup mix

 1/4 cup water

  1 jar (12 ounces) apricot preserves

 1/2 cup Russian or Catalina salad dressing

 1/4 cup packed brown sugar

  1 tablespoon cider vinegar

1 1/2 pounds elk steaks, cut into 1/2-inch strips

  1 teaspoon salt

 1/4 teaspoon pepper

Hot cooked rice

[1] In a bowl, combine soup mix and water; let stand for 15 minutes. Add preserves, salad dressing, brown sugar and vinegar; mix well.

[2] Place elk in a greased 13-in. x 9-in. x 2-in. baking dish. Sprinkle with salt and pepper. Pour apricot mixture over the elk. Cover and bake at 350° for 45 minutes.

[3] Uncover and bake 30-40 minutes longer or until meat is fork-tender. Serve over rice. **Yield:** 4-6 servings.

DOLORES CROCK
CHEYENNE, WYOMING

Wyoming is a paradise for people like us who enjoy hunting. My husband was thrilled when our jobs brought us here over 20 years ago. I've been cooking game since I was a girl, so I use recipes like this enticing elk dish often. It's one of our favorites.

elk parmesan

1 1/2 pounds boneless elk steak

 1/4 to 1/2 teaspoon garlic salt

 1/8 teaspoon pepper

 1/2 cup dry Italian bread crumbs

 1/2 cup grated Parmesan cheese

  2 eggs

 1/4 cup water

 1/2 cup all-purpose flour

 1/4 cup olive oil

1 1/2 cups spaghetti sauce

  6 slices part-skim mozzarella cheese

Hot cooked noodles

Snipped fresh parsley, optional

[1] Cut meat into six pieces; pound with a meat mallet to tenderize. Sprinkle with garlic salt and pepper. Combine bread crumbs and the Parmesan cheese in a bowl. In another bowl, beat eggs with water. Dip both sides of meat into flour, then into egg mixture. Press each side of meat into crumb mixture; refrigerate for 20 minutes.

[2] Heat oil in a large skillet; brown meat on both sides. Place in a greased 13-in. x 9-in. x 2-in. baking pan. Spoon 2 tablespoons spaghetti sauce over each piece. Cover with mozzarella; top with remaining spaghetti sauce. Bake, uncovered, at 350° for 30 minutes or until meat is tender. Serve over noodles; garnish with parsley if desired. **Yield:** 6 servings.

HUNTING & FISHING
tip

Our family favorite is Marinated Venison Steak. We grill this year-round! Our kids prefer this venison steak over beef steak any day. Our marinade for 1 pound of venison steak is 3 tablespoons canola oil, 1 tablespoon lemon juice, 1 tablespoon soy sauce, 1 tablespoon Worcestershire sauce, 2 teaspoons minced garlic and 1/4 teaspoon pepper. I marinate the meat in the refrigerator for 8 hours or overnight.

JAN, MICHIGAN

hearty hunter's stew

- 2 pounds venison or beef chuck, cut in 1-inch cubes
- 2 tablespoons vegetable oil
- 4 1/4 cups water, divided
- 1/2 cup tomato juice
- 2 medium onions, cut into wedges
- 2 celery ribs, sliced
- 1 teaspoon Worcestershire sauce
- 2 bay leaves
- 2 to 3 teaspoons salt
- 1/2 teaspoon pepper
- 6 medium carrots, quartered
- 1 large rutabaga, peeled and cubed
- 6 medium potatoes, peeled and quartered
- 1 cup frozen peas
- 1 tablespoon cornstarch

Baking powder biscuits, optional

[1] In a Dutch oven, brown meat in oil. Add 4 cups water and stir to loosen browned bits from pan. Add tomato juice, onions, celery, Worcestershire sauce, bay leaves, salt and pepper. Cover; reduce heat to simmer. Cook for 2 hours, stirring occasionally. Discard bay leaves. Add carrots, rutabaga and potatoes.

[2] Cover and cook for 40-60 minutes. Stir in the peas; cook for 10 minutes. Combine cornstarch and remaining water until smooth; stir into stew. Cook and stir for 2 minutes or until thickened. Serve with baking powder biscuits if desired. **Yield:** 8 servings.

JOYCE WORSECH CATAWBA, WISCONSIN

Moist, tender meat and thick, rich gravy are the hallmarks of this classic recipe slowly simmered on the stovetop.

HEARTY HUNTER'S STEW

HUNTING & FISHING COOKBOOK

KAREN SMITH
MACKINAW,
ILLINOIS

This cheesy dip is so yummy that even those who don't enjoy venison will dig right in. My grandsons put it in a bowl and eat it with a spoon. I double or triple the recipe when they are coming over to make sure I have enough.

VENISON CHEESE DIP

venison cheese dip

  1 pound ground venison

  3/4 cup chopped onion, divided

  3/4 cup chopped green pepper, divided

  2 tablespoons vegetable oil

  1 pound process cheese (Velveeta), cubed

  1 can (15 ounces) chili without beans

  1 bottle (12 ounces) chili sauce

  1/2 teaspoon garlic salt

  1/2 teaspoon salt

  1/2 teaspoon pepper

  1/2 cup shredded cheddar cheese

Nacho chips

[1] In a large skillet over medium heat, cook the venison, 1/2 cup onion and 1/2 cup green pepper in oil until meat is no longer pink; drain. Stir in the next six ingredients; cook and stir until the cheese is melted.

[2] Transfer to a serving dish. Sprinkle with cheddar cheese and remaining onion and green pepper. Serve with chips. **Yield:** 6 cups.

stuffing-topped venison chops

SUE GRONHOLZ
BEAVER DAM, WISCONSIN

A moist stuffing with apples and raisins is great with pork chops, so I decided to try it with venison chops, too. These venison chops are special enough for company.

  4 venison loin chops (1 1/4 inches thick)

  2 tablespoons vegetable oil

  1 to 1 1/2 cups beef broth

APPLE STUFFING:

  2 cups cubed day-old bread

  1 cup chopped peeled tart apple

  1/4 cup sugar

  1/4 cup raisins

  1/4 cup chopped onion

  1/4 cup butter, melted

  1/4 cup hot water

  1 teaspoon salt

  1/2 teaspoon pepper

  1/8 teaspoon rubbed sage

[1] In a skillet, brown chops in oil on both sides. Transfer to a greased 11-in. x 7-in. x 2-in. baking dish; add enough broth to reach top of chops. In a bowl, combine stuffing ingredients; mix well. Spoon over chops. Cover and bake at 350° for 30 minutes.

[2] Uncover; bake 20-30 minutes longer or until a meat thermometer reads 160°. **Yield:** 4 servings.

spinach venison lasagna

- ¼ cup chopped onion
- 2 tablespoons butter
- 2 cans (8 ounces each) tomato sauce
- 1 teaspoon each Worcestershire sauce and dried basil
- 1 bay leaf
- ¼ teaspoon each garlic powder, ground cloves, ground allspice and dried oregano

WHITE SAUCE:

- 1 can (4 ounces) mushroom stems and pieces, drained
- ¼ cup chopped onion
- ⅓ cup all-purpose flour
- 2 cups milk
- 12 lasagna noodles, cooked and drained
- 2 packages (10 ounces each) frozen chopped spinach, thawed and squeezed dry
- 1 cup (8 ounces) cottage cheese
- 3 cups (12 ounces) shredded mozzarella cheese
- 2 pounds ground venison, cooked and drained
- 1 cup (4 ounces) shredded cheddar cheese

[1] In a large skillet, saute the onion in butter until tender. Stir in the tomato sauce, water, barbecue sauce, Worcestershire sauce, basil, bay leaf, garlic powder, cloves, allspice and oregano. Bring to a boil. Reduce heat. Cover and simmer for 30 minutes.

[2] Meanwhile, in a saucepan, saute mushrooms and onion in butter until tender. Stir in flour. Gradually whisk in milk until blended.

Bring to a boil; cook and stir for 2 minutes or until thickened.

[3] Discard bay leaf. Spread ½ cup tomato sauce into a greased 13-in. x 9-in. x 2-in. baking dish; top with four noodles. Layer with 1 cup spinach, ½ cup cottage cheese, half of white sauce, 1 cup mozzarella cheese, half of venison and ½ cup cheddar cheese. Repeat layers once.

[4] Top with remaining noodles, tomato sauce and mozzarella cheese. Cover; bake at 350° for 35 minutes. Uncover; bake 10-15 minutes longer. Let stand 10 minutes before serving. **Yield:** 8 servings.

JO MITCHELL
MOUNTAIN VIEW,
WYOMING

I often use elk for this satisfying lasagna. You can also make it using ground beef.

HUNTING & FISHING tip

Keep in mind when butchering game to always cut across the grain, never with the grain. This will keep the meat the most tender.

JERRY, WISCONSIN

SPINACH VENISON LASAGNA

HUNTING & FISHING COOKBOOK

DIANE BURGE FRIEDHEIM, MISSOURI

When a family friend shared his hunting bounty with us, I looked for new ways to serve the venison. Even our two children asked for seconds.

venison on caraway rolls

1½ teaspoons active dry yeast

¾ cup warm water (110° to 115°)

1½ teaspoons sugar

2 tablespoons butter, softened

2 tablespoons nonfat dry milk powder

1 egg

1 teaspoon salt

2½ to 3 cups all-purpose flour

1 egg white

1 teaspoon cold water

1 tablespoon rye flour

½ teaspoon coarse salt

½ teaspoon caraway seeds

VENISON BARBECUE:

1 venison roast (3 to 4 pounds)

1 cup water

½ cup ketchup

2 tablespoons onion soup mix

2 teaspoons prepared horseradish

½ teaspoon garlic powder

½ teaspoon dried oregano

½ teaspoon pepper

3 teaspoons cornstarch

1 tablespoon cold water

[1] In a mixing bowl, dissolve yeast in warm water. Add sugar; let stand for 5 minutes. Beat in butter, milk powder, egg, salt and enough all-purpose flour to form a soft dough. Turn onto a floured surface; knead until smooth and elastic, about 4-6 minutes. Place in a greased bowl, turning once to grease top. Cover and let rise in a warm place until doubled, about 40 minutes.

[2] Punch dough down. Turn onto a lightly floured surface; divide into 12 pieces. Shape into 2½-in. circles. Place 2 in. apart on greased baking sheets. Cover and let rise until doubled, about 20-25 minutes.

[3] Beat egg white and cold water; brush over dough. Combine rye flour, coarse salt and caraway seeds; sprinkle over rolls. Bake at 425° for 9-12 minutes or until golden brown. Remove from pans to wire racks.

[4] Place the venison roast in a Dutch oven. In a bowl, combine water, ketchup, soup mix, horseradish and seasonings; pour over roast. Cover and bake at 325° for 2-3 hours or until a meat thermometer reads 160° and meat is tender, turning once.

[5] Remove roast; let stand for 10 minutes. Shred meat with two forks; keep warm. Combine cornstarch and cold water until smooth; stir into pan drippings until blended. Bring to a boil; cook and stir for 2 minutes or until thickened. Return meat to the pan; heat through. Split rolls. Serve meat and gravy on rolls. **Yield:** 12 sandwiches.

deep-dish hunter's pie

1½ pounds potatoes, peeled and cubed

3 garlic cloves, minced

¼ cup milk

1 tablespoon butter

¼ teaspoon dried rosemary, crushed

½ teaspoon salt

VENISON ON CARAWAY ROLLS

CHRISTINA RULIEN MARYSVILLE, WASHINGTON
My husband, an avid hunter, loves the garlic mashed potato topping on this well-seasoned venison dish. It's a special way to use up cooked venison.

DEEP-DISH HUNTER'S PIE

⅛ teaspoon pepper

FILLING:
1 cup sliced fresh mushrooms
1 cup sliced carrots
½ cup chopped onion
¼ cup chopped green pepper
1 tablespoon butter
2 cups cubed cooked venison
1½ cups beef broth
¼ teaspoon dried thyme
⅛ teaspoon ground nutmeg
3 tablespoons all-purpose flour
3 tablespoons cold water
⅓ cup shredded cheddar cheese
2 tablespoons minced parsley

[1] Cook potatoes in boiling water until tender; drain and mash. Add the garlic, milk, butter, rosemary, salt and pepper; set aside.

[2] In a large skillet, saute mushrooms, carrots, onion and green pepper in butter until tender. Add venison, broth, thyme and nutmeg. Bring to a boil. Reduce heat; cover and simmer for 25-30 minutes or until the meat and vegetables are tender.

[3] Combine the flour and water until smooth; stir into skillet. Bring to a boil; cook and stir for 2 minutes or until thickened. Transfer to a greased 2-qt. baking dish. Spread mashed potatoes over the top. Bake, uncovered, at 350° for 30-40 minutes or until bubbly. Sprinkle with cheese. Bake 5 minutes longer or until cheese is melted. Sprinkle with parsley. **Yield:** 6 servings.

HUNTING & FISHING tip

To fix deer cube steak, soak the steaks in milk for about 10 minutes, take them out and coat them with flour. Fry them slowly in butter until golden. Make a mushroom gravy and put the gravy and the cube steaks in a slow cooker for about 4 or 5 hours. It is delicious. ANGELA, WEST VIRGINIA

**GAYLEEN GROTE
BATTLEVIEW,
NORTH DAKOTA**

When we were growing up, this recipe was a family favorite when we had deer meat. Now my children love it, too!

pan-fried venison steak

1	pound venison or beef tenderloin, cut into $1/2$-inch slices
2	cups crushed saltines
2	eggs
3/4	cup milk
1	teaspoon salt
1/2	teaspoon pepper
5	tablespoons vegetable oil

[1] Flatten venison to $1/8$-in. thickness. Place saltines in a shallow bowl. In another shallow bowl, whisk the eggs, milk, salt and pepper. Coat venison with saltines, then dip in egg mixture and coat a second time with saltines.

[2] In a large skillet over medium heat, cook venison in oil in batches for 2-3 minutes on each side or until meat reaches desired doneness. **Yield:** 4 servings.

pioneer stew

**GENE PITTS
WILSONVILLE, ALABAMA**

I learned to cook some years ago while my wife recuperated from surgery. I found that I enjoyed trying different recipes and adapting them to my own taste.

2	tablespoons vegetable oil
2	pounds venison stew meat
3	large onions, coarsely chopped
2	garlic cloves, crushed
1	tablespoon Worcestershire sauce
1	bay leaf
1	teaspoon dried oregano
1	tablespoon salt
1	teaspoon pepper
3	cups water
7	potatoes, peeled and quartered

1 pound carrots, cut into 1-inch pieces

¼ cup all-purpose flour

¼ cup cold water

Bottled browning sauce, optional

[1] Heat oil in a Dutch oven. Brown meat. Add onions, garlic, Worcestershire sauce, bay leaf, oregano, salt, pepper and water. Simmer, covered, 1-½ to 2 hours or until meat is tender.

[2] Add potatoes and carrots. Continue to cook until vegetables are tender, about 30-45 minutes longer.

[3] Mix flour and cold water; stir into stew. Cook and stir until thickened and bubbly. Add browning sauce if desired. Remove bay leaf. **Yield:** 8-10 servings.

classic venison meat loaf

**GRETCHEN SCHADE
PINE GROVE, PENNSYLVANIA**

I caught my fiance eating this meat loaf cold, right out of the fridge! He encouraged me to send in the recipe. If you have a deer hunter in the family, be sure to give this a try.

2 eggs

2 cups soft bread crumbs

½ cup chopped sweet onion

¼ cup packed brown sugar

¼ cup ketchup

1 tablespoon cider vinegar

1 teaspoon garlic powder

½ teaspoon Worcestershire sauce

1 pound ground venison

½ pound bulk pork sausage

4 bacon strips

[1] In a large bowl, combine the first eight ingredients. Crumble venison and sausage over mixture and mix well. Shape into a loaf in a greased 11-in. x 7-in. baking dish. Top with bacon strips.

[2] Bake, uncovered, at 400° for 40-45 minutes or until meat is no longer pink and a meat thermometer reads 160°. Let stand for 5-10 minutes before slicing. **Yield:** 6 servings.

sweet pepper venison stir-fry

¼ cup cornstarch

2 teaspoons sugar

6 tablespoons soy sauce

¼ cup white wine vinegar

½ teaspoon pepper

1 venison tenderloin (about 1 pound), cut into 2-inch strips

1 medium green pepper, julienned

1 medium sweet red pepper, julienned

3 tablespoons vegetable oil

Hot cooked rice

[1] In a small bowl, combine the cornstarch, sugar, soy sauce, vinegar and pepper; stir until smooth. Pour half into a large resealable plastic bag; add venison. Seal bag and turn to coat; refrigerate for 1-2 hours. Cover and refrigerate remaining marinade.

[2] Drain and discard marinade. In a large skillet or wok, stir-fry venison and peppers in oil for 4-6 minutes or until meat is no longer pink and peppers are crisp-tender. Stir reserved marinade; add to the pan. Bring to a boil; cook and stir for 1-2 minutes or until thickened. Serve with rice. **Yield:** 2 servings.

**KATHY GASSER
WAUKESHA,
WISCONSIN**

Every year our friends have a game feed where everyone brings a different wild dish. This stir-fry really knocked their socks off.

SWEET PEPPER VENISON STIR-FRY

**GLORIA LONG
MOREHEAD
CITY, NORTH
CAROLINA**

This satisfying
quiche is loaded
with vegetables
and meat. The
feta cheese pairs
perfectly with
spinach.

spinach
venison quiche

    1 unbaked pastry shell (9 inches)
  1/2 pound ground venison
  1/2 pound sliced fresh mushrooms
  1/2 cup chopped onion
  1/2 cup chopped green pepper
    1 package (10 ounces) frozen
       chopped spinach, thawed and
       squeezed dry
    1 package (4 ounces) crumbled feta
       cheese
    6 eggs
  3/4 cup half-and-half cream
    1 teaspoon pepper
  1/2 teaspoon salt

[1] Line unpricked pastry shell with a double
thickness of heavy-duty foil. Bake at 450° for 8
minutes. Remove foil; bake 5 minutes longer.

[2] Meanwhile, in a large skillet, cook the venison, mushrooms, onion and green pepper for
5-6 minutes or until meat is no longer pink;
drain. Spoon into crust; top with spinach and
feta cheese.

[3] In a bowl, whisk the eggs, cream, pepper
and salt; pour over cheese.

[4] Cover edges loosely with foil. Bake at 350°
for 45-50 minutes or until a knife inserted near
the center comes out clean. Let stand for 5
minutes before cutting. **Yield:** 8 servings.

venison
tortilla lasagna

**DEBRA SCUTT
MASON, MICHIGAN**

I always keep a copy of this recipe around, because every time someone new tries this lasagna,
they want to make it, too. It freezes well and is
excellent for leftovers—if there are any.

SPINACH VENISON QUICHE

1 pound ground venison

1 can (14½ ounces) diced tomatoes with mild green chilies, undrained

1 cup salsa

1 envelope taco seasoning

2 eggs, lightly beaten

2 cups (16 ounces) 4% small-curd cottage cheese

1 teaspoon dried oregano

½ teaspoon ground cumin

10 flour tortillas (8 inches)

1½ cups (6 ounces) shredded cheddar cheese

[1] In a large skillet, cook venison over medium heat until no longer pink; drain. Add the tomatoes, salsa and taco seasoning; cook, stirring occasionally, until heated through. In a small bowl, combine the eggs, cottage cheese, oregano and cumin.

[2] Cut tortillas in half; place half of them in a greased 13-in. x 9-in. baking dish (tortillas will overlap). Top with half of the meat sauce. Spoon cottage cheese mixture over the top. Layer with remaining tortillas and meat sauce.

[3] Cover and bake at 350° for 30 minutes or until heated through. Uncover; sprinkle with cheddar cheese. Bake 5 minutes longer or until cheese is melted. Let stand for 10 minutes before cutting. **Yield:** 12 servings.

apple venison meat loaf

LORRAINE McCLAIN
REPUBLICAN CITY, NEBRASKA

Venison is a nice change of pace at mealtime. This meat loaf doesn't taste gamey, and our guests enjoy it...especially the ones who stay with us during hunting season.

1 egg, beaten

½ cup ketchup

1 tablespoon prepared horseradish

2 cups shredded peeled apples

2 cups unseasoned stuffing cubes

¼ cup finely chopped onion

1 tablespoon ground mustard

2 pounds ground venison

HUNTER'S DELIGHT

In a large bowl, combine the first seven ingredients. Crumble venison over mixture and mix well. Pat into an ungreased 9-in. x 5-in. loaf pan. Bake, uncovered, at 350° for 60-70 minutes or until no pink remains and a meat thermometer reads 160°. **Yield:** 8 servings.

hunter's delight

½ pound sliced bacon, diced

2½ pounds red potatoes, thinly sliced

2 medium onions, sliced

1½ pounds boneless venison steak, cubed

2 cans (14¾ ounces each) cream-style corn

3 tablespoons Worcestershire sauce

1 teaspoon sugar

½ to 1 teaspoon seasoned salt

[1] In a large skillet, cook bacon over medium heat until crisp; drain. Place potatoes and onions in a 5-qt. slow cooker. Top with venison and bacon.

[2] In a large bowl, combine the corn, Worcestershire sauce, sugar and seasoned salt; pour over the top. Cover and cook on low for 6-8 hours or until meat and potatoes are tender. **Yield:** 8 servings.

TERRY PAULL
EAGLE RIVER, WISCONSIN

We live in the North Woods, so we usually have an ample supply of venison. Our mom made this recipe often, and it was always one of our favorites.

Hunting & Fishing COOKBOOK

Young wild ducks have dark, tender meat and can weigh up to 4 pounds. Farm-raised ducks may weigh more.

Wild geese typically weigh between 4 and 14 pounds.

Pheasants are a medium-size game bird. The female, usually about 3 pounds, has more tender, plump and juicy meat than the male, which weighs about 5 pounds.

Quail, known as partridge in some regions of America, are typically 3 to 7 ounces.

Wild turkeys are one of North America's native birds. Compared to their domestic counterparts, wild turkeys are leaner, less meaty, not as tender and have a stronger flavor.

JALAPENO QUAIL APPETIZERS, P. 49
PHEASANT POTPIE, P. 52
ROASTED WILD TURKEY, P. 58

PHEASANT STIR-FRY,
PAGE 54

MARIE REINE
ST. AMANT,
LOUISIANA

My husband's family has enjoyed this satisfying gumbo for many years. Bold seasonings and savory sausage slices enhance the mild meat. John doesn't do much hunting anymore, but we still enjoy this Cajun dish on cool evenings.

RABBIT GUMBO

rabbit gumbo

    1 small onion, chopped
    1 small green pepper, chopped
  1/4 cup vegetable oil
    1 dressed rabbit (about 3 pounds),
       cut into pieces
  1/2 pound smoked sausage, halved
       and cut into 1/4-inch slices
    1 teaspoon salt
  1/2 teaspoon dried thyme
  1/4 teaspoon pepper
  1/4 teaspoon cayenne pepper
  1/2 cup sliced okra

Hot cooked rice

[1] In a Dutch oven, saute onion and green pepper in oil until tender. Add rabbit and enough water to cover. Cover and simmer for 1½ to 2 hours or until meat is very tender. Add sausage, salt, thyme, pepper and cayenne. Simmer, uncovered, for 15-20 minutes.

[2] Remove rabbit; cool. Debone and cut into bite-size pieces; return to pan. Stir in okra; bring to a boil. Serve in bowls over rice. **Yield:** 4-6 servings.

duck breasts with apricot chutney

TASTE OF HOME TEST KITCHEN

When serving this entree as part of a buffet, use a chafing dish or slow cooker to keep it warm. The recipe is for 12 people, so it's good for special occasions. The recipe could also easily be cut in half.

  1½ cups orange juice
  2/3 cup sugar
    2 packages (6 ounces each) dried
       apricots, chopped
  1/2 cup dried cherries
  1/2 cup golden raisins

tip

HUNTING & FISHING

When I have wild turkey, duck or goose breasts, I slice them fairly thin—about ¼ inch—and coat them with a mixture of flour, cornmeal, salt, pepper and red pepper flakes to suit our tastes. I then deep fry or pan fry the slices. The pieces cook quickly and are tender and tasty.

SUZANNE, KENTUCKY

2 teaspoons minced fresh
  gingerroot

¾ teaspoon ground coriander

¾ teaspoon ground cumin

¼ teaspoon salt

¼ teaspoon pepper

⅛ teaspoon ground cloves

2 teaspoons lemon juice

DUCK:

12 duck breasts with skin
   (5 ounces each)

1½ teaspoons salt

¼ teaspoon pepper

2 tablespoons olive oil

ORANGE SAUCE:

¼ teaspoon minced garlic

½ cup Marsala wine

½ teaspoon cornstarch

½ cup orange juice

⅓ cup chicken broth

2 tablespoons grated orange peel

3 tablespoons cold butter

1 tablespoon minced fresh basil

[1] For chutney, in a saucepan, combine orange juice and sugar. Cook and stir over medium heat for 3 minutes or until sugar is dissolved. Add the apricots, cherries, raisins, ginger, coriander, cumin, salt, pepper and cloves. Bring to a boil. Reduce heat to low; cook for 10 minutes or until apricots are tender. Transfer to a bowl; stir in lemon juice. Let stand at room temperature for at least 2 hours.

[2] Season both sides of duck with salt and pepper. In a large skillet, saute duck, skin side down, in oil until skin is browned; turn and cook for 1 minute. Set aside 1 tablespoon drippings. Place duck on a greased rack in a shallow roasting pan. Bake at 350° for 30-35 minutes or until juices run clear and a meat thermometer reads 180°.

[3] For orange sauce, saute garlic in reserved drippings for 1 minute. Add wine; bring to a boil. Cook and stir until reduced by half. In a bowl, combine the cornstarch, orange juice, broth and orange peel until blended. Stir into wine mixture. Bring to a boil. Reduce heat; simmer, uncovered, for 5 minutes.

[4] Remove mixture from the heat. Whisk in butter and basil until smooth. Remove skin from the duck if desired before slicing. Serve duck with the orange sauce and chutney. **Yield:** 12 servings.

grilled wild turkey breast

1 bone-in wild turkey breast
  (about 1½ pounds), split

1 bottle (8 ounces) fat-free honey
  Dijon salad dressing

[1] Place turkey in a large resealable plastic bag; add the salad dressing. Seal bag and turn to coat; refrigerate overnight, turning occasionally.

[2] Drain and discard marinade. Grill turkey, covered, over indirect medium heat for 45-55 minutes or until juices run clear and a meat thermometer reads 170°. **Yield:** 2 servings.

MICHELLE KAASE TOMBALL, TEXAS

With only two ingredients, this is definitely the easiest recipe I have for cooking the wild turkey that my husband, Richard, brings home during spring hunting season. The grilled meat takes on a wonderfully sweet and smoky flavor.

GRILLED WILD TURKEY BREAST

MARY CALENDINE HIDDENITE, NORTH CAROLINA

My husband is an avid hunter. Almost 55 years ago, his aunt gave us this recipe. The tender, flavorful meat combined with the sour cream and seasonings makes a wonderful dish.

hasenpfeffer

- 1 large onion, sliced
- 3 cups white vinegar
- 3 cups water
- 1 tablespoon pickling spice
- 2 teaspoons salt
- ½ teaspoon pepper
- 2 bay leaves
- 8 whole cloves
- 1 dressed rabbit (2½ pounds), cut into serving-size pieces
- ¼ cup all-purpose flour
- 2 to 3 tablespoons butter
- 1 cup (about 8 ounces) sour cream

[1] In a large resealable plastic bag, combine onion, vinegar, water and seasonings. Add rabbit pieces; seal bag and refrigerate for 48 hours, turning occasionally. Remove meat; strain and reserve marinade. Dry meat well; coat lightly with flour.

[2] In a skillet, brown meat in butter. Gradually add 2 to 2½ cups reserved marinade. Cover and bring to a boil. Reduce heat and simmer until tender, about 30 minutes. Remove meat to a warm platter. Add sour cream to pan juices; stir just until heated through. Spoon over the meat and serve immediately. **Yield:** 6 servings.

pheasant in cream sauce

JULIE ANDERSON WAUSAU, WISCONSIN

A savory sauce with garlic and tarragon is a satisfying treatment for baked pheasant. This recipe always brings compliments.

- 1 pheasant or broiler-fryer chicken (2 to 3 pounds), cut up

HASENPFEFFER

1 can (10³/4 ounces) condensed cream of mushroom soup, undiluted

1 can (4 ounces) sliced mushrooms, drained

¹/2 cup apple cider

¹/3 cup chopped onion

4 teaspoons Worcestershire sauce

¹/2 teaspoon salt

1 garlic clove, minced

¹/4 teaspoon dried tarragon

Paprika

[1] Carefully place pheasant in an ungreased 11-in. x 7-in. x 2-in. baking dish. Combine the next eight ingredients; pour over pheasant. Sprinkle generously with paprika.

[2] Bake, uncovered, at 325° for 1¹/2 hours or until a meat thermometer reads 180°, basting occasionally. Sprinkle again with paprika before serving. **Yield:** 3-4 servings.

HEARTY GOOSE SOUP

roast christmas goose

ROSEMARIE FORCUM
WHITE STONE, VIRGINIA

I have such fond childhood memories of Christmas dinner and my mother serving a golden brown Christmas goose. To flavor the meat, Mom stuffed the bird with peeled and quartered fruit that's discarded after baking.

1 goose (10 to 12 pounds)

Salt and pepper

1 medium apple, peeled and quartered

1 medium navel orange, peeled and quartered

1 medium lemon, peeled and quartered

1 cup hot water

[1] Sprinkle the goose cavity with salt and pepper. Place the apple, orange and lemon in the cavity. Place goose breast side up on a rack in a large shallow roasting pan. Prick skin well with a fork. Pour water into pan.

[2] Bake, uncovered, at 350° for 2¹/4 to 3 hours or until a meat thermometer reads 185°. If necessary, drain fat from pan as it accumulates. Cover goose with foil and let stand

for 20 minutes before carving. Discard fruit. **Yield:** 8 servings.

hearty goose soup

2¹/4 cups cubed uncooked goose

1 pound red potatoes, cubed

1 large onion, chopped

1 each medium green, sweet yellow and red pepper, chopped

2 medium carrots, cut into ¹/2-inch slices

1 cup water

3 garlic cloves, minced

2 teaspoons dried basil

Salt and pepper to taste

1 can (15 ounces) tomato sauce

1 can (14¹/2 ounces) Italian stewed tomatoes

2 cups uncooked elbow macaroni

[1] In a 5-qt. slow cooker, combine goose, potatoes, onion, peppers, carrots, water, garlic, basil, salt and pepper. Cover and cook on high for 4 hours or until meat juices run clear and vegetables are tender.

[2] Stir in tomato sauce and tomatoes; cook 1 hour longer. Just before serving, cook macaroni according to package directions; drain. Stir into the soup. **Yield:** 13 servings (about 3 quarts).

LORETTA FENRICH BARNEY LAKE, WASHINGTON

After my son went goose hunting, I was happy to cook what he brought home. So I got ingredients together and came up with this chunky soup. It's chock-full of pasta and vegetables.

**JEAN WILLIAMS
HURTSBORO,
ALABAMA**

We live in an area with many Southern plantations, and quail are abundant. I cook this tasty dish with rich mushroom gravy often when my two boys are home. They think it makes a great meal.

QUAIL IN MUSHROOM GRAVY

quail in mushroom gravy

³/₄ cup all-purpose flour, divided

1 teaspoon salt

¹/₂ teaspoon pepper

6 quail (¹/₃ to ¹/₂ pound each)

¹/₂ cup butter

¹/₂ pound fresh mushrooms, sliced

2 cups chicken broth

2 teaspoons minced fresh thyme or ³/₄ teaspoon dried thyme

Hot cooked wide egg noodles, optional

[1] Combine ¹/₂ cup flour, salt and pepper; coat each quail. Melt butter in skillet; brown the quail. Transfer to an ungreased 2¹/₂-qt. baking dish. In the pan drippings, saute the mushrooms until tender. Add remaining flour and stir to make a smooth paste. Add broth and thyme, stirring constantly. Bring to a boil; boil for 1 minute or until thickened. Pour over the quail.

[2] Cover and bake at 350° for 40-50 minutes or until tender and juices run clear. Serve over noodles if desired. **Yield:** 6 servings.

rabbit fricassee

**AUDREY THIBODEAU
MESA, ARIZONA**

I prefer rabbit cooked this way—moist and tasty, smothered in a tangy lemon sauce that's also a bit peppery.

1 dressed rabbit (about 3 pounds), cut into pieces

¹/₂ cup vegetable oil

2 tablespoons all-purpose flour

1 tablespoon butter, melted

1 teaspoon lemon juice

¹/₂ to 1 teaspoon hot pepper sauce

¹/₂ teaspoon celery salt

tip HUNTING & FISHING

We like to take 2-inch chunks of marinated wild turkey, duck or goose breast and wrap them in bacon with slices of jalapeno pepper and grill them. I finish them with my favorite BBQ sauce just before they come off the grill. This is also a favorite method for doves.

SUZANNE, KENTUCKY

½ teaspoon salt

¼ teaspoon pepper

1 egg

1 cup evaporated milk

[1] In a skillet, brown rabbit in oil; drain. Cover rabbit with boiling water; cover and simmer for 30-40 minutes or until tender. Remove meat and keep warm. Bring cooking liquid to a boil; boil, uncovered, until reduced to 2 cups.

[2] In a bowl, combine flour and butter until smooth; gradually add a small amount of cooking liquid. Return to skillet. Whisk in remaining liquid. Add lemon juice, hot pepper sauce, celery salt, salt and pepper. Bring to a boil, stirring constantly; cook and stir for 2 minutes.

[3] Reduce heat. Combine the egg and milk and gradually whisk into the sauce. Cook for 1 minute or until thickened and mixture reaches 160°. Pour sauce over the top of the rabbit. **Yield:** 4 servings.

jack's stuffed mushrooms

JACK HUNTER
HARLINGEN, TEXAS

Since my son loves stuffed mushrooms, we came up with this wild-game appetizer. We enjoy it before the big meal is served.

12 large fresh mushrooms

3 to 4 whole dove or quail, cooked and deboned

1 cup (4 ounces) shredded cheddar cheese

1 serrano or jalapeno pepper, seeded

Salt and pepper to taste

2 bacon strips, cooked and crumbled

[1] Remove stems from mushrooms; set caps aside. (Discard stems or save for another use.) In a food processor, combine the dove, cheese, serrano, salt and pepper. Cover and pulse until finely chopped.

[2] Stuff mushroom caps with meat mixture. Sprinkle with bacon. Place on a baking sheet. Bake at 400° for 10-15 minutes or until cheese is melted. **Yield:** 1 dozen.

Editor's Note: When cutting or seeding hot peppers, use rubber or plastic gloves to protect your hands. Avoid touching your face.

jalapeno quail appetizers

2 large jalapeno peppers, halved lengthwise and seeded

12 boneless quail breasts (about 1 pound)

12 bacon strips

1 bottle (16 ounces) Italian salad dressing

[1] Cut each jalapeno half into three long strips. Place a strip widthwise in the center of each quail breast; roll up from a short side. Wrap each with a bacon strip and secure with toothpicks. Place in a large resealable plastic bag. Add salad dressing; seal bag and turn to coat. Refrigerate for 8 hours or overnight.

[2] Drain and discard marinade. Grill appetizers, covered, over indirect medium heat for 16-20 minutes or until quail juices run clear and bacon is crisp, turning occasionally. **Yield:** 1 dozen.

Editor's Note: When cutting or seeding hot peppers, use rubber or plastic gloves to protect your hands. Avoid touching your face.

DIANA JOHNSTON KINGSTON, OKLAHOMA

My husband quail hunts every season, and this recipe has become our favorite way to serve the birds. The bacon keeps the meat from drying out, and the jalapeno lends a little zip. I sometimes serve these cute bundles as a main dish.

JALAPENO QUAIL APPETIZERS

**DAWN BRYANT
NORTH PLATTE,
NEBRASKA**

My husband and I do a lot of hunting and eat more wild game than domestic meat. I came up with this recipe for wild rabbit, and the meat cooks up tender and tangy with a fresh, light sauce. I like to serve it with baked potatoes and steamed broccoli.

braised rabbit

    1 dressed rabbit (2½ pounds), cut into serving-size pieces
  ¼ cup olive oil
    1 large onion, halved and thinly sliced
    4 garlic cloves, minced
    2 cups chicken broth
1½ teaspoons dried thyme
  ¼ teaspoon pepper
    1 bay leaf
  ¼ cup all-purpose flour
  ¼ cup lemon juice
    5 tablespoons cold water

[1] In a large skillet over medium heat, cook rabbit in oil until lightly browned; remove and keep warm. In the same skillet, saute onion and garlic until tender. Stir in the broth, thyme, pepper and bay leaf. Return rabbit to pan. Bring to a boil. Reduce heat; cover and simmer for 30-45 minutes or until meat is tender and a meat thermometer reads 160°.

[2] Remove rabbit to a serving platter. Discard bay leaf. Combine the flour, lemon juice and water until smooth; stir into pan juices. Bring to a boil; cook and stir for 2 minutes or until thickened. Serve with rabbit. **Yield:** 4 servings.

BRAISED RABBIT

italian-style duck

**EDNA WATTS
ARLEY, ALABAMA**

Tender duck breasts are smothered in thick tomato sauce and melted mozzarella and cheddar cheeses. With pasta on the side, this attractive entree is special enough to serve when company comes.

    1 small onion, chopped
    1 cup sliced fresh mushrooms
    6 tablespoons butter, divided
    1 can (29 ounces) tomato sauce
  ½ cup grated Parmesan cheese
  ½ cup minced fresh parsley, divided
    1 envelope spaghetti sauce mix
  ½ cup all-purpose flour
1½ teaspoons onion salt
1½ teaspoons garlic salt
    8 boneless skinless duck breast halves
  ½ cup shredded part-skim mozzarella cheese
  ½ cup shredded cheddar cheese
Hot cooked pasta

[1] In a saucepan, saute onion and mushrooms in 2 tablespoons butter until tender. Stir in the tomato sauce, Parmesan cheese, ¼ cup parsley and spaghetti sauce mix. Bring to a boil. Reduce heat; cover and simmer for 15 minutes, stirring occasionally.

[2] In a shallow dish, combine the flour, onion salt and garlic salt; coat duck pieces. In a large skillet, brown duck on both sides in remaining butter. Place in an ungreased 13-in. x 9-in. x 2-in. baking dish. Top with tomato mixture; sprinkle with cheeses.

[3] Bake, uncovered, at 375° for 28-32 minutes or until a meat thermometer reads 180°. Sprinkle with remaining parsley. Serve with pasta. **Yield:** 8 servings.

creamed grouse on toast

    2 quarts water
    1 bay leaf
    4 grouse or squab (¾ to 1 pound each)

CREAMED GROUSE ON TOAST

¹⁄₂ cup chopped onion

¹⁄₂ cup sliced fresh mushrooms

2 tablespoons butter

2 tablespoons all-purpose flour

1 cup chicken broth

2 tablespoons lemon juice

¹⁄₂ teaspoon salt

¹⁄₈ teaspoon pepper

¹⁄₄ cup heavy whipping cream

2 tablespoons minced fresh parsley

Toast or hot cooked rice

Chopped fresh parsley, optional

[1] In a Dutch oven, bring water, bay leaf and grouse to a boil. Reduce heat; cover and simmer until meat is tender. Remove grouse; cool. Debone and cut into pieces. Strain broth; set aside.

[2] In a skillet over medium heat, saute onion and mushrooms in butter until tender. Add flour. Stir in the broth, lemon juice, salt and pepper; bring to a boil. Cook and stir for 2 minutes.

[3] Add grouse and heat through. Add cream and parsley; mix well. Heat through. Serve over toast or rice; garnish with parsley if desired. **Yield:** 4 servings.

HUNTING & FISHING tip

I think game birds are best when boned, the meat cut into strips, lightly coated in flour and crushed crackers, and then gently fried. Remember that they have very little fat and won't necessarily hold up to traditional methods of preparing poultry.

KELLY, MISSOURI

HUNTING & FISHING COOKBOOK

PHEASANT POTPIE

[1] In a large saucepan or Dutch oven, place pheasants, water, quartered onion, celery and garlic; bring to a boil. Reduce heat; cover and simmer for 1 hour or until tender. Remove meat from bones and set aside.

[2] Strain broth, discarding vegetables. Measure 3½ cups broth and place in saucepan. Add lemon juice, salt, pepper, Worcestershire sauce and nutmeg. Remove ½ cup and stir in flour. Bring broth in saucepan to a boil. Add flour mixture; boil 1 minute or until thickened and bubbly.

[3] Add the pearl onions, peas, carrots, pimientos, parsley and pheasant; mix well. Spoon into a 2½-qt. baking dish. Roll pastry to fit dish; place over meat mixture and seal edges to dish. Cut small steam vents in crust. Bake at 425° for 35-40 minutes or until bubbly and golden. **Yield:** 6 servings.

barbecued wild duck

GLORIA WEDO
SLAYTON, MINNESOTA

Our three grown sons still request this finger-licking dish each fall. Basting with the homemade barbecue sauce keeps the poultry nice and moist.

TAWNYA COYNE
HARRISBURG,
PENNSYLVANIA

A hearty meal in itself, this savory pie features delicious pheasant. Here in central Pennsylvania, that game bird isn't as plentiful as in times past, and so this dish is a real treat. I make it for special occasions.

pheasant potpie

2 pheasants (2½ pounds each)

4 cups water

1 medium onion, quartered

1 garlic clove, minced

2 tablespoons lemon juice

1¼ teaspoons salt

½ teaspoon pepper

¼ teaspoon Worcestershire sauce

⅛ teaspoon ground nutmeg

¾ cup all-purpose flour

1 jar (16 ounces) pearl onions, drained

1 package (10 ounces) frozen peas

1½ cups sliced carrots

1 jar (2 ounces) sliced pimientos, drained

¼ cup minced fresh parsley

Pastry for single-crust pie

2 wild ducks (1 pound each), split in half

¼ cup butter

½ cup ketchup

½ cup chopped onion

1 garlic clove, minced

5 teaspoons lemon juice

1 tablespoon brown sugar

1 tablespoon Worcestershire sauce

1 teaspoon salt

½ teaspoon hot pepper sauce

[1] Place ducks in a 13-in. x 9-in. x 2-in. baking dish. Cover and bake at 350° for 1¾ to 2 hours until a meat thermometer reads 180° and meat is tender.

tip
HUNTING & FISHING

To prepare game meat for the freezer, I vacuum seal it. My husband is a meat cutter and that is how we store it. The meat does not get any freezer burn at all.

ANGELA, WEST VIRGINIA

[2] Meanwhile, combine the remaining ingredients in a saucepan; bring to a boil. Reduce heat; cover and simmer for 5 minutes. Baste ducks with sauce during the last 30 minutes of baking time. **Yield:** 4 servings.

slow-cooked goose

EDNA YLIOJA
LUCKY LAKE, SASKATCHEWAN

My husband, Willard, and I own a hunting lodge and host about 16 hunters a week at our camp. The slow cooker makes easy work of fixing this flavorful goose dish, which is a favorite of our guests. The recipe makes lots of savory gravy to serve over mashed potatoes.

$1/2$ cup soy sauce
4 teaspoons vegetable oil
4 teaspoons lemon juice
2 teaspoons Worcestershire sauce
1 teaspoon garlic powder
2 pounds cubed goose breast
$3/4$ to 1 cup all-purpose flour
$1/4$ cup butter
1 can ($10^3/4$ ounces) condensed golden mushroom soup, undiluted
$1^1/3$ cups water
1 envelope onion soup mix
Hot cooked mashed potatoes, noodles or rice

[1] In a large resealable plastic bag, combine the soy sauce, oil, lemon juice, Worcestershire sauce and garlic powder; add goose. Seal bag and turn to coat. Refrigerate for 4 hours or overnight.

[2] Drain and discard marinade. Place flour in another large resealable plastic bag; add goose in batches and shake to coat. In a large skillet over medium heat, melt butter. Brown goose on all sides. Transfer to a slow cooker.

[3] Add soup, water and soup mix. Cover and cook on high for 4-5 hours or until meat is tender. Serve over potatoes, noodles or rice. **Yield:** 4 servings.

rabbit with tarragon sauce

$1/2$ cup all-purpose flour
2 teaspoons dried tarragon
$1^1/2$ teaspoons salt
1 teaspoon pepper
2 rabbits (2 to $2^1/2$ pounds each), cut up
$1/4$ cup butter
$1/4$ cup vegetable oil
2 cups chicken broth

[1] In a large resealable plastic bag, combine flour, tarragon, salt and pepper. Add the rabbit pieces, one at a time, and shake well.

[2] In a large skillet, melt butter; add oil. Saute the rabbit pieces, a few at a time, until browned. Add broth; cover and simmer for 50-60 minutes or until tender. Thicken the pan juices if desired. **Yield:** 8 servings.

YVONNE KESSLER PANGMAN, SASKATCHEWAN

Golden rabbit pieces drizzled with a savory gravy make this a satisfying, stick-to-your-ribs main dish. One of my favorite herbs, tarragon, provides subtle flavor that goes so well with rabbit.

RABBIT WITH TARRAGON SAUCE

CHRIS
SENDELBACH
HENRY, ILLINOIS

Succulent quail with a snappy sauce makes an impressive entree. This dish tastes wonderful over rice or toast points. Sometimes I'll use cinnamon toast to add delicate flavor.

quail with mushroom sauce

- 2 tablespoons lemon juice
- 6 whole quail (5 to 6 ounces each)
- 1/8 teaspoon pepper
- 2 tablespoons vegetable oil
- 2 tablespoons butter
- 3 tablespoons all-purpose flour
- 1 tablespoon minced fresh parsley
- 1 teaspoon dried minced onion
- 2 cups chicken broth
- 1 jar (4 1/2 ounces) sliced mushrooms, drained
- 1/4 cup water
- 1/8 teaspoon hot pepper sauce

Hot cooked rice

[1] Drizzle lemon juice over quail; sprinkle with pepper. In a large skillet, brown quail in oil and butter, turning frequently; remove and set aside.

[2] Stir flour, parsley and onion into the drippings until blended. Gradually stir in broth, mushrooms, water and hot pepper sauce. Bring to a boil. Reduce heat; return quail to pan. Cover and simmer for 20-30 minutes or until meat is tender. Serve with rice. **Yield:** 6 servings.

pheasant stir-fry

(PICTURED ON PAGE 43)

DARLENE KENNING
HUTCHINSON, MINNESOTA

I learned creative ways to prepare game while cooking for hunters at a lodge in Alaska, where my husband was a guide. Everyone enjoyed this savory stir-fry. It looks as good as it tastes.

- 2 tablespoons soy sauce
- 2 tablespoons cornstarch
- 1 tablespoon minced fresh gingerroot or 3/4 teaspoon ground ginger
- 1 tablespoon chicken bouillon granules

QUAIL WITH MUSHROOM SAUCE

1⅓ cups water

1 boneless skinless pheasant breast (about ¾ pound), cut into strips

2 tablespoons vegetable oil, divided

1 cup broccoli florets

1 cup each julienned carrots, celery and onion

1 cup frozen snow peas

Hot cooked white or wild rice

[1] In a small bowl, combine the soy sauce, cornstarch, ginger and bouillon. Add water; set aside. In a skillet or wok over medium-high heat, stir-fry pheasant in 1 tablespoon of oil until no longer pink, about 3-4 minutes. Remove and keep warm.

[2] Add remaining oil to pan. Stir-fry broccoli and carrots for 2 minutes. Add celery, onion and peas; stir-fry until the vegetables are crisp-tender, about 4-5 minutes.

[3] Stir soy sauce mixture and add to the skillet; bring to a boil. Cook and stir for 2 minutes. Return meat to pan and heat through. Serve over rice. **Yield:** 4 servings.

wild duck gumbo

2 wild ducks, cut up

½ cup vegetable oil

⅔ cup all-purpose flour

1 pound smoked sausage, sliced

2 cups chopped onion

1½ cups chopped green pepper

1½ cups sliced celery

2 tablespoons minced fresh parsley

1 tablespoon minced garlic

1 can (14½ ounces) stewed tomatoes

2 bay leaves

2 tablespoons Worcestershire sauce

1½ teaspoons pepper

1 teaspoon salt

1 teaspoon dried thyme

¼ teaspoon cayenne pepper

2 quarts water

Hot cooked rice

WILD DUCK GUMBO

[1] In a Dutch oven over medium heat, brown duck in batches in oil. Remove and set aside. Discard all but ⅔ cup drippings. Add flour to drippings; cook and stir over medium heat until brown, about 12-14 minutes.

[2] Add sausage, onion, green pepper, celery, parsley and garlic. Cook for 10 minutes, stirring occasionally. Add next eight ingredients; mix well.

[3] Add duck; bring to a boil. Reduce heat; cover and simmer 60-75 minutes or until duck is tender.

[4] Remove duck. Cool. Debone and cut into chunks; return to pan. Simmer 5-10 minutes or until heated through. Remove the bay leaves. Serve with rice. **Yield:** 16 servings (4 quarts).

DORIS HEATH BRYSON CITY, NORTH CAROLINA

Our family and friends just love this delightful, rich gumbo—it's such a unique way to serve this wild bird. We like that the meat is tender but not greasy. With all the wonderful spices, this gumbo is a flavorful main dish.

HUNTING & FISHING tip

To grill small-game bird breasts, like dove, marinate them in a mixture that's half water and half wine, lemon juice or vinegar for at least 20 minutes. Drain the meat and sprinkle with Cajun seasoning. Wrap each breast in a half piece of bacon secured with toothpicks and grill.

BECKY, GEORGIA

HUNTING & FISHING COOKBOOK

**DEB MCCOIC
HILLSBORO,
WISCONSIN**

Everyone in my family hunts, so we have an abundance of game. This recipe also works well with wild turkey or grouse and even with chicken if you prefer. I love to make this dish on special occasions and for guests.

PHEASANT AND WILD RICE

pheasant and wild rice

    1 can (10³⁄₄ ounces) condensed cream of mushroom soup, undiluted

    2 soup cans water

    ³⁄₄ cup chopped onion

 2¹⁄₂ teaspoons dried parsley flakes

    2 teaspoons dried oregano

    2 teaspoons garlic powder

    2 teaspoons salt

 1¹⁄₂ teaspoons paprika

    1 teaspoon pepper

    6 bacon strips, cut up

    1 oven cooking bag

    2 cups uncooked wild rice

    ¹⁄₂ pound fresh mushrooms, sliced

    1 large pheasant, halved or 2 small pheasants (about 4 pounds)

[1] In a saucepan, combine first nine ingredients; bring to a boil. Meanwhile, place the bacon in an oven cooking bag. Sprinkle rice and mushrooms over bacon. Add pheasant. Pour soup mixture into bag. Seal and slit according to package directions.

[2] Bake at 325° for 2 to 2¹⁄₂ hours or until a meat thermometer reads 180°. Let the pheasant stand for 10 minutes before carving. **Yield:** 6-8 servings.

quail with creamy mushroom sauce

**JOELANN SYGO
GAYLORD, MICHIGAN**

This golden quail is so moist and tender. The rich cream sauce, dotted with onions and mushrooms, complements the bird nicely.

    2 cups sliced fresh mushrooms

    1 small onion, sliced

    4 tablespoons butter, divided

    1 pound boneless quail breast or boneless skinless chicken breast halves

    1 package (3 ounces) cream cheese, softened

¼ to ½ cup milk

½ cup dry bread crumbs, toasted

[1] In a skillet, saute mushrooms and onion in 2 tablespoons butter. Remove and set aside. In the same skillet, melt remaining butter; saute quail over medium heat for 8 minutes on each side.

[2] Meanwhile, in a small saucepan, heat and stir cream cheese and milk over low heat until smooth. Stir in sauteed mushrooms and onion. Sprinkle bread crumbs over both sides of quail; serve with mushroom sauce. **Yield:** 4 servings.

rice-stuffed squab

1 cup chopped celery

½ cup chopped onion

3 tablespoons butter

1½ cups cooked rice

1½ cups chopped fresh mushrooms

⅓ to ½ cup raisins

6 tablespoons orange juice concentrate, divided

1 tablespoon minced fresh parsley

1½ teaspoons salt, divided

¾ teaspoon dried marjoram

6 dressed squab (about 1 pound each)

¾ cup vegetable oil

[1] In a skillet, saute celery and onion in butter until tender. Add rice, mushrooms, raisins, 3 tablespoons orange juice concentrate, parsley, ¾ teaspoon salt and marjoram. Sprinkle cavities of squab lightly with remaining salt; stuff with rice mixture.

[2] Place on a rack in a roasting pan. Combine oil and remaining orange juice concentrate; brush over squab. Bake, uncovered, at 375° for 1 hour or until meat juices run clear and a meat thermometer inserted into the stuffing reads 165°, basting frequently. **Yield:** 6 servings.

**PEGGY LECZA
BRANFORD,
CONNECTICUT**

For company or family, you'll be proud to serve these golden game birds. The rich-tasting dark meat goes well with the savory rice stuffing, which includes onion, celery, fresh mushrooms and sweet raisins.

RICE-STUFFED SQUAB

HUNTING & FISHING COOKBOOK

TAMMY ROSE GARNAVILLO, IOWA

Since we have avid hunters in our family, I will quite often prepare game. Once it's stuffed with apples and topped with a unique combination of sauces, this wild bird requires no basting and cooks up well.

roasted wild turkey

- 1 wild turkey (10 to 15 pounds)
- 2 large apples, quartered
- 6 to 8 medium red potatoes, quartered
- 2 pounds baby carrots
- 2 medium onions, sliced
- 2 cups water
- 1½ teaspoons seasoned salt
- 1 teaspoon salt
- 1 teaspoon pepper
- ½ cup maple syrup
- ¼ cup French salad dressing
- ¼ cup barbecue sauce
- 2 tablespoons ketchup
- 2 tablespoons steak sauce
- 1 tablespoon lemon juice

[1] Place turkey on a rack in a roasting pan; place apples in turkey cavity. Place potatoes, carrots and onions around turkey. Pour water over vegetables. Combine seasoned salt, salt and pepper; rub over turkey. Combine remaining ingredients; brush over the turkey.

[2] Cover and bake at 325° for 3½ hours or until a meat thermometer reads 180°, basting if desired. Turkey may be uncovered for the last 30 minutes for additional browning if desired. **Yield:** 10-12 servings.

wild goose with giblet stuffing

**LOUISE LAGINESS
EAST JORDAN, MICHIGAN**

This recipe is one of our favorite ways to prepare goose, and it's especially nice for the holidays. My husband does a lot of hunting, so I'm always looking for new ways to fix game.

- 1 dressed wild goose (6 to 8 pounds)

Lemon wedges

Salt

ROASTED WILD TURKEY

LOU BISHOP
PHILLIPS,
WISCONSIN
Pheasant is moist,
tender and flavorful
prepared this way.

BAKED PHEASANT IN GRAVY

HUNTING & FISHING COOKBOOK

STUFFING:
Goose giblets

- 2 cups water
- 10 cups crumbled corn bread
- 2 large Granny Smith apples, chopped
- 1 large onion, chopped
- 1/3 cup minced fresh parsley
- 1 to 2 tablespoons rubbed sage
- 1 teaspoon salt
- 1/4 teaspoon pepper
- 1/4 teaspoon garlic powder

Butter, softened

[1] Rub inside goose cavity with lemon and salt; set aside. In a saucepan, cook giblets in water until tender, about 20-30 minutes. Remove giblets with a slotted spoon and reserve liquid. Chop giblets and place in a large bowl with the corn bread, apples, onion, parsley, sage, salt, pepper and garlic powder. Add enough of the reserved cooking liquid to make a moist stuffing; toss gently.

[2] Stuff the body and neck cavity; truss openings. Place goose, breast side up, on a rack in a shallow roasting pan. Spread with softened butter. Bake, uncovered, at 325° for 25 minutes per pound or until tender and a meat thermometer reads 180°. If goose is an older

bird, add 1 cup of water to pan and cover for the last hour of baking. **Yield:** 6-8 servings.

baked pheasant in gravy

- 1/2 cup all-purpose flour
- 1/2 cup packed brown sugar
- 6 pheasant or grouse breast halves
- 3 tablespoons butter
- 1 can (10 3/4 ounces) condensed cream of celery soup, undiluted
- 1 to 1 1/3 cups water
- 1 cup chicken broth
- 1 can (2.8 ounces) french-fried onions

Mashed potatoes or hot cooked rice

[1] In a large resealable plastic bag, combine flour and brown sugar; add pheasant pieces, one at time, and shake to coat. In a large skillet over medium heat, brown pheasant on both sides in butter. Transfer to a greased 13-in. x 9-in. x 2-in. baking dish.

[2] Combine soup, water and broth until blended; pour over pheasant. Bake, uncovered, at 350° for 40 minutes. Sprinkle with onions. Bake 5-10 minutes longer or until juices run clear. Serve with potatoes or rice. **Yield:** 6 servings.

SHARON
SHAMOSH
ROCKVILLE
CENTER,
NEW YORK

My Uncle Stanley, an avid hunter and fisherman, encouraged me to try game cooking, and this recipe is one of my successes. The tangy orange-cranberry sauce that complements the tender meat makes it ideal for the holidays.

pheasant with cranberry sauce

1 pheasant (2 to 3 pounds)
1/4 teaspoon salt, divided
1/4 teaspoon pepper, divided
2 tablespoons butter, melted
1 package (12 ounces) fresh or frozen cranberries, thawed
1 cup sugar
1 cup orange juice
1/2 teaspoon ground cinnamon
2 tablespoons grated orange peel

[1] Sprinkle cavity of pheasant with 1/8 teaspoon salt and 1/8 teaspoon pepper. Place pheasant on a rack in shallow roasting pan. Brush with butter; sprinkle with remaining salt and pepper.

PHEASANT WITH CRANBERRY SAUCE

[2] Cover and bake at 325° for 45 minutes. Uncover; bake 40-60 minutes longer or until a meat thermometer reads 180°, basting with pan juices frequently.

[3] Meanwhile, in a large saucepan, combine the cranberries, sugar, orange juice and cinnamon. Cook over medium heat for 10-12 minutes or until the berries begin to pop, stirring frequently. Stir in the orange peel. Simmer 5 minutes longer. Cover pheasant with foil and let stand for 10 minutes before carving. Serve pheasant with sauce. **Yield:** 3 servings.

partridge with wild rice

GARY MILLER
RIGGINS, IDAHO

I'm happy to share this flavorful game bird recipe featuring tender partridge on a bed of well-seasoned wild rice. You can use whatever type of bird you have in your area.

1 package (6.7 ounces) mushroom-flavored brown and wild rice mix
1/4 cup all-purpose flour
2 partridge game birds (14 ounces each), split lengthwise
2 tablespoons vegetable oil
1 cup milk
1/4 teaspoon pepper

[1] Prepare rice according to package directions. Place flour in a large resealable plastic bag; add game birds and shake to coat. In a large skillet, cook birds in oil until browned; remove. Add milk and pepper to skillet; cook and stir until heated through.

[2] Place the rice in a greased 9-in. square baking dish. Top with game birds and milk mixture. Bake, uncovered, at 350° for 40-50 minutes or until a meat thermometer reads 180° and meat is tender. **Yield:** 2 servings.

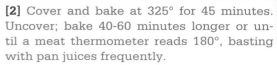

tip HUNTING & FISHING

For moist wild turkey, lay some strips of bacon over the breast meat and cook in an oven bag.

N. McCULLOUGH, PENNSYLVANIA

QUAIL WITH RICE

quail with rice

4 bacon strips, halved

8 quail (about 2 pounds)

1 cup shredded carrots

1/2 cup sliced green onions

1/2 cup minced fresh parsley

2 1/2 cups chicken broth

1 cup uncooked long grain rice

1/2 teaspoon salt

1/4 teaspoon lemon-pepper seasoning

[1] In a large skillet over medium heat, cook bacon until partially done. Remove bacon; drain, reserving 2 tablespoons drippings. Brown quail in drippings. Remove and keep warm.

[2] Saute carrots, onions and parsley in drippings until tender. Add broth, rice, salt and lemon-pepper; bring to a boil. Place quail over rice; place one bacon strip on each. Reduce heat; cover and simmer for 25-30 minutes or until the rice is tender and quail is cooked. **Yield:** 4 servings.

LENORA PICOLET DWIGHT, KANSAS

Quail is a family favorite every fall when my husband goes hunting. It's a special meal, using only one skillet, so there's hardly any cleanup or fuss.

CAROL HEUSCHKEL WINSTED, CONNECTICUT

My husband and I created this lower-fat version as a palate-pleasing alternative to traditional pork sausage. It's moist, flavorful and delicious. We especially enjoy it for breakfast or brunch.

RABBIT BREAKFAST SAUSAGE

rabbit breakfast sausage

1 dressed and boned rabbit (6 pounds), cut up

2 teaspoons salt

1 1/2 teaspoons rubbed sage

1 1/4 teaspoons white pepper

3/4 teaspoon ground nutmeg

1/2 teaspoon ground cinnamon

1 cup finely chopped peeled tart apple

2 tablespoons vegetable oil

[1] In a bowl, combine the first six ingredients; mix well. Cover and refrigerate overnight.

[2] In a meat grinder or food processor, process the mixture in small batches until coarsely ground. Stir in apple. Shape into 16 patties, 3 in. each.

[3] Heat oil in a skillet; cook patties over medium heat for 5 minutes on each side or until sausage is browned and inside is no longer pink. **Yield:** 8 servings.

pheasant in mustard sauce

JOAN MIHALKO
ELKTON, SOUTH DAKOTA

Until I met my husband, an avid hunter, I'd never cooked or eaten pheasant. I tried several different recipes before creating this one using our favorite ingredients.

2 boneless skinless pheasant breast halves

1/4 teaspoon salt

1/8 teaspoon pepper

1 tablespoon vegetable oil

1 tablespoon butter

1/4 cup chopped onion

1 garlic clove, minced

1/2 cup chicken broth

2 tablespoons lemon juice

3 tablespoons Dijon mustard

3/4 teaspoon dried marjoram

Hot cooked rice

[1] Sprinkle pheasant with salt and pepper. In a skillet over medium heat, brown pheasant in oil and butter on both sides, about 6-8 minutes.

[2] Combine onion, garlic, broth, lemon juice, mustard and marjoram; add to skillet. Bring to a boil. Reduce heat; cover and simmer for 15-20 minutes or until pheasant juices run clear. Serve over rice. **Yield:** 2 servings.

wild turkey bake

1 package (6 ounces) long grain and wild rice mix

1 teaspoon chicken bouillon granules

1 cup hot water

3½ cups cubed fully cooked wild turkey

1½ cups chopped celery

1 can (10¾ ounces) condensed cream of mushrooms soup, undiluted

1 can (8 ounces) sliced water chestnuts, drained

1 jar (6 ounces) sliced mushrooms, drained

½ cup chopped onion

¼ cup soy sauce

1 cup soft bread crumbs

2 tablespoons butter, melted

[1] Prepare rice according to package directions; place in a large bowl. Dissolve bouillon in hot water; add to rice. Stir in the turkey, celery, soup, water chestnuts, mushrooms, onion and soy sauce.

[2] Transfer to a greased 3-qt. baking dish. Toss bread crumbs and butter; sprinkle over the top. Bake, uncovered, at 350° for 55-60 minutes or until heated through. **Yield:** 8 servings.

HUNTING & FISHING

Wild turkey meat has the edge over its domestic cousins. Wild turkey has a little over two percent more ~~ein~~, a half percent less fat and slightly less choles- ~~than~~ domestic turkey. In addition, the quantity ~~t~~ is not only generally lower in wild game, but it is healthier since it contains less saturated fat.

NATIONAL WILD TURKEY FEDERATION

Get Fit for Turkey Hunting

Unlike deer or duck hunting, where a hunter generally spends hours sitting still in a tree stand or blind, turkey hunting requires a good deal of walking. Most turkey hunts require the hunter to walk moderate to long distances while scouting or trying to locate the birds.

This can also require traveling up and down hills, around trees, over logs and traversing creeks. The hunter may be in for a formidable workout.

If you have a generally sedentary lifestyle, a few months, or even weeks, of exercise before the season starts could help decrease the risk of health problems in the woods and help you meet the physical challenges of the hunt.

Other things to remember are to rest often and drink plenty of water. Staying hydrated can determine how good you feel during and after the hunt.

National Wild Turkey Federation

**MARGARET HILL
ROANOKE,
VIRGINIA**

Wild rice, turkey and vegetables are combined in a savory sauce and topped with golden crumbs in this hearty dish. Cooked wild turkey can be a little dry, but not when it's prepared this way. I never have leftovers.

WILD TURKEY BAKE

HUNTING & FISHING COOKBOOK

**SUE JURACK
MEQUON,
WISCONSIN**

This duck entree has a fresh orange sauce that's sure to excite your taste buds.

duck a l'orange

- 1 **package (6.2 ounces) fast-cooking long grain and wild rice mix**
- 1 **domestic duck (4 to 6 pounds)**
- ¼ **cup thawed orange juice concentrate**
- 3 **tablespoons honey**
- 2 **tablespoons butter, melted**
- 2 **tablespoons soy sauce**

SAUCE:
- ¼ **cup thawed orange juice concentrate**
- 1 **cup water**
- 1 **tablespoon cornstarch**
- 2 **tablespoons cold water**
- ⅛ **teaspoon salt**

[1] Prepare rice mix according to package directions. Prick skin of duckling well with a fork. Loosely stuff duckling with wild rice mix. Skewer neck openings; tie drumsticks together. Place breast side up on a rack in a shallow roasting pan. In a bowl, combine the orange juice concentrate, honey, butter and soy sauce; set aside.

[2] Bake, uncovered at 350° for 1 hour. Baste with orange juice mixture. Bake 1¼ to 2 hours longer or until a meat thermometer reads 180° for the duckling and 165° for the stuffing, basting occasionally with orange juice mixture. (Drain fat from pan as it accumulates).

[3] Cover loosely with foil if duckling browns to quickly. Cover and let stand for 20 minutes before removing stuffing and carving. Discard any remaining basting sauce.

[4] For orange sauce, in a small saucepan, combine orange juice concentrate and water; bring to a boil. Combine cornstarch and cold water until smooth. Stir into orange sauce; cook and stir for 2 minutes or until thickened. Season with salt. Serve with duck. **Yield:** 4-6 servings.

DUCK A L'ORA

stuffed duckling

JOANNE CALLAHAN
FAR HILLS, NEW JERSEY

I started with a basic bread stuffing and added on-hand ingredients until I came up with this pleasing recipe. The stuffing usually disappears long before the bird is gone!

- 1/2 cup chopped onion
- 1 garlic clove, minced
- 1 tablespoon butter
- 2 cups cubed day-old bread
- 1 cup cooked rice
- 1 teaspoon dried basil
- 1 teaspoon dried rosemary, crushed
- 1 teaspoon rubbed sage
- 1 teaspoon dried parsley flakes
- 1 teaspoon salt, divided
- 1/8 teaspoon pepper
- 1/2 cup raisins
- 1/2 cup chopped pecans
- 1/4 to 1/3 cup chicken broth
- 1 domestic duckling (4 to 5 pounds)

[1] In a large skillet, saute onion and garlic in butter until tender; transfer to a large bowl. Add the bread cubes, rice, basil, rosemary, sage, parsley flakes, 1/2 teaspoon salt and pepper. Add the raisins, pecans and enough broth to moisten; toss gently.

[2] Sprinkle duck cavity with remaining salt. Lightly stuff bread mixture into duck. Place breast side up on a rack in shallow roasting pan. Prick skin well with a fork.

[3] Bake, uncovered, at 350° for 1-3/4 to 2 hours or until a meat thermometer reads 180° for duck and 165° for stuffing. Drain fat as it accumulates during roasting. Cover duck with foil and let stand for 20 minutes before removing stuffing and carving. **Yield:** 4 servings.

HUNTING & FISHING

ip

Ducklings and geese have more fat than other poultry. To re- [remov]e the fat, prick the skin with a sharp tined [fork] before roasting to allow the fat to drain.

TASTE OF HOME TEST KITCHEN

GOOSE WITH APPLE-RAISIN STUFFING

goose with apple-raisin stuffing

- 1 domestic goose (10 to 12 pounds)
- 1 cup chopped celery
- 1 cup chopped onion
- 2 tablespoons butter
- 3 cups chopped peeled apples
- 2 cups raisins
- 8 cups cubed day-old white bread
- 2 to 3 tablespoons sugar
- 1 teaspoon salt
- 2 eggs
- 1/2 cup apple cider
- 1/2 cup water

[1] Sprinkle the inside of the goose with salt. Prick skin well; set aside. In a skillet, saute the celery and onion in butter; transfer to a large bowl. Add the apples, raisins, bread, sugar and salt.

[2] In a small bowl, beat eggs, cider and water. Pour over bread mixture and toss lightly. Stuff into the goose. Place with breast side up on a rack in a large shallow roasting pan.

[3] Bake, uncovered, at 350° for 3 to 3-1/2 hours or until a meat thermometer reads 180°. Drain fat from pan as it accumulates. Remove all dressing. **Yield:** 8-10 servings.

DENISE GOEDEKEN PLATTE CENTER, NEBRASKA

A tempting Thanksgiving goose is a family tradition I've kept up. Paired with moist, lightly sweet apple-raisin stuffing, it's a special main dish that makes us count our blessings.

HUNTING & FISHING COOKBOOK

**DONNA SMITH
FAIRPORT,
NEW YORK**

For over 60 years, this elegant entree has graced my family's holiday table. The zesty stuffing with its nice nutty crunch complements the slices of moist duck, while the hint of orange in the gravy sets it apart.

DUCK WITH ORANGE HAZELNUT STUFFING

duck with orange hazelnut stuffing

  2 **domestic ducklings (4 to 5 pounds each)**

  1 **teaspoon salt**

STUFFING:

  4 **cups coarse soft bread crumbs**

  2 **cups chopped peeled tart apple**

  2 **cups chopped toasted hazelnuts**

  1 **cup chopped celery**

  1/2 **cup chopped onion**

  1/2 **cup orange juice**

  2 **eggs, beaten**

  1/4 **cup butter, melted**

  2 **to 3 tablespoons lemon juice**

  2 **teaspoons grated orange peel**

1 1/2 **teaspoons grated lemon peel**

  1 **teaspoon seasoned salt**

  1/2 **teaspoon pepper**

  1/2 **teaspoon dried thyme**

  1/4 **teaspoon ground nutmeg**

GRAVY:

  3 **tablespoons all-purpose flour**

  1/4 **teaspoon salt**

  1/8 **teaspoon pepper**

  2 **cups chicken broth**

  1/3 **cup orange marmalade**

[1] Sprinkle the inside of ducks with salt; prick skin several times and set aside. Combine the first 15 stuffing ingredients; spoon into ducks.

[2] Place with breast side up on a rack in a large shallow roasting pan. Brush with butter. Bake, uncovered, at 350° for 2 to 2 1/2 hours or until a meat thermometer reads 180° for duck and 165° for stuffing.

[3] Remove all stuffing and keep warm. For gravy, combine 3 tablespoons pan drippings, flour, salt and pepper in a saucepan; stir until smooth. Heat until bubbly, stirring constantly. Gradually add broth. Bring to a boil; cook for 1-2 minutes, stirring constantly. Add the marmalade; stir until smooth.

[4] Serve sauce with ducks and stuffing. **Yield:** 8 servings.

roasted pheasants with oyster stuffing

**GLORIA WARCZAK
CEDARBURG, WISCONSIN**

Bacon-topped pheasants with delicious oyster stuffing: This is a hunter's dream holiday dinner. If you don't have wild pheasant, many meat departments can order it...or you could substitute two broiler-fryer chickens.

- 1 can (8 ounces) whole oysters
- 2 cups herb stuffing mix
- 2 cups corn bread stuffing mix
- 1 can (14$\frac{1}{2}$ ounces) chicken broth, divided
- 1 medium onion, chopped
- $\frac{1}{2}$ cup chopped celery
- $\frac{1}{4}$ cup egg substitute
- 2 pheasants (2 to 3 pounds each)
- 2 tablespoons Worcestershire sauce
- 1 teaspoon poultry seasoning
- 6 bacon strips

[1] Drain oysters, reserving liquid; coarsely chop oysters. In a large bowl, combine the oysters and liquid, stuffing mixes, $\frac{3}{4}$ cup broth, onion, celery and egg substitute. Loosely stuff into pheasants. Skewer or fasten openings. Tie drumsticks together. Place breast side up on a rack in a roasting pan.

[2] Combine the Worcestershire sauce and the remaining broth; spoon over the pheasants. Sprinkle with poultry seasoning. Place three bacon strips over each pheasant.

[3] Bake, uncovered, at 350° for 1$\frac{1}{4}$ to 1$\frac{1}{2}$ hours or until a meat thermometer reads 180° for poultry and 165° for stuffing. Cover and let stand for 10 minutes before removing stuffing and slicing. **Yield:** 6-8 servings.

HUNTING & FISHING

Oyster dressing is a tradition with me. If you put the oysters [thro]ugh the food processor until they're liquefied, [o]yster taste is more evenly distributed.

P.L. LIPKER, FLORIDA

mandarin goose

- 1 domestic goose (12 to 14 pounds)
Salt
- 1 tablespoon all-purpose flour
- 1 tablespoon ground mustard
- $\frac{1}{2}$ cup port wine or $\frac{1}{4}$ cup grape juice plus $\frac{1}{4}$ cup chicken broth
- $\frac{1}{4}$ cup orange juice
- 1 medium onion, quartered
- $\frac{1}{4}$ cup plum or red raspberry jam
- 2 tablespoons cornstarch
- 2 tablespoons cold water
- 1 can (11 ounces) mandarin oranges, drained

[1] Sprinkle inside of goose with salt. Prick skin well; place breast side up on a rack in a large shallow roasting pan. In a small bowl, combine the flour and mustard; stir in wine and orange juice until smooth. Pour over goose. Add onion to pan. Bake, uncovered, at 350° for 3 to 3$\frac{1}{2}$ hours or until a meat thermometer reads 180° (cover with foil during the last hour to prevent goose from overbrowning).

[2] Discard onion. Cover goose and let stand 10-15 minutes before carving. Pour pan drippings into a 2-cup measuring cup; skim off fat. Add enough water to measure 2 cups.

[3] In a large saucepan, combine juices and jam. Combine cornstarch and water until smooth; add to juices. Bring to a boil; cook and stir for 2 minutes or until thickened. Stir in oranges. Serve with goose. **Yield:** 8-10 servings.

**PAULA MAGNUS
REPUBLIC,
WASHINGTON**

With mountains to the east, west and south of us and Canada to the north, we have ample opportunity to hunt. This succulent goose is one of our favorite dishes.

MANDARIN GOOSE

TASTE OF HOME TEST KITCHEN GREENDALE, WISCONSIN

As pretty as a picture with its caramelized seasoning rub, this festive goose is guaranteed to be a holiday showstopper! Best of all, it tastes as delicious as it looks and fills the house with an incredible aroma as it cooks.

spiced roast goose

- 4 cups water, divided
- $^2/_3$ cup plus 1 tablespoon soy sauce, divided
- $^1/_4$ cup chopped celery
- $^1/_4$ cup dried minced onion
- 1 tablespoon sugar
- 1 domestic goose (10 to 12 pounds)

Salt and pepper to taste

- 2 teaspoons ground cinnamon
- 1 teaspoon garlic powder
- 1 teaspoon aniseed
- $^1/_4$ cup cider vinegar
- $^1/_4$ cup honey
- 2 teaspoons cornstarch
- 2 tablespoons cold water

[1] In a large saucepan, combine 2 cups water, $^2/_3$ cup soy sauce, celery, onion and sugar. Bring to a boil, stirring frequently until vegetables are tender. Remove from the heat; allow to cool.

[2] Pour marinade into a large resealable plastic bag. Add goose; seal bag and turn to coat. Refrigerate for 3-4 hours, turning several times.

[3] Drain and discard marinade. Sprinkle goose cavity with salt and pepper. Place on a rack in a shallow roasting pan. Combine the cinnamon, garlic powder and aniseed; rub over goose. Bake, uncovered, at 325° for 30 minutes.

[4] Meanwhile, in a small saucepan, combine the vinegar, honey and remaining water and soy sauce. Bring to a boil. Reduce heat; simmer, uncovered, until reduced by about half.

[5] Baste goose with some of the honey mixture. Bake, uncovered, 30 minutes longer. Cover and bake for $1^1/_2$ to 2 hours or until a meat thermometer reads 180°, basting occasionally with remaining honey mixture. Cover and let stand for 15-20 minutes before carving.

[6] For gravy, strain pan juices into a large measuring cup; skim fat. In a small saucepan, combine cornstarch and cold water until smooth. Stir in pan juices. Bring to a boil; cook and stir for 2 minutes or until thickened. Serve with goose. **Yield:** 6-8 servings.

roasted goose with savory garlic stuffing

**JOLIE STINSON
LEBANON, OREGON**

Looking for an unforgettable entree for Christmas dinner? This is the one! The stuffed bird is moist, tender and so impressive looking on a holiday table.

SPICED ROAST GO

1 medium lemon

1 domestic goose (11 to 13 pounds)

¼ teaspoon salt

¼ teaspoon pepper

3 bacon strips

STUFFING:

2 small onions, finely chopped

2 celery ribs, chopped

8 garlic cloves, minced

¼ cup butter, cubed

1 package (14 ounces) seasoned stuffing cubes

4½ teaspoons dried sage leaves

¾ teaspoon salt

½ teaspoon pepper

½ teaspoon each dried oregano, thyme and Italian seasoning

1¼ cups chicken broth, divided

½ cup egg substitute

[1] Cut lemon in half. Rub inside and outside of goose with cut sides of lemon; discard lemon. Sprinkle inside and outside with salt and pepper. Prick skin well. With fingers, carefully loosen skin from goose breast; place bacon strips under skin. Set aside.

[2] For stuffing, in a large skillet, saute the onions, celery and garlic in butter until tender. Transfer to a large bowl; stir in the stuffing cubes, sage, salt, pepper and herbs. Add 1 cup broth and egg substitute; toss gently. Stuff the goose body and neck cavities loosely; tie drumsticks together.

[3] Place remaining stuffing in a greased 2-qt. baking dish; drizzle with remaining broth. Cover and refrigerate. Remove from the refrigerator 30 minutes before baking.

[4] Place goose breast side up on a rack in a roasting pan. Bake, uncovered, at 425° for 30 minutes. Reduce heat to 350°. Bake, uncovered, 2¾ to 3 hours longer or until juices run clear and a meat thermometer reads 180° for goose and 165° for stuffing, pricking skin occasionally. (Cover loosely with foil if goose browns too quickly.) If necessary, drain fat from pan as it accumulates.

[5] Bake additional stuffing, covered, for 25-30 minutes. Uncover; bake 10 minutes longer or until lightly browned. Cover goose with foil and let stand for 20 minutes before

DUCK WITH CHERRY SAUCE

removing stuffing and carving goose. **Yield:** 12 servings (12 cups stuffing).

duck with cherry sauce

1 domestic duckling (4 to 5 pounds)

1 jar (12 ounces) cherry preserves

1 to 2 tablespoons red wine vinegar

Bing cherries, star fruit and kale, optional

[1] Prick skin of duckling well and place breast side up on a rack in a shallow roasting pan. Tie drumsticks together. Bake, uncovered, at 350° for 2 to 2½ hours or until juices run clear and a meat thermometer reads 180°. (Drain fat from pan as it accumulates.) Cover and let stand 20 minutes before carving.

[2] Meanwhile, for sauce, combine preserves and vinegar in a small saucepan. Cook and stir over medium heat until heated through. Serve with duck. Garnish platter with fruit and kale if desired. **Yield:** 4-5 servings.

SANDY JENKINS ELKHORN, WISCONSIN

My mom prepared this tender roast duck often for Sunday dinner when I was growing up. It was one of my dad's favorite meals. The cherry sauce stirs up easily and makes this duck simply delightful.

Hunting & Fishing
COOKBOOK

For some, there's nothing like a day on the water fishing for relaxation, excitement and good eating!

Before you head out, check with your area's fish and game agency or state department of natural resources to see where you can fish safely.

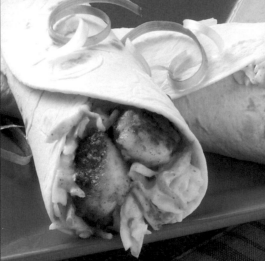

PANFISH CHOWDER, P. 75
WEEKNIGHT CATFISH WRAPS, P. 86
FISH WITH FENNEL, P. 131

FISH ③

**HONEY-FRIED WALLEYE,
PAGE 83**

CATFISH IN GINGER SAUCE

**MARY DIXSON
DECATURE,
ALABAMA**

Whenever I want to serve fish in a flash, I turn to this recipe. The fillets always turn out moist, tender and tasty. For even more flavor, spoon extra sauce over the fish before serving.

catfish in ginger sauce

$1/2$ cup chopped green onions

1 tablespoon vegetable oil

$1/4$ teaspoon ground ginger

1 teaspoon cornstarch

2 tablespoons water

1 cup chicken broth

1 tablespoon soy sauce

1 tablespoon white wine vinegar

$1/8$ teaspoon cayenne pepper

4 catfish fillets (6 ounces each)

[1] In a 2-cup microwave-safe bowl, combine the onions, oil and ginger. Microwave, uncovered, on high for $1^{1/2}$ minutes or until onions are tender.

[2] In small bowl, combine the cornstarch and water until smooth. Stir in the broth, soy sauce, vinegar and cayenne. Stir into onion mixture. Microwave, uncovered, at 70% power for 2-3 minutes, stirring after each minute, until sauce comes to a boil.

[3] Place catfish in a microwave-safe 3-qt. dish; pour sauce over the fish. Cover and microwave on high for 5-6 minutes or until fish flakes easily with a fork. **Yield:** 4 servings.

Editor's Note: This recipe was tested in a 1,100-watt microwave.

mountain trout with butter sauce

**JOSEPH NOAH
CLARKSVILLE, VIRGINIA**

The trout they use in this recipe at the Mast Farm Inn in Valle Crucis, North Carolina, comes straight from a freshwater pond. Even people who don't care for fish love it served this way. We sure enjoy this tempting treatment.

3 pounds mountain trout fillets, cut into 4-ounce portions

Salt and pepper to taste

1 cup all-purpose flour

$1/2$ cup vegetable oil

$1/2$ cup butter

Juice of 2 lemons

$1/2$ cup chicken or brown gravy, optional

[1] Season trout with salt and pepper; dredge with flour. Heat oil in a skillet. Saute trout quickly in hot oil, browning evenly on both sides. Remove trout to a shallow baking pan. Bake at 350° for 5-10 minutes or until fish flakes easily with a fork; keep warm.

[2] Meanwhile, in a saucepan, heat butter until butter begins to brown. Carefully add lemon juice (butter will bubble when juice is added). Blend in gravy if desired. Spoon sauce over fish or serve on the side. **Yield:** 6 servings.

pan-fried trout

**SHIRLEY COLEMAN
MONKTON, VERMONT**

This fish is so tasty yet so easy to prepare. You'll want to serve it often.

2 eggs

8 trout fillets

$2/3$ cup grated Parmesan cheese

2 tablespoons vegetable oil

HUNTING & FISHING

tip

Slather fish fillets in regular prepared mustard. Coat them with flour and deep fry them. You won't really taste the mustard, but it eliminates any fishy taste.

BECKY, GEORGIA

In a shallow bowl, beat eggs. Dip fillets in eggs, then dredge in the Parmesan cheese. Shake off excess. Heat oil in a large skillet over high heat; brown fillets lightly on both sides until fish flakes easily with a fork, about 5-7 minutes. **Yield:** 4 servings.

perch fillets

CONNIE TIBBETTS
WILTON, MAINE

Guests will never guess that lemon-lime soda and pancake mix are the secret ingredients behind these tasty perch fillets in a golden coating.

$1^{1}/_{2}$ cups lemon-lime soda
1 pound perch fillets
2 cups pancake mix
$^{1}/_{4}$ teaspoon pepper

Oil for frying

[1] Pour soda into a shallow bowl; add fish fillets; let stand for 15 minutes. In another shallow bowl, combine pancake mix and pepper. Remove fish from soda and coat with mix.

[2] In a large skillet, heat $^{1}/_{4}$ in. of oil over medium-high heat. Fry fish for 2-3 minutes on each side or until fish flakes with a fork. Drain on paper towels. **Yield:** 4 servings.

feta tomato-basil fish

$^{1}/_{3}$ cup chopped onion
1 garlic clove, minced
2 teaspoons olive oil
1 can ($14^{1}/_{2}$ ounces) Italian diced tomatoes, drained
$1^{1}/_{2}$ teaspoons minced fresh basil or $^{1}/_{2}$ teaspoon dried basil
1 pound walleye, bass or other whitefish fillets
4 ounces crumbled feta cheese

[1] In a saucepan, saute onion and garlic in oil until tender. Add tomatoes and basil. Bring to a boil. Reduce heat; simmer, uncovered, for 5 minutes.

[2] Meanwhile, broil fish 4-6 in. from the heat for 5-6 minutes. Top each fillet with tomato mixture and cheese. Broil 5-7 minutes longer or until fish flakes easily with a fork. **Yield:** 4 servings.

ALICIA SZESZOL
LINDENHURST, ILLINOIS

I rely on my husband for the main ingredient in this fuss-free dish. He fills our freezer after his summer fishing trip.

FETA TOMATO-BASIL FISH

FELICIA
CUMMINGS
RAYMOND,
MAINE

One summer when my husband and I were enjoying our first "getaway" in years, we found ourselves stranded in our cabin cruiser with a dead battery. When hunger set in, my husband rigged up a fishing line, and soon there were two trout sizzling on the portable grill. We eventually made it home all right… and kept the recipe we'd devised.

simple pan-fried trout

    4 lake trout fillets (about 8 ounces each)
    ½ cup grated Parmesan cheese
    ½ cup bacon-flavored crackers, crushed
    ½ cup cornmeal
    ¼ to ½ teaspoon garlic salt
Pinch pepper
    2 eggs
    ½ cup milk
    ½ cup vegetable oil
Lemon wedges and/or snipped fresh chives or parsley, optional

[1] Rinse fish in cold water; pat dry. In a shallow bowl, combine the cheese, cracker crumbs, cornmeal, garlic salt and pepper. In another bowl, beat eggs and milk. Dip fish in the egg mixture, then gently roll in the crumb mixture.

[2] In a skillet, fry fish in oil for 5-7 minutes or until it flakes easily with a fork, turning once. If desired, garnish with lemon, chives and/or parsley. **Yield:** 4 servings.

creole catfish fillets

DAVE BREMSTONE
PLANTATION, FLORIDA

I like to rub catfish fillets with a pleasant mixture of seasonings before cooking them quickly on the grill. The moist fish gets plenty of flavor when served with a spicy sauce and fresh lemon wedges on the side.

    3 tablespoons plain yogurt
    2 tablespoons finely chopped onion
    1 tablespoon mayonnaise
    1 tablespoon Dijon mustard
    1 tablespoon ketchup
    ½ teaspoon dried thyme
    ¼ teaspoon grated lemon peel

SIMPLE PAN-FRIED TROUT

1 teaspoon paprika

1/2 teaspoon onion powder

1/4 teaspoon salt

1/8 teaspoon cayenne pepper

4 catfish fillets (4 ounces each)

4 lemon wedges

[1] In a small bowl, combine the yogurt, onion, mayonnaise, mustard, ketchup, thyme and lemon peel. Cover and refrigerate until serving. In another bowl, combine the paprika, onion powder, salt and cayenne; rub over both sides of fillets.

[2] Grill, covered, in a grill basket coated with nonstick cooking spray over medium-hot heat for 5-6 minutes on each side or until the fish flakes easily with a fork. Serve fillets with lemon wedges and yogurt sauce. **Yield:** 4 servings.

easy fish fillets

THERESA STEWART
NEW OXFORD, PENNSYLVANIA

For folks who want to cook fish in a flash, this recipe is quite a catch. These fillets always turn out moist and flaky.

3/4 cup seasoned bread crumbs

1/3 cup Italian salad dressing

4 catfish fillets (5 ounces each), patted dry

[1] Place bread crumbs in a shallow bowl. Place dressing in another shallow bowl. Dip fish in dressing, then coat with crumbs. Place fish on a rack in a 15-in. x 10-in. x 1-in. baking pan.

[2] Bake uncovered, at 450° for 15-20 minutes or until the fish flakes easily with a fork. **Yield:** 4 servings.

panfish chowder

6 bacon strips, cut into 1-inch pieces

2/3 cup chopped onion

1/2 cup chopped celery

3 medium potatoes, peeled and cubed

2 cups water

1/2 cup chopped carrots

PANFISH CHOWDER

2 tablespoons minced fresh parsley

1 tablespoon lemon juice

1/2 teaspoon dill weed

1/4 teaspoon garlic salt

1/8 teaspoon pepper

1 pound panfish fillets (perch, sunfish or crappie), cut into 1-inch chunks

1 cup half-and-half cream

[1] In a 3-qt. saucepan, cook the bacon until crisp. Remove bacon and set aside; discard all but 2 tablespoons of drippings. Saute onion and celery in drippings until tender. Add the next eight ingredients.

[2] Simmer until vegetables are tender, about 30 minutes. Add fish and bacon; simmer for 5 minutes or just until fish flakes easily with a fork. Add cream and heat through. **Yield:** 4-6 servings.

CYNDI FLISS
BEVENT, WISCONSIN

With my husband being an avid hunter and fisherman, I can never have enough new fish and wild game recipes. We especially enjoy this rich chowder. It's a hearty dish with big chunks of fish, potatoes and bacon in a tempting, creamy broth.

HUNTING & FISHING COOKBOOK

DENNIS
DORNFELDT
SHEBOYGAN,
WISCONSIN

Your favorite fisherman would be proud to find his catch fried with this golden coating. I've gotten raves each time I've made this fish.

CRACKER-COATED
FRIED PERCH

cracker-coated fried perch

  2 eggs

  1/2 cup milk

  2 cups butter-flavored cracker crumbs

  1/2 teaspoon garlic salt

  1/4 teaspoon dried oregano

  1/4 teaspoon dried tarragon

  1/4 teaspoon pepper

  1 pound lake perch fillets

Vegetable oil

[1] In a shallow bowl, beat eggs and milk. In another bowl, combine cracker crumbs, garlic salt, oregano, tarragon and pepper. Cut perch into serving-size pieces; dip in egg mixture, then coat with crumbs.

[2] Heat oil in a skillet over medium heat. Fry fish for several minutes on each side or until it flakes easily with a fork. **Yield:** 4 servings.

cream cheese-stuffed catfish

ANNELIESE DEISING
PLYMOUTH, MICHIGAN

Flaky fish fillets and strips of bacon are wrapped around a rich cream cheese filling, making an entree that's sure to pamper you and a guest. It's become a favorite of mine.

  4 bacon strips

  1/2 cup soft bread crumbs

  4 1/2 teaspoons cream cheese, softened

  2 teaspoons lemon juice, divided

 **HUNTING & FISHING**

For a side dish that inspires second helpings to go with your fish entree, stir a can of tiny shrimp (rinsed and drained) into your favorite coleslaw.

ANN, MINNESOTA

1½ teaspoons finely chopped onion

1½ teaspoons finely chopped celery

1½ teaspoons dried parsley flakes

½ teaspoon dried thyme

¼ teaspoon pepper, divided

⅛ teaspoon salt

2 catfish fillets (6 ounces each)

[1] In a skillet, cook bacon over medium heat until cooked but not crisp. Remove to paper towels; keep warm.

[2] In a bowl, combine the bread crumbs, cream cheese, 1½ teaspoons lemon juice, onion, celery, parsley, thyme, ⅛ teaspoon pepper and salt. Sprinkle catfish fillets with remaining lemon juice and pepper.

[3] Spread crumb mixture over each fillet; roll from one end. Wrap two strips of bacon around each fillet and secure with toothpicks. Place in a greased 8-in. square baking dish. Bake at 350° for 25-30 minutes or until fish flakes easily with a fork. Remove toothpicks before serving. **Yield:** 2 servings.

baked parmesan perch

CAROL GAUS
ITASCA, ILLINOIS

Let compliments be your catch of the day when you serve this crispy, breaded fish. It's so easy to prepare this fish in the oven.

2 tablespoons dry bread crumbs

1 tablespoon grated Parmesan cheese

1 tablespoon paprika

1 teaspoon dried basil

1 pound perch or fish fillets of your choice

1 tablespoon butter, melted

In a shallow bowl, combine the bread crumbs, Parmesan cheese, paprika and basil. Brush fish fillets with butter, then dip into the crumb mixture. Place in a greased baking pan. Bake, uncovered, at 475° for about 10 minutes or until fish flakes easily with a fork. **Yield:** 4 servings.

catfish cakes

1½ pounds catfish fillets

2 eggs, beaten

1 large potato, peeled, cooked and mashed

1 large onion, finely chopped

1 to 2 tablespoons chopped fresh parsley

2 to 3 drops hot pepper sauce

1 garlic clove, minced

1 teaspoon salt

½ teaspoon pepper

½ teaspoon dried basil

2 cups finely crushed butter-flavored crackers

Vegetable oil

Tartar sauce, optional

[1] Poach or bake catfish fillets. Drain and refrigerate. Flake cooled fish into a large mixing bowl. Add eggs, potato, onion, parsley, hot pepper sauce, garlic, salt, pepper and basil; mix well. Shape into eight patties; coat with cracker crumbs.

[2] Heat a small amount of oil in a large skillet. Cook patties, a few at a time, until browned on both sides and heated through. Serve with tartar sauce if desired. **Yield:** 8 servings.

JAN CAMPBELL
PURVIS,
MISSISSIPPI

These cakes are crispy on the outside and moist and flavorful on the inside—a real treat! I like to serve them with hush puppies and coleslaw. I developed the recipe to put to good use all the catfish we catch at our lake cabin.

CATFISH CAKES

KATHERINE
NELSON
PALMDALE,
CALIFORNIA

I got the idea for this recipe from my brother-in-law, Brett, a fabulous "experimental" cook. Even the pickiest of eaters will crave more of this dish, so you might want to double the recipe!

cajun catfish with fruit salsa

6 catfish fillets (6 ounces each)

3 tablespoons butter, melted

2 tablespoons Cajun seasoning

SALSA:

2 medium navel oranges, peeled, sectioned and diced

1 cup diced cantaloupe

1/2 cup diced honeydew

2 tablespoons lime juice

[1] Brush both sides of fillets with butter; sprinkle with Cajun seasoning. Place on a broiler pan; broil 6 in. from heat for 8-10 minutes or until fish flakes easily with a fork.

[2] For salsa, in a small bowl, combine the remaining ingredients. Serve with fish. **Yield:** 6 servings.

herbed fish fillets

SUE KROENING
MATTOON, ILLINOIS

This simple treatment complements the mild flavor of fresh fish and makes a memorable meal.

2 tablespoons lemon juice

1 tablespoon butter, melted

1/2 teaspoon dried thyme

1/2 teaspoon grated lemon peel

1/4 teaspoon salt

1/4 teaspoon paprika

1/8 teaspoon garlic powder

4 snapper, orange roughy, catfish or trout fillets (6 ounces each)

Combine the first seven ingredients; dip fillets. Grill, covered, over hot heat for 10 minutes or until fish flakes easily with a fork. **Yield:** 4 servings.

CAJUN CATFISH WITH FRUIT SALSA

HUNTING & FISHING COOKBOOK

campfire trout dinner

WENDY MCGOWAN
POULSBO, WASHINGTON

There's nothing that tastes better than fresh trout cooked this way over a campfire. It's a wonderful reward for a day spent fishing.

    4 pan-dressed trout (1 pound each)
    8 lemon slices
    2 medium onions, sliced into eight
       wedges
    8 bacon strips, partially cooked
    4 medium carrots, thinly sliced
    1 tablespoon dried marjoram
  1/4 teaspoon salt
  1/8 teaspoon pepper
    1 to 2 tablespoons butter, cut up
    4 lemon wedges

[1] Place each trout on a double thickness of heavy-duty foil (about 20-in. x 18-in.). Place 2 lemon slices and 4 onion wedges in each trout and wrap with 2 slices of bacon. Fold foil around trout and seal tightly.

[2] Place carrots on a double thickness of heavy-duty foil (about 12-in. square) and sprinkle with the marjoram, salt and pepper. Dot with butter. Fold foil around carrots and seal tightly. Grill, covered, over medium heat for 20-25 minutes or until fish flakes easily with a fork and carrots are tender. Serve trout with carrots and lemon wedges. **Yield:** 4 servings.

lemon-batter fish

  1 1/2 cups all-purpose flour, divided
      1 teaspoon baking powder
    3/4 teaspoon salt
    1/2 teaspoon sugar
      1 egg, beaten
    2/3 cup water
    2/3 cup lemon juice, divided
      2 pounds perch fillets or walleye
         fillets, cut into bite-size pieces
Oil for frying
Lemon wedges, optional

[1] In a shallow bowl, combine 1 cup flour, baking powder, salt and sugar; set aside.

LEMON-BATTER FISH

Combine the egg, water and 1/3 cup lemon juice; stir into dry ingredients until smooth. In separate shallow bowls, place remaining lemon juice and remaining flour. Dip fillets in lemon juice, then flour and coat with the batter.

[2] Heat 1 in. of oil in a skillet. Fry fish, a few at a time, over medium-high heat for 2-3 minutes on each side or until the fish flakes easily with a fork. Carefully drain on paper towels. Garnish with lemon wedges if desired. **Yield:** 5 servings.

JACKIE HANNAHS MUSKEGON, MICHIGAN

My husband ranks this recipe as one of his favorites. A lot of fishing takes place in our area, which makes this a good choice for a regional recipe.

HUNTING & FISHING tip

We cook whole trout on the grill. No sauce is needed, just a little salt and pepper, and close the lid. When done, put the trout on a plate and run a knife down its back, then put the knife under the back bone at the head of the fish, and lift up and away. The one side will come off easily. Then put the fish on another plate and lift the back bone alone, and the other piece will be filleted.

KAREN, WASHINGTON

BAKED FISH

**LYNN MATHIEU
GREAT MILLS,
MARYLAND**

I created this quick recipe after enjoying a seafood dish with Parmesan cheese sprinkled on top at a restaurant. The cheese added extra zip and gave me the idea to try it at home.

baked fish

½ pound panfish fillets (perch, trout or other whitefish)

4 teaspoons grated Parmesan cheese

½ teaspoon dill weed

[1] Place fish in a 10-in. pie plate that has been coated with cooking spray. Sprinkle with Parmesan cheese and dill weed.

[2] Bake, uncovered, at 350° for 8-10 minutes or until the fish flakes easily with a fork. **Yield:** 2 servings.

savory cajun-style catfish

**DOLORES BARNAS
BLASDELL, NEW YORK**

These nicely spiced fillets are sure to win you a boatload of compliments! I got the original recipe from a chef in the culinary arts department of a college where I used to work.

4½ teaspoons paprika

1 teaspoon onion powder

1 teaspoon dried oregano

1 teaspoon pepper

½ teaspoon white pepper

½ teaspoon dried thyme

¼ teaspoon cayenne pepper

4 catfish fillets (6 ounces each)

Refrigerated butter-flavored spray

[1] In a shallow bowl, combine the first seven ingredients. Spritz both sides of fish with butter-flavored spray. Dip one side of each fillet in spice mixture; place spice side down in a large skillet coated with butter-flavored spray.

[2] Cook over medium-high heat for 8-10 minutes or until fish flakes easily with a fork, turning once. **Yield:** 4 servings.

Editor's Note: This recipe was tested with I Can't Believe It's Not Butter Spray.

fisherman's specialty

**BRUCE HEADLEY
GREENWOOD, MISSOURI**

A friend at work shared some of his fresh catch prepared in this simple way. After one bite, I knew it was the best fried fish I'd ever tasted. Whenever I catch bass, crappie or bluegill, my wife uses this recipe. The fillets come out moist and not at all fishy tasting. Our family won't eat fish any other way.

2 eggs

2 teaspoons lemon-pepper seasoning, divided

6 bluegill or perch fillets (2 to 3 ounces each)

1 cup crushed saltines (about 30 crackers)

Vegetable oil

tip · HUNTING & FISHING

Cooking fish on the road in an RV, or if you are tent camping, can be smelly and a mess to clean up. If you've caught fresh fish, this cooking method is hard to beat: Wrap seasoned, fresh fish fillets in two layers of regular aluminum foil or one layer of heavy-duty foil and carefully seal all the seams. Chill the fish for an hour or two. Place the foil packet right on the hot coals. A 2-pound fish will take about 20 to 25 minutes to cook. Platter the fish, toss the foil, pour the wine and enjoy!

BECKY, GEORGIA

In a small shallow bowl, beat eggs and $1^{1}/_{2}$ teaspoons lemon-pepper. Dip fillets in egg mixture, then coat with cracker crumbs. Sprinkle with remaining lemon-pepper. In a skillet, heat $^{1}/_{4}$ in. of oil. Fry fillets for 3-4 minutes on each side or until fish flakes easily with a fork. **Yield:** 3 servings.

catfish with pecan butter

DIXIE TERRY
GORVILL, ILLINOIS

Two Southern favorites—catfish and pecans—are combined deliciously in this tempting recipe.

- 1 cup butter, softened
- $^{1}/_{2}$ cup chopped pecans, toasted
- 1 teaspoon lemon juice

Dash hot pepper sauce

- 2 eggs, lightly beaten
- 1 cup milk
- 1 cup cornmeal
- $^{1}/_{2}$ cup all-purpose flour
- 1 teaspoon garlic powder
- 1 teaspoon paprika
- 1 teaspoon pepper
- $^{1}/_{2}$ teaspoon onion powder
- $^{1}/_{2}$ teaspoon dried oregano
- $^{1}/_{2}$ teaspoon dried thyme
- $^{1}/_{4}$ teaspoon salt
- $^{1}/_{4}$ teaspoon cayenne pepper
- 6 catfish fillets (6 ounces each)

Vegetable oil for frying

Lemon wedges

[1] In a food processor, combine the first four ingredients; cover and process until smooth. Set aside.

[2] In a shallow dish, combine the eggs and milk. In another shallow dish, combine the cornmeal, flour and seasonings. Dip fillets in egg mixture, then coat with the flour mixture.

[3] In a large skillet, heat $^{1}/_{4}$ in. oil over medium heat. Fry fillets in batches for 5-6 minutes on each side or until fish flakes easily with a fork. Remove from the skillet and keep warm. Serve with pecan butter and lemon wedges. **Yield:** 6 servings.

baked trout fillets

- 1 pound trout fillets
- 1 cup (8 ounces) sour cream
- $^{1}/_{4}$ cup grated Parmesan cheese
- 1 tablespoon lemon juice
- 1 tablespoon finely chopped onion
- $^{1}/_{2}$ teaspoon salt

Paprika

[1] Place fish in a greased shallow 3-qt. baking dish. In a small bowl, combine the sour cream, Parmesan cheese, lemon juice, onion and salt; spread over fish. Sprinkle with paprika.

[2] Bake, uncovered, at 350° for 20-25 minutes or until fish flakes easily with a fork. **Yield:** 4 servings.

MARY ZIMMERMAN SPRING LAKE, MICHIGAN

Moist, tender trout is draped in a creamy Parmesan cheese coating that makes this dish elegant enough to serve company. I picked up this recipe at the campground where we once stayed. I also use the delicious sour cream mixture on salmon.

BAKED TROUT FILLETS

MRS. W. D.
BAKER
STARKVILLE,
MISSISSIPPI

Mississippi is the nation's largest producer of farm-raised catfish. My family loves this dish and asks for it often. One reason I like it is it's so simple to prepare.

catfish parmesan

- ³/₄ cup dry bread crumbs
- 3 tablespoons grated Parmesan cheese
- 2 tablespoons chopped fresh parsley
- ½ teaspoon salt
- ¼ teaspoon paprika
- ⅛ teaspoon each pepper, dried oregano and basil
- 6 fresh or frozen catfish fillets (3 to 5 ounces each)
- ½ cup butter, melted

In a shallow bowl, combine the bread crumbs, Parmesan cheese, parsley and seasonings. Dip catfish in butter, then in crumb mixture. Arrange catfish in a greased 13-in. x 9-in. x 2-in. baking dish. Bake, uncovered, at 375° for 20-25 minutes or until fish flakes easily with a fork. **Yield:** 6 servings.

bacon honey walleye

LINDA NEUMANN
ALGONAC, MICHIGAN

The texture and flavor of the walleye is only enhanced by this recipe's savory-sweet topping. It takes only a few minutes to grill.

- 16 bacon strips, partially cooked
- 4 walleye fillets (2½ pounds)
- 1 cup thinly sliced onion
- ¼ cup butter, melted
- 2 tablespoons honey
- ½ teaspoon salt
- ¼ teaspoon pepper

[1] Fold four 18-in. x 15-in. pieces of heavy-duty foil in half; fold up edges to make pans about 12 in. x 7 in. Divide bacon among pans; top with fish and onion. Drizzle with butter and honey; season with salt and pepper.

CATFISH PARMESAN

[2] Grill, covered, over medium heat for 12-15 minutes or until fish flakes easily with a fork. Cut fillets in half; serve each with two bacon strips. **Yield:** 8 servings.

honey-fried walleye

(PICTURED ON PAGE 71)

SHARON COLLIS
COLONA, ILLINOIS

We fish on most summer weekends, so we have lots of fresh fillets. Everyone who tries this crisp, golden fish loves it. It's my husband's favorite. Honey gives the coating a deliciously different twist.

1 egg
1 teaspoon honey
1 cup coarsely crushed saltines (about 22 crackers)
$\frac{1}{3}$ cup all-purpose flour
$\frac{1}{4}$ teaspoon salt
$\frac{1}{4}$ teaspoon pepper
4 to 6 walleye fillets (about $1\frac{1}{2}$ pounds), skin removed

Vegetable oil

Additional honey

Lemon or lime slices, optional

[1] In a shallow bowl, beat egg and honey. In another bowl, combine the cracker crumbs, flour, salt and pepper. Dip fillets into egg mixture, then coat with crumb mixture.

[2] In a large skillet, heat $\frac{1}{4}$ in. of oil; fry fish over medium-high heat for 3-4 minutes on each side or until fish flakes easily with a fork. Drizzle with honey; garnish with lemon or lime slices if desired. **Yield:** 4-6 servings.

catfish with shrimp salsa

2 tablespoons Cajun or blackened seasoning
$\frac{1}{2}$ teaspoon ground cumin
$\frac{1}{2}$ teaspoon ground coriander
4 catfish fillets (6 ounces each)
2 to 3 tablespoons vegetable oil

SALSA:
1 medium green pepper, diced
$\frac{3}{4}$ cup diced onion
1 celery rib, diced

CATFISH WITH SHRIMP SALSA

1 jalapeno pepper, seeded and chopped
2 garlic cloves, minced
1 tablespoon butter
$1\frac{1}{2}$ cups fresh or frozen corn
3 plum tomatoes, seeded and chopped
2 packages (5 ounces each) frozen cooked salad shrimp, thawed
$\frac{1}{2}$ teaspoon Cajun or blackened seasoning

Dash hot pepper sauce

[1] Combine the Cajun seasoning, cumin and coriander; rub over catfish fillets. In a large skillet, fry fillets in oil over medium-high heat for 4-5 minutes on each side or until fish flakes easily with a fork. Remove and keep warm.

[2] In the same skillet, saute the green pepper, onion, celery, jalapeno and garlic in butter until tender. Add the corn, tomatoes and shrimp; cook and stir for 4-5 minutes or until corn is tender. Stir in Cajun seasoning and hot pepper sauce. Serve with catfish. **Yield:** 4 servings.

Editor's Note: When cutting or seeding hot peppers, use rubber or plastic gloves to protect your hands. Avoid touching your face.

DENISE WALL
RIDGEWAY,
SOUTH
CAROLINA

Catfish are plentiful in the freshwater lake by my house. This is one of my favorite recipes. Cajun seasoning, cumin and coriander spice up the fillets nicely. The colorful corn and shrimp salsa makes an excellent accompaniment.

HUNTING & FISHING COOKBOOK

PERLENE HOEKEMA LYNDEN, WASHINGTON

We sometimes send our delicious Washington salmon all the way to Michigan for my sister to use in this family-favorite dish! The tasty topping can be used on other types of fish, too. Fresh thyme from your garden really sparks the flavor.

LEMON HERBED SALMON

lemon herbed salmon

2¹/₂	cups fresh bread crumbs
4	garlic cloves, minced
¹/₂	cup chopped fresh parsley
6	tablespoons grated Parmesan cheese
¹/₄	cup chopped fresh thyme or 1 tablespoon dried thyme
2	teaspoons grated lemon peel
¹/₂	teaspoon salt
6	tablespoons butter, melted, divided
1	salmon fillet (3 to 4 pounds)

[1] In a shallow bowl, combine bread crumbs, garlic, parsley, Parmesan cheese, thyme, lemon peel and salt; mix well. Add 4 tablespoons butter; toss lightly to coat. Set aside.

[2] Pat salmon dry. Place skin side down in a greased baking dish. Brush with remaining butter; cover with crumb mixture. Bake at 350° for 20-25 minutes or until salmon flakes easily with a fork. **Yield:** 8 servings.

honey-mustard grilled trout

CHARLENE CRONIN KENNER, LOUISIANA

This easy-to-prepare dish is a must-have with my family. We like the honey-mustard sauce so much, I make a double batch and keep some in the fridge to use as a dressing.

¹/₄	cup mayonnaise
1	tablespoon cider vinegar
1	tablespoon prepared mustard
1	tablespoon honey
¹/₈	teaspoon cayenne pepper
4	large onions, cut into ¹/₂-inch slices
6	trout fillets (6 ounces each)

[1] Coat grill rack with nonstick cooking spray before starting the grill. In a bowl, combine the first five ingredients. Place onions cut side down on grill rack with sides touching. Arrange fillets on onion slices.

[2] Cover and grill over medium-hot heat for 5 minutes. Baste with mustard mixture. Cook

5-6 minutes longer or until fish flakes easily with a fork, basting frequently. Discard onion slices. **Yield:** 6 servings.

oven-fried fish

GARY SACHO
DE PERE, WISCONSIN

I'm always pleased to cook up the day's catch of fresh fish using this tasty recipe. The moist fillets are nicely flavored.

- 1/2 cup condensed cream of onion soup, undiluted
- 1 tablespoon milk
- 3/4 pound perch, bluegill or catfish fillets

Dash pepper

- 2 tablespoons butter, melted
- 1 1/2 teaspoons lemon juice
- 3/4 cup crushed sour cream & onion potato chips

[1] In a shallow bowl, combine onion soup and milk. Dip fillets in soup mixture; place in an 11-in. x 7-in. x 2-in. baking dish coated with nonstick cooking spray. Sprinkle with pepper.

[2] Combine butter and lemon juice; drizzle over fillets. Top with crushed chips. Bake, uncovered, at 350° for 17-20 minutes or until fish flakes easily with a fork. **Yield:** 2 servings.

walleye delight

CONNIE REILLY
STANCHFIELD, MINNESOTA

I love fish and think grilling is one of the best ways to prepare it. The combination of lemon juice, basil and other seasonings is fantastic.

- 1 pound walleye, pike, perch or trout fillets
- 2 teaspoons butter, softened
- 1 tablespoon lemon juice
- 1 tablespoon snipped fresh basil or 1/2 to 1 teaspoon dried basil
- 1 teaspoon lemon-pepper seasoning
- 1/2 teaspoon garlic salt
- 4 ounces fresh mushrooms, sliced

[1] Coat an 18-in. x 18-in. piece of heavy-duty foil with nonstick cooking spray. Place fillets on foil. Spread with butter. Sprinkle with lemon juice, basil, lemon-pepper and garlic salt. Top with mushrooms. Bring opposite edges of foil together; fold down several times. Fold remaining edges toward fish and seal tightly.

[2] Grill, covered, over hot heat for 10-14 minutes, turning once, or until fish flakes easily with a fork. **Yield:** 4 servings.

lemon dill walleye

- 1 large onion, halved and thinly sliced
- 1 tablespoon butter
- 4 cups water
- 1 tablespoon snipped fresh dill or 1 teaspoon dill weed
- 3/4 cup milk
- 2 medium lemons, thinly sliced
- 1/8 teaspoon pepper
- 2 pounds walleye, cod, halibut or orange roughy fillets

[1] In a large skillet, saute onion in butter until tender. Add water and dill; bring to a boil. Reduce heat; simmer, uncovered, for 4-5 minutes. Add milk; stir in lemons and pepper. Top with fillets. Cover and simmer for 12-15 minutes or until fish flakes easily with a fork.

[2] Transfer fish to a serving platter and keep warm. Strain cooking liquid, reserving lemons, onion and dill; serve with fish. **Yield:** 8 servings.

DAWN PIASTA
DAUPHIN,
MANITOBA

In our area, walleye is popular and abundant. In this light entree, the fish is moist and nicely enhanced with lemon and dill.

LEMON DILL WALLEYE

**MONICA PERRY
BOISE, IDAHO**

I tuck catfish "nuggets" and a convenient coleslaw mix into tortillas with tasty results. The fish gets a slight kick from the Creole seasoning.

weeknight catfish wraps

- 1½ cups coleslaw mix
- 2 tablespoons finely chopped onion
- ⅛ teaspoon pepper
- 1 teaspoon Creole or Cajun seasoning, divided
- ¼ cup coleslaw salad dressing
- 2 tablespoons pancake mix
- ½ pound catfish fillets, cut into 2-inch pieces
- 1 teaspoon canola oil
- 4 flour tortillas (6 inches), warmed

[1] In a small bowl, combine the coleslaw mix, onion, pepper and ¼ teaspoon seasoning. Stir in dressing. Cover and refrigerate for at least 30 minutes.

[2] In a resealable plastic bag, combine the pancake mix and remaining seasoning. Add fish and toss to coat. In a small skillet, cook fish in oil over medium heat for 6 minutes or until lightly browned on each side and fish flakes easily with a fork. Spoon coleslaw mixture onto tortillas; top with fish and roll up. **Yield:** 2 servings.

veggie-topped fillets

**JOAN SHIRLEY
TREGO, MONTANA**

These easy-to-prepare fillets are baked in a mild tomato-flavored sauce.

- 4 walleye or sole fillets (6 ounces each)
- ¾ teaspoon salt, divided
- ⅛ teaspoon pepper
- 1½ cups V8 juice
- ½ cup chopped celery
- ½ cup chopped onion
- ¼ cup chopped green pepper
- 1 tablespoon lemon juice

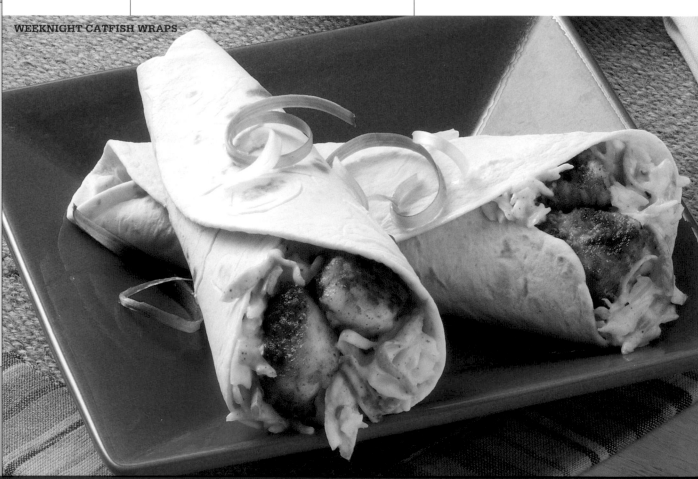

WEEKNIGHT CATFISH WRAPS

1 teaspoon sugar

1 tablespoon butter

Hot cooked rice, optional

[1] Place fillets in a 13-in. x 9-in. x 2-in. baking dish coated with nonstick cooking spray; sprinkle with ½ teaspoon salt and pepper. In a saucepan, combine the V8 juice, celery, onion, green pepper, lemon juice, sugar and remaining salt; bring to a boil.

[2] Cook over medium-low heat for 5-6 minutes or until vegetables are tender. Pour over fish; dot with butter.

[3] Bake, uncovered, at 350° for 10-15 minutes or until fish flakes easily with a fork. Serve with rice if desired. **Yield:** 4 servings.

golden catfish fillets

SHARON STEVENS
WEIRTON, VIRGINIA

My grandmother always made these crisp fillets from Granddad's fresh catch from the Ohio River. You should immediately refrigerate cleaned, fresh fish and use them within 2 days.

3 eggs

¾ cup all-purpose flour

¾ cup cornmeal

1 teaspoon garlic powder

½ teaspoon salt

½ teaspoon pepper

5 catfish fillets (6 ounces each)

Oil for frying

[1] In a shallow bowl, beat eggs until foamy. In another shallow bowl, combine the flour, cornmeal and seasonings. Dip fillets in eggs, then coat with cornmeal mixture.

[2] Heat ¼ in. of oil in a large skillet; fry fish over medium-high heat for 3-4 minutes on each side or until fish flakes easily with a fork. **Yield:** 5 servings.

vegetable trout bake

4 small red potatoes, cut into 1-inch pieces

1 cup cut fresh green beans (2-inch pieces)

8 to 10 frozen pearl onions

VEGETABLE TROUT BAKE

½ teaspoon salt, divided

4 garlic cloves, minced, divided

2 trout fillets (6 ounces each)

¼ cup pitted Greek or ripe olives, halved

3 teaspoons minced fresh parsley, divided

¼ teaspoon pepper

2 plum tomatoes, chopped

¼ cup white wine

[1] In a large saucepan, combine the potatoes, beans and onions; cover with water. Add ¼ teaspoon salt. Bring to a boil; reduce heat. Cover and cook for 10-15 minutes or until beans and onions are crisp-tender; drain.

[2] Place vegetables in a single layer in a shallow 2-qt. baking dish coated with nonstick cooking spray. Top with half of the garlic. Place trout skin side down over vegetables. Sprinkle with olives, 1½ teaspoons parsley, pepper and remaining salt and garlic. Top with tomatoes and remaining parsley.

[3] Pour wine over the top. Cover and bake at 400° for 35-40 minutes or until fish flakes easily with a fork. **Yield:** 2 servings.

ELIZABETH YARNELL
DENVER, COLORADO

I love how easy this dish is to prepare. If you don't care for trout, use salmon or chicken breasts. Instead of green beans and tomatoes, try eggplant and broccoli florets. Try your own variations and have fun.

JOYCE
SZYMANSKI
MONROE,
MICHIGAN

We live close to Lake Erie, which is nicknamed the "Walleye Capital of the World." I came up with this fantastic recipe as a way to serve that succulent fish.

baked walleye

- ³/₄ cup chopped onion
- ³/₄ cup chopped green pepper
- ³/₄ cup chopped celery
- 1 tablespoon dried parsley flakes
- ¹/₂ teaspoon garlic powder
- ¹/₂ teaspoon pepper
- ¹/₂ teaspoon seasoned salt
- 1 cup V8 juice
- 1 pound walleye fillets

[1] In a saucepan, combine first eight ingredients; bring to a boil. Reduce heat; simmer, uncovered, until vegetables are crisp-tender, stirring occasionally, about 5 minutes. Place fish in a greased 13-in. x 9-in. baking pan.

[2] Pour vegetable mixture over the fish. Cover and bake at 350° for 30 minutes or until fish flakes easily with a fork. **Yield:** 4 servings.

trout amandine

BONNIE SUE GREENE
MESA, COLORADO

I catch wonderful trout here, and this is a simple yet delicious way to prepare it.

- 2 teaspoons salt
- ¹/₂ teaspoon pepper
- 4 pan-dressed trout (about 1 pound each)
- 2 eggs
- ¹/₂ cup half-and-half cream
- ¹/₂ cup all-purpose flour
- ¹/₂ cup slivered almonds
- 3 tablespoons butter, divided
- 3 to 4 tablespoons lemon juice
- ¹/₂ teaspoon dried tarragon
- ¹/₄ cup olive oil

[1] Sprinkle salt and pepper in the cavity of each trout. In a shallow bowl, beat eggs and cream. Dip trout in egg mixture, then roll in flour. In a small skillet over low heat, saute the almonds in 2 tablespoons butter until lightly browned. Add lemon juice and tarragon; heat through. Remove from the heat and keep warm.

[2] Meanwhile, in a skillet over medium heat, combine oil and remaining butter. Fry the trout for 8-10 minutes; carefully turn and fry 8 minutes longer or until it flakes easily with a fork. Top trout with almond mixture. **Yield:** 4 servings.

catfish with parsley sauce

LEE BAILEY
BELZONI, MISSISSIPPI

There's lots of flavor in this tempting dish. The golden fillets have a bit of zip, and the pesto-like parsley sauce is a delicious, fresh-tasting addition.

SAUCE:
- 2 cups tightly packed fresh parsley leaves
- ¹/₂ cup olive oil
- ¹/₂ cup chopped pecans
- 1 garlic clove, minced
- ¹/₂ cup grated Romano cheese

BAKED WALLEYE

BARBECUED TROUT

½ cup grated Parmesan cheese

2 tablespoons butter, cut into pieces

FILLETS:

1 cup all-purpose flour

½ to 1 teaspoon cayenne pepper

1 teaspoon salt

6 catfish fillets (6 to 8 ounces each)

1 to 2 tablespoons vegetable oil

1 to 2 tablespoons butter

[1] In a food processor or blender, process parsley until coarsely chopped. Add remaining sauce ingredients; process until smooth. Refrigerate. Combine the flour, cayenne pepper and salt in a bowl. Dredge each fillet; shake off excess.

[2] In a skillet, heat 1 tablespoon each of oil and butter. Fry fillets for 4-5 minutes or until golden brown. Turn fillets; add remaining oil and butter if necessary. Divide the sauce and spread evenly on the cooked side of each fillet. Cover and cook for 5 minutes or until fish flakes easily with a fork. **Yield:** 6 servings.

barbecued trout

6 pan-dressed trout

⅔ cup soy sauce

½ cup ketchup

2 tablespoons lemon juice

2 tablespoons vegetable oil

1 teaspoon dried rosemary, crushed

Lemon wedges, optional

[1] Place trout in a single layer in a plastic bag or glass dish. Combine soy sauce, ketchup, lemon juice, oil and rosemary; pour two-thirds of marinade into bag or dish. Cover (or close bag) and let stand for 1 hour, turning once. Set aside remaining marinade for basting.

[2] Discard marinade from fish. Place fish in a single layer in a well-greased hinged wire grill basket. Grill, covered, over medium heat for 8-10 minutes or until fish is browned on bottom. Turn and baste with reserved marinade; grill 5-7 minutes longer or until fish flakes easily with a fork. Serve with lemon if desired. **Yield:** 6 servings.

VIVIAN WOLFRAM MOUNTAIN HOME, ARKANSAS

This delicious recipe came from a friend. The sauce really gives the fish a wonderful flavor. Even those who aren't fond of fish will like it prepared this way.

**VAL KEITHLEY
HAMMOND,
INDIANA**

A friend gave me this recipe, and it's been a family favorite since the first time I made it.

CATFISH CREOLE

catfish creole

¼ **cup each chopped onion, celery and green pepper**

2 **garlic cloves, minced**

2 **teaspoons olive oil**

¾ **cup chicken broth**

1 **tablespoon tomato paste**

½ **teaspoon salt**

½ **teaspoon each dried basil, oregano and thyme**

⅛ **teaspoon each white, black and cayenne pepper**

Dash paprika

½ **cup diced fresh tomato**

1 **pound catfish or orange roughy fillets**

Hot cooked rice

Minced fresh parsley

[1] In a small skillet, saute the onion, celery, green pepper and garlic in oil until tender.

Add the broth, tomato paste and seasonings; bring to a boil. Reduce heat; simmer, uncovered, for 5 minutes or until heated through. Stir in tomato.

[2] Arrange the fillets in a greased 13-in. x 9-in. x 2-in. baking dish; top with vegetable mixture. Bake, uncovered, at 375° for 15-20 minutes or until fish flakes easily with a fork. Serve over rice; sprinkle with parsley. **Yield:** 4 servings.

tip

HUNTING & FISHING

To make a casserole out of I pound of any kind of fresh or frozen fish fillets, grease a 13- x 9-inch pan, then line the bottom with the fish. Spread a condensed can of cream of shrimp soup over the fish. Combine a sleeve of crushed butter-flavored crackers with a stick of melted butter and sprinkle the crumbs over the soup. Bake it at 350° for 30 to 40 minutes or until bubbly.

DELORES, SOUTH CAROLINA

stuffed mountain trout

LORETTA WALTERS
OGDEN, UTAH

You can substitute any whole fish in this recipe, but I like it best when it's made with fresh-caught trout from our local mountain streams.

    2 trout (10 to 11 ounces each)
    4 tablespoons plus 1$\frac{1}{2}$ teaspoons lemon juice, divided
    3 teaspoons dill weed, divided
    2 teaspoons lemon-pepper seasoning, divided
    1 small onion, chopped
    1 tablespoon butter
  $\frac{1}{2}$ cup minced fresh parsley
    2 cups soft bread crumbs

[1] Place trout in a 13-in. x 9-in. x 2-in. baking dish coated with nonstick cooking spray. Sprinkle 3 tablespoons lemon juice, 1$\frac{1}{2}$ teaspoons dill and 1$\frac{1}{2}$ teaspoons lemon-pepper in the fish cavities and over outside of fish; set aside.

[2] In a nonstick skillet, saute onion in butter until tender. Add the parsley and remaining dill and lemon-pepper. Stir in bread crumbs; heat through. Sprinkle with remaining lemon juice; stir gently until moistened. Stuff into fish cavities. Bake, uncovered, at 400° for 25-30 minutes or until fish flakes easily with a fork. **Yield:** 4 servings.

southwestern fried perch

JIM LORD
MANCHESTER, NEW HAMPSHIRE

This is one of my favorite ways to prepare perch. Taco seasoning and cornmeal make the coating zesty and unique.

    1 envelope taco seasoning
    1 pound lake perch fillets
    1 egg
  $\frac{1}{2}$ cup yellow cornmeal
  $\frac{1}{4}$ cup all-purpose flour
    3 tablespoons vegetable oil

[1] Place taco seasoning in a large resealable bag; add perch fillets, one at a time, and shake to coat. In a shallow bowl, lightly beat the egg. Combine cornmeal and flour in another shallow bowl. Dip fillets in egg, then coat with cornmeal mixture. Place in a single layer on a plate; refrigerate for 15 minutes.

[2] In a large skillet, heat oil over medium-high heat. Fry fillets for 2-3 minutes on each side or until fish flakes easily with a fork. **Yield:** 4 servings.

baked parmesan fish

  $\frac{1}{3}$ cup grated Parmesan cheese
    2 tablespoons all-purpose flour
  $\frac{1}{2}$ teaspoon paprika
  $\frac{1}{4}$ teaspoon salt
  $\frac{1}{8}$ teaspoon pepper
    1 egg
    2 tablespoons milk
    4 catfish or orange roughy fillets (4 ounces each)

In a shallow bowl, combine the Parmesan cheese, flour, paprika, salt and pepper. In another bowl, beat egg and milk. Dip fish fillets into egg mixture, then coat with the Parmesan mixture. Arrange in a greased 13-in. x 9-in. x 2-in. baking dish. Bake, uncovered, at 350° for 25-30 minutes or until fish flakes easily with a fork. **Yield:** 4 servings.

CAROLYN BRINKMEYER CENTENNIAL, COLORADO

Here's an easy way to work an elegant fish dish into your menu. I sometimes sprinkle the golden fillets with slivered or sliced almonds before baking. My husband, daughter and I love this tasty way to eat fish.

BAKED PARMESAN FISH

HUNTING & FISHING COOKBOOK

SUSAN WRIGHT CHAMPAIGN, ILLINOIS

I enjoyed a similar gumbo at a local restaurant and duplicated it pretty closely. I lightened it up a bit, but no one in my family seemed to mind.

southern seafood gumbo

- 1 medium onion, chopped
- 2 celery ribs with leaves, chopped
- 1 medium green pepper, chopped
- 3 garlic cloves, minced
- 1 tablespoon olive oil
- 1 bottle (46 ounces) spicy hot V8 juice
- 1 can (14$\frac{1}{2}$ ounces) diced tomatoes, undrained
- $\frac{1}{4}$ teaspoon cayenne pepper
- 1 package (16 ounces) frozen sliced okra, thawed
- 1 pound catfish fillets, cut into $\frac{3}{4}$-inch cubes
- $\frac{3}{4}$ pound uncooked medium shrimp, peeled and deveined
- 3 cups cooked long grain rice

SOUTHERN SEAFOOD GUMBO

[1] In a large saucepan, saute the onion, celery, green pepper and garlic in oil until tender. Stir in the V8 juice, tomatoes and cayenne; bring to a boil. Reduce heat; cover and simmer for 10 minutes.

[2] Stir in okra and catfish; cook 8 minutes longer. Add the shrimp; cook about 7 minutes longer or until shrimp turn pink. Place rice in individual serving bowls; top with gumbo. **Yield:** 12 servings.

seafood-stuffed rainbow trout

MYRONIUK TRACY EDMONTON, ALBERTA

This is a special way to serve fresh rainbow trout, stuffed with a mixture of scallops, shrimp, rice, bacon and vegetables. But don't wait for a special occasion to serve it—it's easy to put together and put in the oven.

- 4 tablespoons butter, melted, divided
- 1 tablespoon lemon juice
- 2 pan-dressed trout (about 12 ounces each)
- $\frac{1}{4}$ teaspoon pepper
- $\frac{1}{4}$ cup cooked long grain rice
- 2 bacon strips, cooked and crumbled
- 2 tablespoons each chopped onion and diced sweet red pepper
- 15 frozen cooked salad shrimp, thawed
- 4 sea scallops, diced
- 1 tablespoon vegetable oil
- 2 medium lemons, thinly sliced

[1] Combine 2 tablespoons butter and the lemon juice; brush over trout cavities. Sprinkle with pepper; set aside.

[2] In a small skillet, saute the rice, bacon, onion, red pepper, shrimp and scallops in oil for 5 minutes or until scallops are firm and opaque. Spoon into fish cavities. Top with lemon slices.

[3] Brush remaining butter over a sheet of heavy-duty foil; wrap fish in foil and seal tightly. Place on a baking sheet. Bake at 425° for 25-28 minutes or until fish flakes easily with a fork. **Yield:** 4 servings.

spicy catfish with tomatoes

MARLA ANTHONY
LOGANVILLE, GEORGIA

I came up with this recipe after trying something similar at a catfish house in the mountains of northern Georgia. My husband and I both appreciate this healthy, flavor-packed dish.

1 catfish fillet (about ¹/₂ pound)

¹/₄ teaspoon salt

¹/₈ teaspoon pepper

Dash to ¹/₈ teaspoon cayenne pepper

1 cup canned Mexican diced tomatoes with juice

1 to 2 green onions, thinly sliced

Hot cooked white or brown rice, optional

[1] Sprinkle fish with salt, pepper and cayenne. In a nonstick skillet, cook fish over medium for about 3 minutes on each side or until lightly browned. Top with tomatoes and sprinkle with green onions. Bring to a boil. Reduce heat; simmer, uncovered, for about 2 minutes.

[2] Cover skillet and simmer 2-3 minutes longer or until liquid is reduced and fish flakes easily with a fork. Serve with rice if desired. **Yield:** 2 servings.

stuffed walleye

4 bacon strips, halved

¹/₄ cup chopped onion

2 celery ribs, finely chopped

1 can (6 ounces) crabmeat, drained, flaked and cartilage removed or 1 cup imitation crabmeat, flaked

¹/₄ cup butter

4 cups crushed seasoned stuffing

1¹/₂ cups boiling water

¹/₂ teaspoon salt

¹/₈ teaspoon pepper

¹/₈ teaspoon cayenne pepper

4 walleye fillets (about 8 ounces each)

[1] In a skillet, cook the bacon over medium heat for 3-5 minutes or until it begins to crisp; drain on paper towels. In the same skillet,

STUFFED WALLEYE

saute onion, celery and crab in butter until vegetables are tender. Transfer to a large bowl; add the stuffing, water, salt, pepper and cayenne; toss to moisten.

[2] Place fillets in a greased 15-in. x 10-in. x 1-in. baking pan. Spoon stuffing mixture over fillets; top each with two pieces of bacon.

[3] Bake, uncovered, at 425° for 20-25 minutes or until fish flakes easily with a fork and bacon is cooked. **Yield:** 4 servings.

KIM LEONARD
KALAMAZOO,
MICHIGAN

Walleye is the No.1 game fish in the Midwest. It's a thrill to catch and tastes great, too. This recipe, created by my husband, is a favorite of my family.

HUNTING & FISHING **tip**

I marinate fish fillets for 30 minutes in a mixture of half water and half lemon juice with a little salt before cooking. They have wonderful flavor.

DORIS, INDIANA

HUNTING & FISHING COOKBOOK

**NANCY KELLEY
NASHVILLE,
TENNESSEE**

Five ingredients are all you need to prepare this terrific trout dish. I'm sure it will become a family favorite at your house, too.

trout meuniere

4 trout fillets (6 ounces each)

1$\frac{1}{3}$ cups crushed saltines

4 tablespoons butter, divided

1 package (2$\frac{1}{4}$ ounces) sliced almonds

2 tablespoons lemon juice

[1] Coat both sides of fillets with crushed saltines. In a large skillet, melt 3 tablespoons butter over medium-high heat. Cook fillets for 3-5 minutes on each side or until fish flakes easily with a fork. Remove and keep warm.

[2] In the same skillet, cook and stir the almonds in remaining butter until lightly toasted. Stir in the lemon juice. Serve over trout. **Yield:** 4 servings.

catfish soup

**RUBY WILLIAMS
BOGALUSA, LOUISIANA**

My soup makes a very appetizing meal for two. I don't care for leftovers, and this recipe makes just enough. It's a hit at my house!

1 large onion, chopped

$\frac{1}{4}$ cup chopped celery

4 garlic cloves, minced

2 teaspoons vegetable oil

1$\frac{1}{2}$ cups chopped, seeded and peeled tomatoes

1 cup water

2 bay leaves

1 strip orange peel (about 2 inches x 1 inch)

1 tablespoon minced fresh parsley

$\frac{3}{4}$ to 1 teaspoon salt

$\frac{1}{4}$ teaspoon dried thyme

$\frac{1}{8}$ teaspoon coarsely ground pepper

Dash cayenne pepper

1 catfish fillet or firm whitefish of your choice (about $\frac{1}{2}$ pound), cubed

[1] In a saucepan, saute the onion, celery and garlic in oil for 3 minutes. Stir in the tomatoes, water, bay leaves, orange peel, parsley and seasonings. Bring to a boil. Reduce heat; cover and simmer for 20 minutes.

[2] Stir in catfish; return to a boil. Reduce heat; cover and simmer for 5 minutes or until fish flakes easily with a fork. Discard bay leaves and orange peel. **Yield:** 2 servings.

TROUT MEUNIERE

stuffed trout

SHIRLEY COLEMAN
MONKTON, VERMONT

This is an easy recipe that's special enough for company. It's a delicious treatment for your fresh trout.

- 2 bacon strips, cooked and crumbled
- 1/2 cup fresh coarse bread crumbs
- 1/4 cup chopped onion
- 2 tablespoons chopped fresh parsley
- 1/8 teaspoon salt
- 1/8 teaspoon pepper
- 4 dressed trout (1/2 pound each)

In a medium bowl, combine the first six ingredients; mix well. Stuff 1/4 cup into cavity of each trout. Place on a lightly greased rack in a shallow roasting pan. Bake at 350° for 35-40 minutes or until fish flakes easily with a fork. **Yield:** 4 servings.

CAJUN-STYLE CATFISH

walleye veracruz

ROBERT & LINDA NAGLE
PARK RAPIDS, MINNESOTA

Living in Minnesota lake country, we've naturally had to come up with a variety of recipes for fresh walleye. This is a favorite of ours that has Mexican flair. We sprinkle the fish with lemon pepper, then top it with sliced onion, green pepper, tomato and black olives.

- 4 walleye or catfish fillets (6 ounces each)
- 2 teaspoons lemon-pepper seasoning
- 1 medium red onion, sliced and separated into rings
- 1 medium green pepper, sliced into rings
- 1 large tomato, sliced
- 1/4 cup sliced ripe olives

[1] Place the fillets in a 13-in. x 9-in. x 2-in. baking dish coated with nonstick cooking spray. Sprinkle with lemon-pepper. Layer with the onion, green pepper, tomato and olives.

[2] Cover and bake at 350° for 25-30 minutes or until fish flakes easily with a fork. **Yield:** 4 servings.

cajun-style catfish

- 1/2 cup chopped onion
- 1/2 cup chopped celery
- 1/2 cup chopped green pepper
- 1 tablespoon olive oil
- 1 can (14 1/2 ounces) diced tomatoes and green chilies, undrained
- 1/2 cup sliced fresh mushrooms
- 1 can (2 1/4 ounces) sliced ripe olives, drained
- 1/2 teaspoon garlic powder
- 4 catfish fillets (6 ounces each)
- 1/4 cup grated Parmesan cheese

[1] In a large skillet, saute the onion, celery and green pepper in oil until tender. Add the tomatoes, mushrooms, olives and garlic powder. Bring to a boil. Reduce heat; simmer mixture, uncovered, for 10 minutes or until slightly thickened.

[2] Place the catfish in an ungreased 13-in. x 9-in. x 2-in. baking dish. Top with vegetable mixture; sprinkle with Parmesan cheese. Bake, uncovered, at 400° for 15-20 minutes or until fish flakes easily with a fork. **Yield:** 4 servings.

IRENE CLIETT
CEDAR BLUFF,
MISSISSIPPI

This dish features the green pepper, onion and celery combination common to Cajun dishes, but it's not too spicy. It's a colorful and flavorful way to serve our locally raised catfish.

HUNTING & FISHING COOKBOOK

SESAME DILL FISH

**LINDA HESS
CHILLIWACK,
BRITISH
COLUMBIA**

A tangy yogurt, dill and sesame seed coating make the most delicious fish. I know you'll love it and how quick it is to fix, too.

sesame dill fish

½ cup dry bread crumbs

¼ cup sesame seeds

½ teaspoon dill weed

¼ teaspoon salt

¾ cup plain yogurt

1 pound catfish or other whitefish fillets

¼ cup vegetable oil

Lemon wedges, optional

[1] In a shallow bowl, combine bread crumbs, sesame seeds, dill and salt. Place yogurt in another bowl; stir until smooth. Dip fillets in yogurt; shake off excess, then dip them in crumb mixture.

[2] Heat oil in a large nonstick skillet. Fry fillets over medium-high heat for 2-3 minutes on each side or until fish flakes easily with a fork. Serve with lemon wedges if desired. **Yield:** 4 servings.

trout with mushrooms

**KATHY KITTELL
LENEXA, KANSAS**

A mild lemon sauce accented by fresh mushrooms complements these tender trout fillets. When fish is on sale, I buy plenty to serve to my large brood, because it always gets eaten right away.

½ pound fresh mushrooms, sliced

6 tablespoons butter, divided

2 tablespoons minced fresh parsley

⅓ cup all-purpose flour

¼ teaspoon salt

4 trout fillets (about 6 ounces each)

⅓ cup heavy whipping cream

½ teaspoon lemon juice

[1] In a large skillet, saute mushrooms in 2 tablespoons butter until tender. Stir in parsley. Remove mushrooms to a serving platter; keep warm. Combine flour and salt in a shallow dish; coat fillets with flour mixture on both sides.

[2] Add 2 tablespoons butter to the skillet. Cook trout over medium heat for 8-10 minutes on each side or until fish flakes easily with a fork; arrange over mushrooms.

[3] For sauce, melt remaining butter in a small saucepan. Gradually stir in cream and lemon juice. Bring to a boil for 3-4 minutes or until slightly thickened, stirring constantly. Serve over trout and mushrooms. **Yield:** 4 servings.

salsa catfish

**TERESA HUBBARD
RUSSELLVILLE, ALABAMA**

Give your fish a Southwestern kick with this change-of-pace preparation. My sister doesn't like seafood, so I figured I'd disguise it with a mix of interesting tastes and textures. Everyone was surprised by the slightly crunchy tortilla chip coating.

1 cup finely crushed baked tortilla chips

½ to 1 teaspoon chili powder

3 tablespoons lemon juice

1 tablespoon canola oil

4 catfish fillets (4 ounces each)

1 cup salsa, warmed

[1] In a shallow bowl, combine tortilla chip crumbs and chili powder. In another bowl, combine lemon juice and oil. Dip fish in lemon mixture, then coat with crumb mixture.

[2] Place in a 13-in x 9-in. x 2-in. baking dish coasted with nonstick cooking spray. Sprinkle with any remaining crumbs. Bake at 450° for 8-10 minutes or until fish flakes easily with a fork. Serve with salsa. **Yield:** 4 servings.

trout baked in cream

ANN NACE
PERKASIE, PENNSYLVANIA

Here's a quick and delicious way to serve trout. It's definitely one of our family's favorites.

- 6 trout fillets (about 3$\frac{1}{2}$ ounces each)
- 2 tablespoons lemon juice
- 1 teaspoon dill weed
- $\frac{1}{2}$ teaspoon salt
- $\frac{1}{8}$ teaspoon pepper
- 1 cup heavy whipping cream
- 2 tablespoons seasoned bread crumbs

Place trout in a greased 13-in. x 9-in. x 2-in. baking dish. Sprinkle with lemon juice, dill, salt and pepper. Pour cream over all. Sprinkle with bread crumbs. Bake, uncovered, at 350° for 11-15 minutes or until fish flakes easily with a fork. **Yield:** 4-6 servings.

lime broiled catfish

- 1 tablespoon butter
- 2 tablespoons lime juice
- $\frac{1}{2}$ teaspoon salt, optional
- $\frac{1}{4}$ teaspoon pepper
- $\frac{1}{4}$ teaspoon garlic powder
- 2 catfish fillets (6 ounces each)

Lime slices or wedges, optional

Fresh parsley, optional

[1] Melt butter in a saucepan. Stir in lime juice, salt if desired, pepper and garlic powder; mix well. Remove from the heat and set aside. Place fillets in a shallow baking dish. Brush fillets generously with lime-butter sauce.

[2] Broil for 5-8 minutes or until fish flakes easily with a fork. Remove to a warm serving dish; spoon pan juices over each fillet. Garnish with lime and parsley if desired. **Yield:** 2 servings.

NICK NICHOLSON
CLARKSDALE, MISSISSIPPI

To serve a reduced-calorie dish that is ready in about 15 minutes, I came up with this recipe. I think the lime juice adds fresh flavor to the mild taste of the fish.

LIME BROILED CATFISH

HUNTING & FISHING COOKBOOK

NORMA
DESROCHES
WARWICK,
RHODE ISLAND

I've lived in Rhode Island for over 35 years and love the fresh seafood dishes served here. This is a favorite of mine. My mother-in-law gave me the recipe.

NEW ENGLAND FISH BAKE

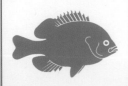

new england fish bake

- 4 medium potatoes, peeled
- 1 teaspoon all-purpose flour
- 1 small onion, sliced into rings
- 1/2 teaspoon salt
- 1/4 teaspoon pepper
- 3/4 cup milk, divided
- 1 1/2 pounds freshwater fish (trout, catfish or pike) or cod fillets
- 3 tablespoons grated Parmesan cheese, optional
- 2 tablespoons minced fresh parsley or 2 teaspoons dried parsley flakes
- 1/4 teaspoon paprika

[1] Place potatoes in a saucepan and cover with water; bring to a boil. Cook until almost tender; drain. Slice 1/8 in. thick; place in a greased shallow 2-qt. baking dish. Sprinkle with flour. Top with onion; sprinkle with salt and pepper. Pour half of the milk over potatoes. Place fish on top; pour remaining milk over the fish. Sprinkle with Parmesan cheese if desired.

[2] Cover and bake at 375° for 20-30 minutes or until fish flakes easily with a fork. Sprinkle with parsley and paprika. **Yield:** 3-4 servings.

trout chowder

LINDA KESSELRING
CORNING, NEW YORK

This hearty chowder cooks conveniently in a slow cooker so I can spend more time fishing and less in the kitchen. Broccoli adds fresh taste and lively color to the rich, cheesy broth.

- 1 medium onion, chopped
- 1 tablespoon butter
- 2 cups milk
- 1 cup ranch salad dressing
- 1 pound boneless trout fillets, skin removed
- 1 package (10 ounces) frozen broccoli cuts, thawed
- 1 cup cubed or shredded cheddar cheese
- 1 cup cubed or shredded Monterey Jack cheese
- 1/4 teaspoon garlic powder

Paprika, optional

[1] In a skillet, saute onion in butter until tender. Transfer to a slow cooker; add milk, dressing, fish, broccoli, cheeses and garlic powder.

[2] Cover and cook on high for 1$\frac{1}{2}$-2 hours or until soup is bubbly and fish flakes easily with a fork. Sprinkle with paprika if desired. **Yield:** 6 servings.

southwestern catfish

BRUCE CRITTENDEN
CLINTON, MISSISSIPPI

Catfish fillets are rubbed with a blend that includes chili powder, cumin, coriander, cayenne and paprika, then topped with homemade salsa. A green salad, garlic bread and baked sweet potatoes round out the meal nicely.

- 3 medium tomatoes, chopped
- $\frac{1}{4}$ cup chopped onion
- 2 jalapeno peppers, seeded and finely chopped
- 2 tablespoons white wine vinegar
- 3 teaspoons salt, divided
- 3 teaspoons paprika
- 3 teaspoons chili powder
- 1 to 1$\frac{1}{2}$ teaspoons ground cumin
- 1 to 1$\frac{1}{2}$ teaspoons ground coriander
- $\frac{3}{4}$ to 1 teaspoon cayenne pepper
- $\frac{1}{2}$ teaspoon garlic powder
- 4 catfish fillets (6 ounces each)

[1] For salsa, in a bowl, combine the tomatoes, onion, jalapenos, vinegar and 1 teaspoon salt. Cover and refrigerate for at least 30 minutes.

[2] Combine paprika, chili powder, cumin, coriander, cayenne, garlic powder and remaining salt; rub over catfish.

[3] Coat grill rack with nonstick cooking spray before starting the grill. Grill fillets, uncovered, over medium heat for 5 minutes on each side or until fish flakes easily with a fork. Serve with salsa. **Yield:** 4 servings.

Editor's Note: When cutting or seeding hot peppers, use rubber or plastic gloves to protect your hands. Avoid touching your face.

baked walleye with vegetables

- 1 small onion, thinly sliced
- 1 tablespoon olive oil
- 2 small zucchini, julienned
- 1 cup sliced fresh mushrooms
- $\frac{1}{4}$ teaspoon pepper
- $\frac{1}{8}$ teaspoon garlic powder
- 2 tablespoons lemon juice
- 2 tablespoons grated Parmesan cheese, divided
- 4 walleye fillets (about 6 ounces each)
- 1 tablespoon butter, melted

[1] In a nonstick skillet, cook onion in oil over medium heat for about 2 minutes. Stir in zucchini and mushrooms; cook and stir 2 minutes longer. Sprinkle with pepper and garlic powder; stir in lemon juice. Cool and stir 30 seconds longer. Remove from heat; stir in 1 teaspoon Parmesan cheese.

[2] Place fillets in a 13-in. x 9-in. x 2-in. baking dish coated with nonstick cooking spray. Top each fillet with about $\frac{1}{4}$ cup onion mixture. Drizzle with butter and sprinkle with remaining Parmesan cheese. Bake, uncovered, at 375° for 18-22 minutes or until the fish flakes easily with a fork. **Yield:** 4 servings.

SONDRA OSTHEIMER BOSCOBEL, WISCONSIN

Mushrooms, zucchini and onions taste just as good with fish as they do with beef and venison. You'll want to share this excellent entree with company.

BAKED WALLEYE WITH VEGETABLES

ELIZABETH
LEBLANC
BOURG,
LOUISIANA

You'll be "hooked" once you try these homemade fish sandwiches. The golden cornmeal breading coats the fillets nicely, and the sauce is tangy. One taste, and you'll know you've got a great meal on the line.

saucy fish sandwiches

1 cup mayonnaise
1/3 cup ketchup
1 teaspoon dried parsley flakes
1 teaspoon dried minced onion
1/2 teaspoon Worcestershire sauce
1/4 to 1/2 teaspoon hot pepper sauce
1/8 teaspoon garlic powder
1/2 cup all-purpose flour
1/2 cup yellow cornmeal
1 teaspoon salt
1/8 teaspoon pepper
1/8 teaspoon cayenne pepper
1 egg
1/2 cup milk
6 panfish or cod fillets (about 1 pound)
Vegetable oil
6 hamburger buns, split
Lettuce leaves

[1] In a small bowl, combine the first seven ingredients; cover and chill at least 1 hour. In a shallow bowl, combine the flour, cornmeal, salt, pepper, and cayenne pepper. Beat egg and milk. Cut fish to fit buns; dip fillets into egg mixture, then coat with flour mixture.

[2] In a large skillet, fry fish in a small amount of oil for 5-10 minutes or until it flakes easily with a fork and is golden brown on both sides. Serve on buns with lettuce and sauce. **Yield:** 6 servings.

zippy cajun baked catfish

WENDY STENMAN
GERMANTOWN, WISCONSIN

This is our favorite way to serve catfish. I've made this with half of the spices at first. When my family got older, I doubled the spices.

2 tablespoons canola oil
2 teaspoons garlic salt
2 teaspoons dried thyme
2 teaspoons paprika
1/2 teaspoon cayenne pepper
1/2 teaspoon hot pepper sauce
1/4 teaspoon pepper
4 catfish fillets (8 ounces each)

[1] In a small bowl, combine the first seven ingredients; brush over both sides of fish.

[2] Place fish in a 13-in. x 9-in. x 2-in. baking dish coated with nonstick cooking spray. Bake at 450° for 10-13 minutes or until fish flakes easily with a fork. **Yield:** 4 servings.

catfish coating mix

JEAN KOMLOS
PLYMOUTH, MICHIGAN

This is such a tasty treatment for catfish. With notes on how to use it, this mix makes an excellent gift for an avid fisherman.

1 3/4 cups dry bread crumbs
3/4 cup cornflakes
3/4 cup grated Parmesan cheese
1 1/2 teaspoons salt
1 1/2 teaspoons paprika
3/4 teaspoon dried thyme

SAUCY FISH SANDWICHES

TANGY LEMON CATFISH

CAROL MINGIA
GREENSBORO,
NORTH
CAROLINA

My husband turns
up his nose at any
fish dish I prepare,
except this one. In
fact, this one makes
his eyes light up!

³/4 teaspoon pepper

ADDITIONAL INGREDIENTS FOR CATFISH:
  ¹/3 cup milk
  1¹/2 pounds catfish fillets, cut into 4-inch strips

In a foood processor, combine first seven ingredients; cover and process until blended. Store in an airtight container in the refrigerator for up to 4 months. **Yield:** about 3 cups.

To prepare catfish: In a shallow dish, place milk. In another shallow dish, place 1 cup coating mixture. Dip fish in milk, then coat with bread crumb mixture. Carefully place in a greased 15-in. x 10-in. x 1-in. baking pan. Bake at 450° for 15-20 minutes or until fish flakes easily with a fork, carefully turning once. **Yield:** 6 servings.

tangy lemon catfish

  2 tablespoons lemon juice
  1 garlic clove, minced
¹/4 teaspoon salt
Dash dried oregano

¹/2 pound catfish or whitefish fillets
¹/4 cup cornmeal
  2 tablespoons all-purpose flour
1¹/2 teaspoons canola oil
1¹/2 teaspoons butter

TARTAR SAUCE:
¹/4 cup mayonnaise
  1 tablespoon finely chopped dill pickle
  2 teaspoons finely chopped onion
  2 teaspoons minced fresh dill or ³/4 teaspoon dill weed

[1] In a resealable plastic bag, combine the lemon juice, garlic, salt and oregano; add fillets. Seal bag and turn to coat; refrigerate for 30-60 minutes, turning several times.

[2] Drain and discard marinade. In a shallow bowl, combine cornmeal and flour. Coat fillets with cornmeal mixture. In a skillet, cook fillets in oil and butter for 5 minutes on each side or until golden brown and fish flakes easily with a fork.

[3] Meanwhile, for tartar sauce, in a bowl, combine the mayonnaise, pickle, onion and dill. Serve with fish. **Yield:** 2 servings.

TASTE OF HOME TEST KITCHEN

Fishing for a new way to serve salmon that's special enough for company? Try this elegant entree. A generous topping of bread crumbs, almonds, green onion and seasonings give moist salmon a tasty treatment.

BAKED SALMON WITH CRUMB TOPPING

baked salmon with crumb topping

- 1 cup soft whole wheat bread crumbs
- 1/3 cup sliced almonds, coarsely chopped
- 1 tablespoon finely chopped green onion
- 1 1/2 teaspoons minced fresh thyme or 1/2 teaspoon dried thyme
- 1/2 teaspoon salt
- 1/8 teaspoon pepper
- 2 tablespoons butter, melted
- 1 salmon fillet (2 pounds)

[1] In a bowl, combine the bread crumbs, almonds, onion, thyme, salt and pepper; mix well. Add butter and toss lightly; set aside.

[2] Pat salmon dry. Place skin side down in a 15-in. x 10-in. x 1-in. baking pan coated with nonstick cooking spray. Spritz salmon with nonstick cooking spray; cover with crumb mixture. Bake, uncovered, at 350° for 20-25 minutes or until fish flakes easily with a fork. **Yield:** 8 servings.

salmon with orange-kiwi salsa

MARIA DAVIS
FLOWER MOUND, TEXAS

When I first tried this wonderful marinated baked salmon, I knew I had to have the recipe. The citrusy salsa is as pretty as it is tasty.

- 1/2 cup white wine or chicken broth
- 1/2 cup unsweetened red grapefruit juice
- 4 garlic cloves, minced
- 1 to 2 teaspoons dill weed

tip

HUNTING & FISHING

In general, I pound of whole fish yields I serving. One pound of fish steaks or fillets equals 3 to 4 servings. Prepare fresh fish within I to 2 days after it's caught. It should be pan-dressed, washed in cold water, blotted with paper towels, placed in an airtight container or heavy-duty plastic bag, and refrigerated in the coldest part of your refrigerator. TASTE OF HOME TEST KITCHEN

4 salmon fillets (6 ounces each)

SALSA:

1 cup chopped orange

1 cup chopped kiwifruit

1 large onion, chopped

1 jalapeno pepper, seeded and diced

[1] In a large resealable plastic bag, combine the first four ingredients; add salmon. Seal bag and turn to coat; refrigerate for 2 hours. In a bowl, combine salsa ingredients. Cover and refrigerate until serving.

[2] Drain marinade and place in a saucepan. Bring to a boil; boil for 1 minute. Gently place salmon in a 13-in. x 9-in. x 2-in. baking dish. Pour marinade over salmon. Cover and bake at 375° for 20-25 minutes or until fish flakes easily with a fork. Serve with fruit salsa. **Yield:** 4 servings.

Editor's Note: When cutting and seeding hot peppers, use rubber or plastic gloves to protect your hand. Avoid touching your face.

lemony salmon and pasta

1 whole garlic bulb

1 tablespoon water

3 tablespoons olive oil, divided

5 tablespoons Cajun seasoning

3 tablespoons honey

1 salmon fillet (2 pounds), cut into 2-inch pieces

3 plum tomatoes, quartered

1 medium sweet red pepper, cut into 1/4-inch strips

1 medium sweet yellow pepper, cut into 1/4-inch strips

1 large red onion, sliced

8 ounces uncooked penne or medium tube pasta

LEMON SAUCE:

1/3 cup butter, cubed

1/4 cup olive oil

3 tablespoons lemon juice

1 to 2 garlic cloves, minced

2 teaspoons grated lemon peel

1 tablespoon minced fresh parsley

1/2 teaspoon salt

Dash dried tarragon

Dash cayenne pepper

1/3 cup pitted ripe olives

1/4 cup sunflower kernels, toasted

[1] Cut top off garlic bulb, leaving root end intact. Place cut side up in a small ungreased baking dish; drizzle water around the garlic. Slowly drizzle 1 tablespoon oil into center of bulb. Cover and bake at 350° for 50-60 minutes or until garlic is very soft. Cool for 5 minutes. Squeeze softened garlic from skins; set aside.

[2] Combine the Cajun seasoning, honey and remaining oil; spoon half over the salmon. In a bowl, combine tomatoes, peppers and onion; add remaining honey mixture and toss to coat. Place salmon and vegetables on a greased broiler pan. Broil 3-4 in. from the heat for 6-8 minutes or until fish flakes easily with a fork and vegetables are crisp-tender.

[3] Meanwhile, cook pasta according to package directions. In a saucepan, combine the first nine sauce ingredients; cook and stir until butter is melted. Drain the pasta. In a large serving bowl, gently toss pasta, lemon sauce, softened garlic, salmon and vegetables. Sprinkle with olives and sunflower kernels. **Yield:** 8 servings.

PENNY CHILDS FERNDALE, WASHINGTON

My family made this up as we went along one night. There are endless possibilities for this dish, but I wrote down this version because we all liked it so much.

LEMONY SALMON AND PASTA

**RITA FUTRAL
OCEAN SPRING,
MISSISSIPPI**

I created this recipe for a catfish cooking contest by modifying a recipe for shrimp and spaghetti, which I also developed.

catfish with lemon-butter sauce

   3/4 cup butter

   8 ounces fresh mushrooms, sliced

   1 garlic clove, minced

   1/2 cup chicken broth or dry white wine

   2 tablespoons lemon juice

   1/4 to 1/3 cup chopped fresh parsley

   1 teaspoon salt

   1/2 teaspoon pepper

1 1/2 pounds catfish fillets, cut into bite-size pieces

 16 ounces spaghetti, cooked and drained

   1/2 cup grated Parmesan cheese

Lemon slices or wedges, optional

Additional parsley, optional

[1] In a large skillet, melt butter over medium heat. Cook mushrooms and garlic, stirring occasionally, for 5 minutes. Add broth or wine, lemon juice, parsley, salt and pepper; cook 3 minutes, stirring occasionally.

[2] Add catfish; simmer, uncovered, for 6-8 minutes or until fish flakes easily with a fork. (Butter sauce will be thin.) Serve over spaghetti. Sprinkle with Parmesan cheese. Garnish with lemon and parsley if desired. **Yield:** 6-8 servings.

lemon-pepper catfish

**REGINA ROSENBERRY
GREENCASTLE, PENNSYLVANIA**

Nothing beats a late supper of grilled catfish after a hard day's work.

   6 tablespoons lemon juice

   1/4 cup butter, melted

   2 teaspoons Worcestershire sauce

   4 catfish fillets (about 5 ounces each)

CATFISH WITH LEMON-BUTTER SAUCE

¹/₂ teaspoon salt

¹/₂ teaspoon lemon-pepper seasoning

[1] In a large resealable plastic bag, combine lemon juice, butter and Worcestershire sauce. Add catfish; seal bag and turn to coat. Refrigerate 30 minutes, turning occasionally.

[2] Coat grill rack with nonstick cooking spray before starting the grill. Drain and discard marinade. Sprinkle catfish with salt and lemon-pepper. Grill, covered, over medium heat for 4-6 minutes on each side or until fish flakes with a fork. **Yield:** 4 servings.

spinach catfish skillet

LEE BREMSON
KANSAS CITY, MISSOURI

Nestled in a skillet with colorful, nutritious carrots and spinach, this catfish fillet comes out perfectly moist. Preparing this no-fuss skillet supper is as easy as heating a frozen dinner—and it tastes so much better!

10 baby carrots

2 teaspoons vegetable oil

¹/₄ cup thinly sliced onion

1 catfish fillet (about 6 ounces)

1 package (6 ounces) fresh baby spinach

2 tablespoons white wine vinegar

¹/₄ teaspoon sugar

[1] In a skillet, stir-fry carrots in oil for 1-2 minutes or until crisp-tender. Add onion; cook and stir for 1 minute. Add catfish; cook for 2-3 minutes on each side. Add spinach. Sprinkle with vinegar and sugar.

[2] Cover and cook for 5 minutes or until fish flakes easily with a fork. Remove to a warm serving dish; spoon pan juices over fillet. **Yield:** 1 serving.

FISH FILLETS ITALIANO

fish fillets italiano

¹/₄ cup chopped onion

1 garlic clove, minced

2 teaspoons olive oil

1 cup diced zucchini

¹/₂ cup sliced fresh mushrooms

¹/₂ teaspoon dried oregano

¹/₄ teaspoon dried basil

1 can (8 ounces) tomato sauce

1 tablespoon tomato paste

³/₄ **pound cod, perch or haddock fillets**

2 **tablespoons shredded Parmesan cheese**

[1] In a skillet, saute onion and garlic in oil until tender. Add the zucchini, mushrooms, oregano and basil. Cook for 3 minutes or until tender. Stir in tomato sauce and paste. Cook 8-10 minutes longer or until heated through.

[2] Place fillets in an ungreased 11-in. x 7-in. x 2-in. baking dish; top with vegetable mixture. Bake, uncovered, at 350° for 20 minutes or until fish flakes easily with a fork. Sprinkle with Parmesan cheese. **Yield:** 2 servings.

MARGARET RISINGER
PACIFICA, CALIFORNIA

My husband is an avid fisherman, so we enjoy a lot of fresh ocean fish. I found this recipe in a cookbook but adjusted it to serve two and changed the seasonings. Served with rice and a salad, it makes a delicious low-fat entree.

HUNTING & FISHING COOKBOOK

HUNTING & FISHING tip

Wrap fresh fish in freezer paper, heavy-duty foil or heavy-duty plastic bags for long-term storage in the freezer. Freeze leaner fish, such as catfish and rainbow trout, for up to 6 months. Freeze oily fish, such as salmon and lake trout, for up to 3 months. TASTE OF HOME TEST KITCHEN

catfish with savory strawberry sauce

HEATHER SAPP
ARLINGTON, VIRGINIA

This mouthwatering fish is sure to be the hit of your next special dinner. The tangy sauce is excellent with the sweet catfish.

4 catfish fillets (6 ounces each)
1/4 teaspoon salt
1/4 teaspoon pepper
1 teaspoon hot pepper sauce
1/4 cup strawberry spreadable fruit
2 tablespoons red wine vinegar
1 tablespoon seafood sauce
3/4 teaspoon soy sauce
1/2 teaspoon grated horseradish
1 garlic clove, minced
1/3 cup cornmeal
1/3 cup all-purpose flour
1 tablespoon olive oil

[1] Place fillets in a shallow dish. Sprinkle with the salt, pepper and hot pepper sauce; set aside. In a small saucepan, combine the strawberry spreadable fruit, vinegar, seafood sauce, soy sauce, horseradish and garlic. Cook until heated through.

[2] Meanwhile, in a large resealable plastic bag, combine cornmeal and flour. Add one catfish fillet at a time and shake to coat.

[3] In a large nonstick skillet, cook catfish in oil over medium-high heat for 2-3 minutes on each side or until fish flakes easily with a fork. Drain on paper towels. Serve with strawberry sauce. **Yield:** 4 servings.

catfish po'boys

MILDRED SHERRER
FORT WORTH, TEXAS

A zesty cornmeal mixture coats catfish strips in these filling sandwiches.

2 tablespoons mayonnaise
1 tablespoon sour cream
1 tablespoon white wine vinegar
1 teaspoon sugar
2 cups broccoli coleslaw mix

CRUNCHY-COATED WALLEYE

SONDRA OSTHEIMER BOSCOBEL, WISCONSIN

Your fresh lake fish will go to wonderful use in this recipe, which produces crunchy, golden fillets. Delicious!

crunchy-coated walleye

1/3 cup all-purpose flour
1 teaspoon paprika
1/2 teaspoon salt
1/4 teaspoon pepper
1/4 teaspoon onion powder
1/4 teaspoon garlic powder
2 eggs
2 1/4 pounds walleye, perch or pike fillets
1 1/2 cups mashed potato flakes
1/3 cup vegetable oil
Tartar sauce and lemon wedges, optional

[1] In a shallow bowl, combine flour, paprika, salt, pepper, onion powder and garlic powder. In another bowl, beat the eggs. Dip both sides of fillets in flour mixture and eggs, then coat with potato flakes.

[2] In a skillet, fry fillets in oil for 5 minutes on each side or until fish flakes easily with a fork. Serve with tartar sauce and lemon if desired. **Yield:** 4 servings.

1 pound catfish fillets, cut into
2¹/₂-inch strips

2 tablespoons milk

¹/₄ cup cornmeal

2 teaspoons Cajun seasoning

¹/₂ teaspoon salt

¹/₈ teaspoon cayenne pepper

2 teaspoons olive oil

4 kaiser rolls, split

[1] In a small bowl, whisk the mayonnaise, sour cream, vinegar and sugar until smooth. Add coleslaw mix; toss. Set aside. In a shallow bowl, toss the catfish with milk. In a large resealable plastic bag, combine cornmeal, Cajun seasoning, salt and cayenne. Add catfish, a few pieces at a time, and shake to coat.

[2] In a large nonstick skillet, heat oil over medium heat. Cook catfish for 4-5 minutes on each side or until fish flakes easily with a fork and coating is golden brown. Spoon coleslaw onto rolls; top with catfish. **Yield:** 4 servings.

crispy catfish

³/₄ cup finely crushed saltines (about 22 crackers)

1 teaspoon seasoned salt

¹/₂ teaspoon celery salt

¹/₂ teaspoon garlic salt

4 catfish fillets (about 8 ounces each)

¹/₃ cup butter, melted

In a shallow dish, combine the first four ingredients. Pat fillets dry; dip in butter, then coat with crumb mixture. Coat grill rack with cooking spray before starting grill. Grill fillets, covered, over medium-hot heat for 10 minutes or until fish flakes easily with a fork, carefully turning once. **Yield:** 4 servings.

**RHONDA DIETZ
GARDEN CITY,
KANSAS**
Grilling is my family's favorite way to fix suppers. Because my husband savors fresh fish off the grill, this recipe quickly became one of his most requested.

CRISPY CATFISH

**RITA FUTRAL
OCEAN SPRING,
MISSISSIPPI**

Temperatures here on the Gulf Coast are moderate year-round, so we grill out a lot. My husband, Larry, came up with this recipe by experimenting. Our whole family likes the unique taste of this dish.

greek grilled catfish

6 catfish fillets (8 ounces each)

Greek seasoning to taste

4 ounces feta cheese, crumbled

1 tablespoon dried mint

2 tablespoons olive oil

Fresh mint leaves or parsley, optional

Cherry tomatoes, optional

[1] Sprinkle both sides of fillets with Greek seasoning. Sprinkle each fillet with 1 rounded tablespoon feta cheese and $\frac{1}{2}$ teaspoon mint. Drizzle 1 teaspoon olive oil over each. Roll up fillets and secure with toothpicks.

[2] Grill over medium heat for 20–25 minutes or until fish flakes easily with a fork. Or, place fillets in a greased baking dish and bake at 350° for 30-35 minutes or until fish flakes easily with fork. Garnish with mint leaves or parsley and cherry tomatoes if desired. **Yield:** 6 servings.

coconut-crusted perch

**NORMA THURBER
JOHNSTON, RHODE ISLAND**

A coconut breading lends tropical taste to tender perch served with a sweet-sour sauce for dipping. I've made this dish for my family for years. It's good with any whitefish.

$\frac{1}{2}$ cup apricot preserves

$\frac{1}{4}$ cup ketchup

$\frac{1}{4}$ cup light corn syrup

2 tablespoons lemon juice

$\frac{1}{4}$ teaspoon ground ginger

2 cups crushed butter-flavored crackers (about 50 crackers)

1 cup flaked coconut

2 eggs

2 tablespoons evaporated milk

$\frac{1}{2}$ teaspoon salt

GREEK GRILLED CATFISH

3 pounds perch fillets

1 cup vegetable oil, divided

[1] For sweet-sour sauce, combine the preserves, ketchup, corn syrup, lemon juice and ginger in a small saucepan. Bring to a boil. Reduce heat; simmer, uncovered, for 5 minutes or until slightly thickened. Remove from the heat and keep warm.

[2] In a shallow dish, combine the cracker crumbs and coconut. In another shallow dish, whisk the eggs, milk and salt. Dip each fillet in egg mixture, then coat with crumb mixture.

[3] In a large skillet, cook fish in 3 tablespoons oil in batches over medium-high heat for 1-2 minutes on each side or until fish flakes easily with a fork, adding oil as needed. Serve with sweet-sour sauce. **Yield:** 8 servings.

BAKED FISH AND RICE

flavorful catfish fillets

**ELLEN MUNNIK
CHESTERFIELD, MICHIGAN**

This is the best catfish ever. It's fast to prepare, and the cayenne adds a little zip. The golden cornmeal and herb coating keeps the fillets moist and gives them traditional appeal without the fat that comes from frying.

1/4 cup buttermilk

2 teaspoons Dijon mustard

1/2 cup cornmeal

1/2 teaspoon dried thyme

1/2 teaspoon pepper

1/4 to 1/2 teaspoon cayenne pepper

1 pound catfish fillets

Lemon wedges, optional

[1] In a shallow bowl, whisk buttermilk and mustard until smooth. In another bowl, combine the cornmeal and seasonings. Dip fillets into buttermilk mixture, then into cornmeal mixture. Place 1 in. apart on a wire rack coated with nonstick cooking spray. Place rack on a baking sheet.

[2] Broil fish 4 in. from the heat for 3-4 minutes on each side or until fish flakes easily with a fork. Serve with lemon if desired. **Yield:** 4 servings.

baked fish and rice

1 1/2 cups boiling chicken broth

1/2 cup uncooked long grain rice

1/4 teaspoon Italian seasoning

1/4 teaspoon garlic powder

1 package (10 ounces) frozen chopped broccoli, thawed and drained

1 tablespoon grated Parmesan cheese

1 can (2.8 ounces) french-fried onions, divided

1 pound fresh or frozen fish fillets, thawed

Dash paprika

1/2 cup shredded cheddar cheese

[1] In a greased 11-in. x 7-in. x 2-in. baking dish, combine the broth, rice, Italian seasoning and garlic powder. Cover and bake at 375° for 10 minutes. Add the broccoli, Parmesan cheese and half of the onions. Top with fish fillets; sprinkle with paprika.

[2] Cover and bake 20-25 minutes longer or until the fish flakes easily with a fork. Uncover; sprinkle with cheddar cheese and remaining onions. Bake 3 minutes longer or until cheese is melted. **Yield:** 4 servings.

**JO GROTH,
PLAINFIELD,
IOWA**

I just recently tried this simple-to-fix meal in one, and it was an instant hit here at our house. Fish and rice are a tasty change of pace from regular meat-and-potato fare.

HUNTING & FISHING COOKBOOK

GLAZED SALMON FILLET

½ cup finely chopped red onion

⅓ cup minced lovage or celery leaves

¼ cup lemon juice

1 tablespoon grated lemon peel

½ teaspoon salt

½ teaspoon hot pepper sauce

SALMON:

1 egg

2 tablespoons milk

1 cup dry bread crumbs

½ cup grated Parmesan cheese

4 salmon fillets (6 ounces each)

3 tablespoons vegetable oil

[1] In a large bowl, gently toss the compote ingredients. Cover and let stand at room temperature for 1 hour.

[2] In a shallow bowl, whisk the egg and milk. In another shallow bowl, combine bread crumbs and Parmesan cheese. Pat salmon dry with paper towels. Dip in milk mixture, then coat with crumb mixture.

[3] In a large nonstick skillet, cook the salmon in oil over medium-high heat until fish flakes easily with a fork, turning once. Serve with compote. **Yield:** 4 servings.

artichoke olive salmon

MICHELE SALAZAR
PLAIN CITY, OHIO

After I enjoyed a salmon fillet smothered with artichoke hearts, olives and diced tomatoes at an Italian restaurant, I decided to create this recipe at home. My husband loves it.

1 salmon fillet (20 ounces)

1 cup stuffed olives, chopped

1 can (4¼ ounces) chopped ripe olives

1 can water-packed artichoke hearts, rinsed and drained

1 can (14½ ounces) diced tomatoes, drained

Cut salmon into four pieces. Place on a piece of heavy-duty foil (about 18 in. x 15 in.). Top each piece with olives, artichokes and tomatoes. Fold foil around salmon and seal tightly. Place on a baking sheet. Bake at 350° for

SHERRY WEST
NEW RIVER,
ARIZONA

I love to cook and usually try a new recipe at least once a week. This salmon has wonderful flavor. I've served it to company several times, and they always love it.

glazed salmon fillet

¼ cup soy sauce

2 tablespoons brown sugar

¼ teaspoon crushed red pepper flakes

¼ teaspoon ground ginger

⅛ teaspoon sesame oil

1 salmon fillet (1½ pounds)

In a small bowl, combine the first five ingredients. If grilling the salmon, coat grill rack with nonstick cooking spray before starting the grill. Grill salmon, covered, over medium heat or broil 4-6 in. from the heat for 5-6 minutes on each side or until fish flakes easily with a fork, basting frequently with glaze. **Yield:** 6 servings.

parmesan salmon fillets

TASTE OF HOME TEST KITCHEN

This tasty pan-fried salmon with a salsa-like compote makes a colorful entree any time of year. If you can't find lovage leaves, use celery leaves instead.

TOMATO LOVAGE COMPOTE:

2 large tomatoes, seeded and chopped

35-40 minutes or until fish flakes easily with a fork. **Yield:** 4 servings.

snowcapped salmon

ELLA HOSMER
CENTRAL, ALASKA

The name of this recipe is suggestive of my state's wondrous beauty. Alaska is known for its salmon, and this is one of my favorite ways to prepare it. The recipe also works well with other kinds of fish.

    1 tablespoon all-purpose flour
    4 salmon fillets (6 ounces each)
    2 egg whites
    1 cup mayonnaise
    1 teaspoon ground mustard
    1/4 cup grated Parmesan cheese

[1] Sprinkle flour over salmon fillets. Place in a greased 11-in. x 7-in. x 2-in. baking dish. In a small mixing bowl, beat egg whites until stiff peaks form.

[2] In another bowl, combine the mayonnaise and mustard; fold in egg whites. Spoon over salmon. Sprinkle with cheese. Bake, uncov-ered, at 350° for 25-30 minutes or until fish flakes easily with a fork. **Yield:** 4 servings.

Editor's Note: Reduced-fat or fat-free mayon-naise is not recommended for this recipe.

basil caesar salmon

    4 salmon fillets (8 ounces each)
    1/4 cup creamy Caesar salad dressing
Pepper to taste
    1 cup Caesar salad croutons, crushed
    1/2 cup grated Parmesan cheese
    2 teaspoons dried basil
    2 tablespoons olive oil

Place salmon in a greased 15-in. x 10-in. x 1-in. baking pan. Spoon the salad dressing over fillets; sprinkle with pepper. Combine the croutons, Parmesan cheese and basil; sprinkle over fillets and gently press into dressing. Drizzle with oil. Bake, uncovered, at 350° for 15-20 minutes or until fish flakes easily with a fork. **Yield:** 4 servings.

LAURIE LACLAIR
NORTH RICHLAND
HILLS, TEXAS

Since I love both salmon and Caesar salad, I created this delish fish dish. It's hard to believe it takes so little effort to prepare such a showy company entree.

BASIL CAESAR SALMON

HUNTING & FISHING COOKBOOK

HONEY WALLEYE

**KITTY MCCUE
ST. LOUIS PARK,
MINNESOTA**

Our state is known as the "Land of 10,000 Lakes," so fishing is a favorite recreation here. This recipe is a quick way to prepare all the fresh walleye that's hooked by the anglers in our family.

honey walleye

- 1 egg
- 2 teaspoons honey
- 2 cups crushed butter-flavored crackers (about 45 to 50)
- 1/2 teaspoon salt
- 4 to 6 walleye fillets (1 1/2 to 2 pounds)
- 1/3 to 1/2 cup vegetable oil

Lemon wedges, optional

[1] In a shallow bowl, beat egg; add honey. In a large resealable plastic bag, combine crackers and salt. Dip fish in egg mixture, then shake in bag until coated.

[2] In a skillet, cook fillets in oil for 3-5 minutes on each side or until golden and fish flakes easily with a fork. Serve with lemon wedges if desired. **Yield:** 4-6 servings.

hearty walleye sandwiches

**CARMEN HENDERSON
HEREFORD, TEXAS**

Our family likes to fish, so I'm always looking for different ways to prepare our catch. This one has turned out to be a family favorite.

- 1 walleye fillet (about 12 ounces), cut in half
- 1 tablespoon lemon juice
- 1/4 teaspoon salt
- 1/8 to 1/4 teaspoon pepper
- 1/4 cup cornmeal
- 4 bacon strips
- 1 tablespoon butter, softened
- 2 submarine buns, split
- 1/4 cup mayonnaise
- 1 garlic clove, minced

Lettuce leaves

Tomato slices

[1] Sprinkle fillet with lemon juice, salt and pepper. Coat with cornmeal and set aside. In a skillet, cook bacon over medium heat until crisp. Remove to paper towels; drain, reserving 2 tablespoons drippings.

[2] In the same skillet, cook fillet in reserved drippings for about 4 minutes on each side or until fish flakes easily with a fork. Meanwhile, butter cut sides of buns. Place buttered side up on a baking sheet. Toast under broiler for about 1 minute or until golden brown.

[3] In a small bowl, combine the mayonnaise and garlic; spread on buns. Top with lettuce, tomato slices and fish. **Yield:** 2 servings.

fisherman's crispy coating

TAMMI FREIH
LAKEWOOD, CALIFORNIA

My father is an avid fisherman and frequently acts as the chef on fishing trips he takes with his buddies. To please that group—and to get us kids to eat fish at home—he created this pleasantly mild, crispy coating.

- 1 egg
- 1 cup milk
- 1 cup crisp rice cereal, crushed
- 1/4 cup all-purpose flour
- 1/4 cup cornmeal
- 1 1/2 teaspoons lemon-pepper seasoning
- 1/4 teaspoon seasoned salt
- 1/8 teaspoon onion salt
- 1/8 teaspoon garlic salt
- 4 walleye or other whitefish fillets (1 3/4 to 2 pounds)

Oil for frying

[1] In a shallow bowl, whisk together the egg and milk. In a large resealable plastic bag, combine the cereal, flour, cornmeal and seasonings. Dip the fish fillets into egg mixture, then coat with cereal mixture.

[2] In a large skillet, heat 1/4-in. of oil over medium-high heat. Fry the fillets for 5-7 minutes on each side or until fish flakes easily with a fork. **Yield:** 4 servings.

italian-style walleye

CATHY LUESCHEN
COLUMBUS, NEBRASKA

Herbs and melted cheese dress up fillets in this recipe. When I want a quick fish dinner, this is the recipe I turn to.

- 4 to 6 walleye fillets (about 1 1/2 pounds)
- 1 can (15 ounces) tomato sauce
- 2 tablespoons chopped fresh parsley
- 1 teaspoon Italian seasoning
- 1/2 teaspoon dried basil
- 1/4 teaspoons salt
- 1/8 teaspoon pepper

- 1 cup (4 ounces) shredded part-skim mozzarella cheese

[1] Place walleye in a greased shallow 3-qt. or 13-in. x 9-in. x 2-in baking dish. Combine the tomato sauce, parsley, Italian seasoning, basil, salt and pepper; pour over the fish.

[2] Bake, uncovered, at 350° for 15 minutes. Sprinkle with mozzarella cheese. Bake 5-10 minutes longer or until fish flakes easily with a fork. **Yield:** 4-6 servings.

broiled fish

- 4 snapper, catfish, trout or orange roughy fillets (1 1/2 to 2 pounds)
- 6 tablespoons butter, melted, divided
- 1 tablespoon all-purpose flour

Paprika

Juice of 1 lemon

- 1 tablespoon minced fresh parsley
- 2 teaspoons Worcestershire sauce

[1] Place fish on a broiler rack that has been coated with nonstick cooking spray. Brush tops of fish with 3 tablespoons of the butter; dust with flour and sprinkle with paprika. Broil 5-6 in. from the heat for 5 minutes or until fish just begins to brown.

[2] Combine lemon juice, parsley, Worcestershire sauce and remaining butter; pour over the fish. Broil 5 minutes longer or until fish flakes easily with a fork. **Yield:** 4 servings.

ANN BERG
CHESAPEAKE, VIRGINIA

Mother's secret in preparing this recipe was to butter the fish first before dusting it with flour. That seals in the moisture of the fish, which makes it succulent and absolutely delicious.

BROILED FISH

HUNTING & FISHING COOKBOOK

**MARGARET GARBERS
VAN HORNE, IOWA**

All the fishermen at your house will be pleased to turn over their catch for this tasty recipe. The seasoned crumb mixture produces a crispy coating for baked fillets that really stays on.

bluegill parmesan

1/4 cup butter, melted
1/2 cup dry bread crumbs
1/3 cup grated Parmesan cheese
2 tablespoons minced fresh parsley
1 teaspoon salt
1/2 teaspoon paprika
1/4 teaspoon dried oregano
1/4 teaspoon dried basil
1/4 teaspoon pepper
1 pound fresh or frozen bluegill fillets, thawed

Place butter in a shallow dish. In another shallow dish, combine the bread crumbs, the Parmesan cheese and seasonings. Dip fillets in butter, then coat with crumb mixture. Place in a greased 15-in. x 10-in. x 1-in. baking pan. Bake, uncovered, at 350° for 20 minutes or until the fish flakes easily with a fork. **Yield:** 4 servings.

crab-stuffed catfish

**JOY MCCONAGHY
MOLINE, ILLINOIS**

My family was not big on fish until I made this dish. I stuff catfish fillets with crabmeat, cheese, seasoned bread crumbs and mayonnaise.

1 can (6 ounces) crabmeat, drained, flaked and cartilage removed or 1 cup imitation crabmeat, flaked
3 tablespoons seasoned bread crumbs
2 tablespoons shredded Monterey Jack cheese
2 tablespoons butter, melted
1 1/2 teaspoons mayonnaise
1/8 teaspoon salt, optional
1/8 teaspoon pepper
Dash cayenne pepper
2 catfish or whitefish fillets (6 ounces each)
1/8 teaspoon paprika

BLUEGILL PARMESAN

In a bowl, combine the first eight ingredients. Cut each fillet in half widthwise; place two halves in a greased 8-in. square baking dish. Press crab mixture onto fillets; top with remaining halves. Sprinkle with paprika. Bake, uncovered, at 425° for 22-26 minutes or until fish flakes easily with a fork. **Yield:** 2 servings.

italian catfish fillets

CHERI LEFKOWITCH
NORWALK, CONNECTICUT

A tangy red sauce adds pizzazz to the catfish fillets in this simple entree. I've been preparing this recipe for years, and my family loves it.

> 1 can (8 ounces) tomato sauce
> 2 teaspoons olive oil
> 1 teaspoon zesty Italian salad dressing mix
> 1/4 teaspoon salt
> 1/8 teaspoon pepper
> 4 catfish fillets (6 ounces each)
> 3 tablespoons shredded Romano cheese

[1] In a bowl, combine the first five ingredients. Pour half of the sauce into an 11-in. x 7-in. x 2-in. baking dish coated with nonstick cooking spray. Arrange fish over sauce. Top with remaining sauce.

[2] Bake, uncovered, at 375° for 20 minutes. Sprinkle with cheese. Bake 5 minutes longer or until fish flakes easily with a fork and cheese is melted. **Yield:** 4 servings.

oven-fried catfish

KAY BELL
PALESTINE, TEXAS

You can't beat this easy method for making the very best catfish. It's a favorite of mine.

> 1 cup crushed cornflakes
> 3/4 teaspoon celery salt
> 1/4 teaspoon onion powder
> 1/4 teaspoon paprika
> 1/8 teaspoon pepper
> 6 catfish fillets (6 ounces each)
> 1/3 cup butter, melted

INSTEAD OF FRYING FISH

[1] In a shallow bowl, combine the cornflakes, celery salt, onion powder, paprika and pepper. Brush the fish fillets with butter; coat with crumb mixture.

[2] Place in a greased 13-in. x 9-in. x 2-in. baking dish. Bake, uncovered, at 350° for 25 minutes or until fish flakes easily with a fork. **Yield:** 6 servings.

instead of frying fish

> 1 pound walleye, perch or pike fillets
> 1/4 cup milk
> 1 cup crushed potato chips
> 1/4 cup grated Parmesan cheese
> 1/4 teaspoon dried thyme
> 1 tablespoon dry bread crumbs
> 2 tablespoons butter, melted

[1] Cut fish into serving-size pieces. Place milk in a shallow bowl. In another shallow bowl, combine potato chips, Parmesan cheese and thyme. Dip fish in milk, then coat with the potato chip mixture. Sprinkle a greased 8-in. square baking dish with bread crumbs.

[2] Place fish over crumbs; drizzle with butter. Bake, uncovered, at 475° for 12-14 minutes or until the fish flakes easily with a fork. **Yield:** 4 servings.

SHARON FUNFSINN
MENDOTA, ILLINOIS

This quick recipe is one I discovered over 20 years ago in a fund-raiser cookbook. Since my husband is an avid fisherman, I've put it to good use over the years. The crispy potato chip coating bakes up toasty brown, and the fillets stay nice and moist.

HUNTING & FISHING COOKBOOK

**DIXIE HARMON
BAINVILLE,
MONTANA**

Fresh salmon is a real treat for us. So when I have the opportunity to cook with a whole salmon, I love to make this elegant entree.

baked whole salmon

- ¾ cup white wine or chicken broth
- ¾ cup chopped celery leaves
- 1 small onion, minced
- 2 lemon slices
- 8 fresh basil leaves
- 2 teaspoons dried tarragon
- 1 teaspoon dried rosemary, crushed
- ¼ teaspoon dried thyme
- 1 whole salmon (about 10 pounds)
- 1½ teaspoons salt

WINE SAUCE:

- 2 green onions, chopped
- ½ cup butter
- 6 tablespoons all-purpose flour
- 2⅓ cups water
- 2⅓ cups white wine or chicken broth
- 2 egg yolks, lightly beaten
- ½ cup heavy whipping cream

Salt and pepper to taste

[1] In a saucepan over medium heat, combine the first eight ingredients. Bring to a boil. Reduce heat; simmer, uncovered, 30 minutes.

[2] Remove head and tail from salmon if desired. Place a double thickness of heavy-duty foil on a baking sheet (longer than the length of the fish). Grease foil. Place salmon on foil; sprinkle the cavity with salt. Pour herb sauce over fish. Fold foil over fish and seal tightly. Bake at 375° for 60-75 minutes or until fish flakes easily with a fork.

[3] Place the salmon on a serving platter and keep warm. Strain cooking juices, reserving ⅓ cup. In a large saucepan, saute the green onions in butter until tender. Stir in the flour until blended. Gradually stir in the water, wine or broth and reserved cooking juices. Bring to a boil; cook and stir for 2 minutes or until thickened.

BAKED WHOLE SALMON

[4] Reduce heat. Stir a small amount of hot liquid into egg yolks; return all to pan, stirring constantly. Add cream, salt and pepper. Cook and stir until mixture reaches 160°. Serve with the salmon. **Yield:** 12-14 servings.

salmon chowder

MARY LOU PEARCE
VICTORIA, BRITISH COLUMBIA

We live near some of the best salmon fishing in the world. I came up with this chowder that uses salmon in place of shellfish.

   2 cups diced peeled potatoes
1 1/2 cups fresh or frozen mixed
      vegetables
   1 large onion, chopped
 1/2 teaspoon celery seed
   2 cups water
   6 plum tomatoes, peeled, seeded
      and chopped
   3 tablespoons butter
   3 tablespoons all-purpose flour
 1/4 teaspoon salt
Dash pepper
   2 cups milk
   2 cups cubed cooked salmon

[1] In a Dutch oven, combine the potatoes, vegetables, onion, celery seed and water. Bring to a boil. Reduce heat; cover. Simmer for 20 minutes or until vegetables are tender. Add the tomatoes; simmer 5 minutes longer.

[2] In saucepan, melt butter. Stir in the flour, salt and pepper until smooth. Gradually add milk. Bring to a boil; cook and stir for 2 minutes or until thickened. Add to the vegetable mixture with salmon; heat through. **Yield:** 8 servings.

HUNTING & FISHING **tip**

Use a sharp, flexible knife to remove skin from a fish fillet. Position the fillet with the tail end closest to you, skin side down. Starting at the tail end, make a small 45-degree angle cut in the meat to, but not through, the skin. Using that cut as a starting point, insert knife and angle it flat against the skin. Hold the skin taut and slide knife along the skin, separating it from the fillet. As you push the knife away, pull the skin toward you.   TASTE OF HOME TEST KITCHEN

PECAN-CRUSTED SALMON

pecan-crusted salmon

   2 salmon fillets (6 ounces each)
   2 tablespoons mayonnaise
 1/2 cup finely chopped pecans
 1/3 cup seasoned bread crumbs
   2 tablespoons grated Parmesan
      cheese
   1 tablespoon minced fresh parsley
   1 tablespoon butter, melted
CUCUMBER SAUCE:
 1/2 cup chopped seeded peeled
      cucumber
 1/2 cup vanilla yogurt
 1/2 teaspoon snipped fresh dill
      or 1/4 teaspoon dill weed
 1/8 teaspoon garlic powder

[1] Place salmon skin side down in a greased 11-in. x 7-in. x 2-in. baking dish. Spread 1 tablespoon mayonnaise over each fillet. Combine the pecans, bread crumbs, Parmesan cheese, parsley and butter; spoon over salmon. Bake at 425° for 10-15 minutes or until fish flakes easily with a fork.

[2] Meanwhile, in a small bowl, combine the cucumber sauce ingredients. Serve with the salmon. **Yield:** 2 servings.

CHERYL BYDOWDKI
PUNTA GORDA, FLORIDA

This nutty coating and cool sauce turn ordinary salmon into something special. My husband was thrilled the first time I served it, and has raved about it every time since!

CATFISH WITH SPICED FRUIT SALSA

KAREN MARTIS
MERRILLVILLE,
INDIANA

I frequently serve fish fillets because they're good for my family's health and easy to prepare. I added homemade fruit salsa to this meal because it's fresh and light; perfect for the spicy fish.

catfish with spiced fruit salsa

> 4 catfish fillets (6 ounces each)
> 2 teaspoons vegetable oil
> 2 teaspoons ground coriander
> 1 teaspoon ground cumin
> 1/4 teaspoon ground cinnamon
> 1/4 teaspoon cayenne pepper
> 3/4 teaspoon salt
> 1/2 cup dried tropical fruit
> 1/3 cup unsweetened apple juice
> 1 tablespoon cider vinegar
> 1 tablespoon 100% apricot spreadable fruit
> 2 tablespoons minced fresh parsley

[1] Rub both sides of fillets with oil. Combine the coriander, cumin, cinnamon and cayenne; set aside 1/2 teaspoon. Add salt to remaining spice mixture; rub over both sides of fillets.

[2] In a saucepan, combine the tropical fruit, apple juice, vinegar and reserved spice mixture. Bring to a boil; stir in spreadable fruit. Remove from the heat; let stand for 5 minutes.

[3] In a large nonstick skillet coated with nonstick cooking spray, cook fillets over medium-high heat for 3-4 minutes on each side or

until fish flakes easily with a fork. Serve with the fruit salsa; sprinkle with parsley. **Yield:** 4 servings.

catfish jambalaya

MRS. BILL SAUL
MACON, MISSISSIPPI

My family owns a catfish processing plant, so I frequently fix that fish for meals. This colorful, zippy main dish is a great favorite of ours.

> 2 cups chopped onion
> 1/2 cup chopped celery
> 1/2 cup chopped green pepper
> 2 garlic cloves, minced
> 1/4 cup butter, optional
> 1 can (10 ounces) diced tomatoes and green chilies, undrained
> 1 cup sliced fresh mushrooms
> 1/4 teaspoon cayenne pepper
> 1/2 teaspoon salt, optional
> 1 pound catfish fillets, cubed

Hot cooked rice, optional

Sliced green onions, optional

[1] In a saucepan over medium-high heat, saute onion, celery, green pepper and garlic in butter until tender, about 10 minutes. Add tomatoes, mushrooms, cayenne and salt if desired; bring to a boil.

[2] Add catfish. Reduce heat; cover and simmer until fish flakes easily with a fork, about 10 minutes. If desired, serve with rice and top with green onions. **Yield:** 4 servings.

tasty oven-fried catfish

PHYLLIS EARLY
HOLLAND, MICHIGAN

This moist baked catfish gets its crisp golden coating from cornflake crumbs. The fillets are nicely seasoned with celery salt, onion powder and paprika.

> 4 catfish fillets (6 ounces each)
> 1 cup cornflake crumbs
> 1 teaspoon celery salt
> 1/2 teaspoon onion powder
> 1/4 teaspoon paprika
> 1/8 teaspoon pepper

1 egg white

2 tablespoons milk

[1] Pat fish dry with paper towels. In a shallow bowl, combine the cornflake crumbs, celery salt, onion powder, paprika and pepper.

[2] In another bowl, beat the egg white and milk. Dip fillets into egg white mixture, then coat with crumb mixture.

[3] Place in a 13-in. x 9-in. x 2-in. baking dish coated with nonstick cooking spray. Bake, uncovered, at 350° for 25-30 minutes or until fish flakes easily with a fork. **Yield:** 4 servings.

cajun baked catfish

2 tablespoons yellow cornmeal

2 teaspoons Cajun seasoning or blackening seasoning

1/2 teaspoon dried thyme

1/2 teaspoon dried basil

1/4 teaspoon garlic powder

1/4 teaspoon lemon-pepper seasoning

2 catfish fillets (6 ounces each)

1/4 teaspoon paprika

In a shallow bowl, combine the cornmeal, Cajun seasoning, thyme, basil, garlic powder and lemon-pepper. Add catfish and turn to coat. Place on a baking sheet coated with nonstick cooking spray. Sprinkle with paprika. Bake at 400° for 20-25 minutes or until fish flakes easily with a fork. **Yield:** 2 servings.

JIM GALES GLENDALE, WISCONSIN

This well-seasoned fish nets me compliments from family and friends whenever I serve it. The fish is moist and flaky, and the coating is crisp, crunchy and flecked with paprika.

CAJUN BAKED CATFISH

HUNTING & FISHING COOKBOOK

perch with cucumber relish

- 2/3 cup chopped seeded cucumber
- 1/2 cup chopped radishes
- 2 tablespoons white vinegar
- 1 teaspoon canola oil
- 1/4 teaspoon sugar
- 1/4 teaspoon dried tarragon
- 1/8 teaspoon salt
- 2 tablespoons butter
- 4 perch or tilapia fillets (6 ounces each)

For relish, in a small bowl, combine the first seven ingredinets; set aside. In a large skillet, melt butter over medium-high heat. Cook fillets for 3-4 minutes on each side or until fish flakes easily with a fork. Serve with relish. **Yield:** 4 servings.

poached perch with broccoli

ALYCE REED
ELYRIA, OHIO

We live near Lake Erie and love to fish, and we consider this our favorite perch recipe. Everyone who tastes it loves the tender fillets served with broccoli in a creamy garlic sauce.

- 1 pound fresh broccoli, cut into spears
- 3/4 cup water
- 1 small onion, sliced
- 1 bay leaf
- 1 teaspoon salt
- 1/2 teaspoon dried tarragon
- 2 pounds perch fillets

GARLIC SAUCE:
- 1 cup mayonnaise

PERCH WITH CUCUMBER RELISH

1 egg white

2 tablespoons milk

[1] Pat fish dry with paper towels. In a shallow bowl, combine the cornflake crumbs, celery salt, onion powder, paprika and pepper.

[2] In another bowl, beat the egg white and milk. Dip fillets into egg white mixture, then coat with crumb mixture.

[3] Place in a 13-in. x 9-in. x 2-in. baking dish coated with nonstick cooking spray. Bake, uncovered, at 350° for 25-30 minutes or until fish flakes easily with a fork. **Yield:** 4 servings.

cajun baked catfish

2 tablespoons yellow cornmeal

2 teaspoons Cajun seasoning or blackening seasoning

1/2 teaspoon dried thyme

1/2 teaspoon dried basil

1/4 teaspoon garlic powder

1/4 teaspoon lemon-pepper seasoning

2 catfish fillets (6 ounces each)

1/4 teaspoon paprika

In a shallow bowl, combine the cornmeal, Cajun seasoning, thyme, basil, garlic powder and lemon-pepper. Add catfish and turn to coat. Place on a baking sheet coated with nonstick cooking spray. Sprinkle with paprika. Bake at 400° for 20-25 minutes or until fish flakes easily with a fork. **Yield:** 2 servings.

JIM GALES GLENDALE, WISCONSIN

This well-seasoned fish nets me compliments from family and friends whenever I serve it. The fish is moist and flaky, and the coating is crisp, crunchy and flecked with paprika.

CAJUN BAKED CATFISH

TRACI WYNNE BEAR, DELAWARE

You can use this recipe with any thick fish fillet, but I suggest catfish or haddock. The Cajun flavor is great!

skillet-grilled catfish

¼ cup all-purpose flour

¼ cup cornmeal

1 teaspoon onion powder

1 teaspoon dried basil

½ teaspoon garlic salt

½ teaspoon dried thyme

¼ to ½ teaspoon white pepper

¼ to ½ teaspoon cayenne pepper

¼ to ½ teaspoon pepper

4 catfish fillets (6 to 8 ounces each)

¼ cup butter

[1] In a large resealable bag, combine the first nine ingredients. Add catfish, one fillet at a time, and shake to coat.

[2] Place a large cast-iron skillet on a grill rack over medium-hot heat. Melt butter in the skillet; add catfish. Grill, covered, for 6-8 minutes on each side or until fish flakes easily with a fork. **Yield:** 4 servings.

trout-stuffed red potatoes

BONNIE GOMEZ RIO RANCHO, NEW MEXICO

Hollowed-out small red potatoes serve as "cups" to hold a creamy trout filling, seasoned with lemon, dill and a dash of hot pepper sauce. My husband, who's a chef, prepared these for the State of Colorado Potato Commissioners and they were a hit. He smokes the trout that we catch, but you can also substitute baked trout or salmon in this recipe.

12 tiny red potatoes (about 1½-inch diameter)

¼ cup mayonnaise

¼ cup sour cream

2 tablespoons finely chopped green onion

1 teaspoon snipped fresh dill

¼ teaspoon lemon juice

⅛ teaspoon salt

⅛ teaspoon pepper

Dash hot pepper sauce, optional

HUNTING & FISHING COOKBOOK

1 cup flaked smoked trout

Fresh dill sprigs

[1] Place potatoes in a saucepan and cover with water. Bring to a boil. Reduce heat; cover and cook for 10-15 minutes or until tender. Drain. Cut potatoes in half horizontally. Cut a thin slice from the bottom of each potato to level if necessary. Scoop out the pulp with a melon baller, leaving a thick shell.

[2] In a bowl, mash the pulp. Stir in the mayonnaise, sour cream, onion, dill, lemon juice, salt, pepper and hot pepper sauce if desired. Fold in trout. Pipe into potato shells. Garnish with dill sprigs. **Yield:** 2 dozen.

parmesan catfish

LETTIE SIMON
BATON ROUGE, LOUISIANA

This moist baked fish has a slightly crunchy coating with a mild Parmesan flavor. Even my kids love this delicious, easy-to-fix recipe.

$\frac{1}{2}$ cup all-purpose flour

$\frac{1}{4}$ cup grated Parmesan cheese

3 tablespoons cornmeal

1 teaspoon paprika

$\frac{1}{4}$ teaspoon salt

$\frac{1}{4}$ teaspoon pepper

1 egg white

$\frac{1}{4}$ cup milk

4 catfish fillets (6 ounces each)

[1] In a shallow dish, combine the flour, Parmesan cheese, cornmeal, paprika, salt and pepper; set aside. In another shallow dish, beat egg white and milk. Dip fillets in milk mixture, then in flour mixture.

[2] Place in a 13-in. x 9-in. x 2-in. baking dish coated with nonstick cooking spray. Bake, uncovered, at 350° for 35-40 minutes or until fish flakes easily with a fork. **Yield:** 4 servings.

southern pecan catfish

1 cup finely chopped pecans, divided

$\frac{1}{2}$ cup cornmeal

1 teaspoon salt, divided

1 teaspoon pepper, divided

4 catfish fillets (6 ounces each)

$\frac{1}{2}$ cup butter, divided

$\frac{1}{2}$ cup heavy whipping cream

2 tablespoons lemon juice

1 to 2 tablespoons minced fresh parsley

[1] In a shallow bowl, combine $\frac{1}{2}$ cup pecans, cornmeal, $\frac{1}{2}$ teaspoon salt and $\frac{1}{2}$ teaspoon pepper. Coat catfish with pecan mixture. In a large skillet, melt $\frac{1}{4}$ cup butter over medium-high heat; fry fillets for 6-7 minutes on each side or until fish flakes easily with a fork. Remove and keep warm.

[2] In the same skillet, melt remaining butter over medium heat. Add remaining pecans; cook and stir for 1 minute. Add the cream, lemon juice and remaining salt and pepper; cook and stir for 1 minute. Stir in the parsley. Spoon over catfish. **Yield:** 4 servings.

MARY ANN GRIFFIN SAGINAW, MICHIGAN

For this super-fast recipe, I coat catfish in pecans, then top it with a thick, rich cream sauce. It looks like you spent all day on it, but it's actually so speedy to prepare. Garnish it with lemon wedges, parsley or chopped pecans.

SOUTHERN PECAN CATFISH

**MILDRED
SHERRER
FORT WORTH,
TEXAS**

I give fish a healthy flavor lift with homemade relish. Tangy vinegar and tarragon lend zest to the tasty condiment, and chopped cucumber and radishes add garden-fresh color.

perch with cucumber relish

- $2/3$ cup chopped seeded cucumber
- $1/2$ cup chopped radishes
- 2 tablespoons white vinegar
- 1 teaspoon canola oil
- $1/4$ teaspoon sugar
- $1/4$ teaspoon dried tarragon
- $1/8$ teaspoon salt
- 2 tablespoons butter
- 4 perch or tilapia fillets (6 ounces each)

For relish, in a small bowl, combine the first seven ingredinets; set aside. In a large skillet, melt butter over medium-high heat. Cook fillets for 3-4 minutes on each side or until fish flakes easily with a fork. Serve with relish. **Yield:** 4 servings.

poached perch with broccoli

**ALYCE REED
ELYRIA, OHIO**

We live near Lake Erie and love to fish, and we consider this our favorite perch recipe. Everyone who tastes it loves the tender fillets served with broccoli in a creamy garlic sauce.

- 1 pound fresh broccoli, cut into spears
- $3/4$ cup water
- 1 small onion, sliced
- 1 bay leaf
- 1 teaspoon salt
- $1/2$ teaspoon dried tarragon
- 2 pounds perch fillets

GARLIC SAUCE:
- 1 cup mayonnaise

PERCH WITH CUCUMBER RELISH

1 tablespoon lemon juice

1 garlic clove, minced

$1/2$ teaspoon ground mustard

$1/4$ teaspoon salt

$1/4$ teaspoon pepper

[1] Place broccoli in a steamer basket. Place in a saucepan over 1 in. of water; bring to a boil. Cover and steam until crisp-tender; set aside and keep warm.

[2] In a large skillet, combine the water, onion, bay leaf, salt and tarragon; bring to a boil. Reduce heat; add perch fillets in batches. Cover and cook until fish is firm and flakes easily with a fork. Remove fish and onions with a slotted spoon; keep warm. Discard bay leaf.

[3] In a bowl, combine all of the sauce ingredients. stir in 2-4 tablespoons cooking liquid until sauce reaches desired consistency. Arrange the broccoli on a serving platter; top with the fish, onions and garlic sauce. **Yield:** 4-6 servings.

cornmeal catfish fillets

TAMMY MOORE-WORTHINGTON
ARTESIA, NEW MEXICO

This is my best way to prepare fresh fish. The fillets cook up moist with an irresistible crisp, golden coating. Whether your fish comes from a nearby lake or the grocery store, it makes a terrific meal.

1 egg white

1 cup milk

1 cup cornmeal

$3/4$ teaspoon salt

$1/4$ teaspoon garlic powder

$1/4$ to $1/2$ teaspoon cayenne pepper

$1/8$ teaspoon pepper

4 catfish fillets (8 ounces each)

Vegetable oil

Lemon or lime wedges, optional

[1] In a shallow bowl, beat the egg white until foamy; add milk and mix well. In another shallow bowl, combine the cornmeal, salt, garlic powder, cayenne and pepper. Dip fillets in milk mixture, then coat with cornmeal mixture.

[2] Heat $1/4$ in. of oil in a large skillet; fry fish over medium-high for 3-4 minutes on each side

SALSA FISH

or until it flakes easily with a fork. Garnish with lemon or lime if desired. **Yield:** 4 servings.

salsa fish

2 pounds walleye, bass or perch fillets

1 cup seasoned bread crumbs

1 tablespoon vegetable oil

$1^1/2$ cups salsa

2 cups (8 ounces each) shredded part-skim mozzarella cheese

Coat fillets with bread crumbs. In a large skillet, brown fillets on both sides in oil. Transfer to a greased 13-in. x 9-in. x 2-in. baking dish. Top with salsa and cheese. Bake, uncovered, at 400° for 7-10 minutes or until fish flakes easily with a fork. **Yield:** 6 servings.

DIANE GRAJEWSKI NORTH BRANCH, MICHIGAN

My family loves outdoor activities, especially fishing. I give their catch of the day unexpected zip with salsa. It dresses up these golden crumb-coated fillets and keeps them moist and tender.

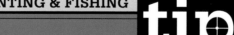

HUNTING & FISHING tip

Overcooked fish loses its flavor and becomes tough. As a general guideline, fish is cooked 10 minutes for every inch of thickness.

For fish fillets, check for doneness by gently inserting a fork at an angle into the thickest portion of the fish. When the meat is opaque and flakes into sections, it is cooked completely.

Whole fish or steaks are done when the flesh is opaque and is easily removed from the bones. The juices in cooked fish are milky white.

TASTE OF HOME TEST KITCHEN

HUNTING & FISHING COOKBOOK

MARINATED CATFISH FILLETS

salmon in lime sauce

HELEN VAIL
GLENSIDE, PENNSYLVANIA

I marinate salmon in a lime and vegetable mixture, then tuck individual portions into foil packets. I like to serve this fish with grilled skewers of corn-on-the-cob rounds, mushrooms and cherry tomatoes.

  1 small tomato, chopped
  1 small sweet red pepper, chopped
  2 green onions, thinly sliced
$2/3$ cup lime juice
  2 tablespoons vegetable oil
$1/2$ teaspoon grated lime peel
$1/4$ to $1/2$ teaspoon cayenne pepper
  1 salmon fillet ($1^1/2$ pounds)

[1] In a large resealable plastic bag, combine the first seven ingredients; mix well. Cut salmon into four pieces; place in the bag. Seal and turn to coat; refrigerate for 30 minutes.

[2] Drain and discard marinade from fish and vegetables. Place each piece of salmon and about $1/3$ cup vegetable mixture on a piece of double-layered heavy-duty foil (about 18 in. square). Fold foil around the mixture and seal tightly. Grill, covered, over medium heat for 15-20 minutes or until salmon flakes easily with a fork. **Yield:** 4 servings.

easy smoked salmon

NORMA FELL
BOYNE CITY, MICHIGAN

I discovered this recipe years ago, and it has become my favorite way to prepare salmon. This cold salmon is great at a party served with crackers.

  1 salmon fillet (about 2 pounds)
  2 tablespoons brown sugar
  2 teaspoons salt
$1/2$ teaspoon pepper
  1 to 2 tablespoons Liquid Smoke

[1] Place salmon skin side down in an 11-in. x 7-in. x 2-in. baking pan coated with nonstick cooking spray. Sprinkle with brown sugar, salt and pepper. Drizzle with Liquid Smoke. Cover and refrigerate for 4-8 hours.

PAULETTA BOESE
MACON, MISSISSIPPI

Recently, we hosted a group of young people from Canada. Since we wanted to give them a true taste of the South, we served this catfish. They loved it.

marinated catfish fillets

  6 catfish fillets (about 8 ounces each)
  1 bottle (16 ounces) Italian salad dressing
  1 can ($10^3/4$ ounces) condensed tomato soup, undiluted
$3/4$ cup vegetable oil
$3/4$ cup sugar
$1/3$ cup white vinegar
$3/4$ teaspoon celery seed
$3/4$ teaspoon salt
$3/4$ teaspoon pepper
$3/4$ teaspoon ground mustard
$1/2$ teaspoon garlic powder

[1] Place fillets in a large resealable plastic bag, add salad dressing. Seal bag; refrigerate for 1 hour, turning occasionally. Drain and discard marinade. Combine remaining ingredients; mix well. Remove 1 cup for basting. (Refrigerate remaining sauce for another use.)

[2] Grill fillets, covered, over medium-hot heat for 3 minutes on each side. Brush with the basting sauce. Continue grilling for 6-8 minutes or until fish flakes easily with a fork, turning once and basting several times. **Yield:** 6 servings.

[2] Drain and discard liquid. Bake, uncovered, at 350° for 35-45 minutes or until fish flakes easily with a fork. Cool to room temperature. Cover and refrigerate for 8 hours or overnight. **Yield:** 16 servings.

grilled salmon caesar salad

   2 **salmon fillets (1 pound each)**
   3 **cups cubed French bread**
   1 **tablespoon olive oil**
 1/4 **teaspoon garlic powder**
   1 **bunch romaine, torn**
   2 **cups small cherry tomatoes**

DRESSING:
   3 **tablespoons olive oil**
   2 **tablespoons lemon juice**
 41/2 **teaspoons mayonnaise**
 21/4 **teaspoons sugar**
   2 **garlic cloves, minced**
 1/2 **teaspoon salt**
 1/8 **teaspoon pepper**
   1 **tablespoon grated Parmesan cheese**

[1] Coat grill rack with nonstick cooking spray before starting the grill. Place salmon skin side down on grill. Grill, covered, over medium-hot heat for 15-20 minutes or until fish flakes easily with a fork. Cool.

[2] For croutons, toss the bread cubes, oil and garlic powder in a bowl. In a nonstick skillet, saute bread cubes for 5-6 minutes or until golden brown, stirring occasionally. Remove from the heat; set aside.

[3] Flake salmon into chunks. In a large bowl, combine romaine and tomatoes. In a small bowl, combine the oil, lemon juice, mayonnaise, sugar, garlic, salt and pepper. Pour over salad and toss to coat. Add the salmon, croutons and Parmesan cheese; toss gently. **Yield:** 6 servings.

CLARA BARRETT MADISON, FLORIDA

Flaky grilled salmon, lettuce, tomatoes and homemade garlic croutons star in this attractive salad. A Caesar-style dressing, seasoned to please with lemon juice and grated Parmesan cheese, coats this colorful dish.

GRILLED SALMON CAESAR SALAD

HUNTING & FISHING COOKBOOK

**BARBARA PARKS
RENTON,
WASHINGTON**

This soup is a tasty way to prepare heart-healthy salmon. Even though it uses 2% milk, it tastes rich. Serve it with a green salad and crusty, whole grain bread.

salmon bisque

- 1 small sweet red pepper
- 1 salmon fillet (8 ounces)
- 1/2 cup finely chopped carrot
- 1 tablespoon chopped shallot
- 1 tablespoon vegetable oil
- 2 garlic cloves, minced
- 3 tablespoons all-purpose flour
- 1 can (14-1/2 ounces) chicken broth
- 2 cups 2% milk
- 1 teaspoon seafood seasoning
- 1/4 teaspoon Liquid Smoke, optional

[1] Broil red pepper 4 in. from the heat until skin blisters, about 5 minutes. With tongs, rotate pepper a quarter turn. Broil and rotate until all sides are blistered and blackened. Immediately place pepper in a bowl; cover and let stand for 15-20 minutes. Peel off and discard charred skin. Remove stems and seeds. Set roasted pepper aside.

[2] Broil salmon 4 in. from the heat for 7-10 minutes on each side or until fish flakes easily with a fork. Break salmon into small pieces; set aside.

[3] In a large saucepan, saute the carrot and shallot in oil until tender. Add garlic; saute 1 minute longer. Stir in flour until blended. Gradually add broth. Bring to a boil; cook and stir for 1-2 minutes or until thickened.

[4] Transfer to a blender; add roasted pepper. Cover and puree until smooth. Return to the pan. Stir in the milk, seafood seasoning, Liquid Smoke if desired and salmon; heat through. **Yield:** 4 servings.

fried bluegill fillets

**DOUG WRIGHT
MAIZE, KANSAS**

The secret to this recipe is dipping the fish fillets twice into the eggs and the crumb mixture. This makes the fish so crispy.

SALMON BISQUE

1 cup seasoned bread crumbs

1 cup grated Parmesan cheese

1/2 teaspoon salt

1/2 teaspoon lemon-pepper seasoning

1/4 teaspoon pepper

6 eggs

1 1/2 pounds bluegill or crappie fillets

1/2 cup vegetable oil, divided

[1] In a shallow bowl, combine the first five ingredients. In another bowl, whisk the eggs. Dip fillets in eggs, then coat with crumb mixture. Dip again in eggs and crumb mixture.

[2] In a large skillet over medium-high heat, cook fillets in batches in 2 tablespoons oil for 2-3 minutes on each side or until fish flakes easily with a fork, adding oil as needed. **Yield:** 6 servings.

new england clam chowder

AGNES WARD
STRATFORD, ONTARIO

I left a cruise ship with a great souvenir...the recipe for this splendid chowder! It's a traditional soup that stands the test of time.

12 fresh cherrystone clams

3 cups cold water

2 bacon strips, diced

1 small onion, chopped

2 medium potatoes, peeled and finely chopped

1/4 teaspoon salt

1/4 teaspoon pepper

2 tablespoons all-purpose flour

1 cup milk

1/2 cup half-and-half cream

[1] Tap clams; discard any that do not close. Place clams and water in a large saucepan. Bring to a boil. Reduce heat; cover and simmer for 5-6 minutes or until clams open.

[2] Remove meat from clams; chop meat and set aside. Strain liquid through a cheesecloth-lined colander; set aside.

[3] In a large saucepan, cook bacon over medium heat until crisp. Using a slotted spoon, remove to paper towels. Saute onion in drippings until tender.

BAKED HORSERADISH SALMON

[4] Return bacon to the pan; add clam meat and reserved liquid. Stir in the potatoes, salt and pepper. Bring to a boil. Reduce heat; cover and simmer for 10-12 minutes or until potatoes are tender.

[5] Combine flour and milk until smooth; gradually stir into soup. Bring to a boil; cook and stir for 2 minutes or until thickened. Gradually stir in cream; heat through (do not boil). **Yield:** 1 3/4 quarts.

baked horseradish salmon

1 salmon fillet (1 pound)

1 tablespoon butter, melted

1 tablespoon prepared horseradish, drained

2 teaspoons lemon juice

1/4 teaspoon garlic powder

1/8 teaspoon pepper

[1] Place salmon skin side down in an 11-in. x 7-in. baking dish coated with cooking spray. In a small bowl, combine the butter, horseradish, lemon juice, garlic powder and pepper; spread over salmon.

[2] Bake, uncovered, at 375° for 20-25 minutes or until fish flakes easily a fork. **Yield:** 4 servings.

JAMES OCKERMAN FLORAL CITY, FLORIDA

I never liked salmon until my husband, Jim, created this healthy, delicious entree. Now, all we have to do is mention that we're having Jim's salmon for dinner, and we have happy guests!

3

HUNTING & FISHING COOKBOOK

**LEE BREMSON
KANSAS CITY,
MISSOURI**

A flavorful pesto helps keep the fish moist, and toasted bread crumbs give the entree a nice finishing touch. I like to use basil and parsley from the garden for this easy dish.

PESTO SALMON

pesto salmon

> 1 slice bread
> 1/4 cup lightly packed fresh basil
> 2 tablespoons packed fresh parsley
> 2 1/2 teaspoons olive oil
> 1/2 teaspoon pine nuts
> 1/4 teaspoon minced garlic

Dash salt

Dash coarsely ground pepper

> 2 salmon fillets (6 ounces each)

[1] For pesto, tear bread into pieces; place in a miniature food processor. Pulse until fine crumbs form. Set aside 1 tablespoon. To the remaining bread crumbs, add the basil, parsley, oil, pine nuts, garlic, salt and pepper; cover and process until finely chopped.

[2] Place salmon on a baking sheet coated with cooking spray. Spread with pesto. Sprinkle with reserved bread crumbs. Bake at 400° for 20-22 minutes or until fish flakes easily with a fork and crumbs are lightly browned. **Yield:** 2 servings.

campfire fried fish

**TASTE OF HOME TEST KITCHEN
GREENDALE, WISCONSIN**

This classic recipe will have you cooking up a shore lunch in no time. Fry up whatever type of fish you've caught that day.

> 2 eggs
> 3/4 cup all-purpose flour
> 1/2 cup cornmeal
> 1 teaspoon salt
> 1 teaspoon paprika
> 3 pounds walleye, bluegill or perch fillets

Canola oil

[1] In a shallow bowl, whisk eggs. In a large resealable plastic bag, combine the flour, cornmeal, salt and paprika. Dip fillets in eggs, then roll in flour mixture.

[2] Add 1/4 in. of oil to a large cast-iron skillet; place skillet on grill rack over medium-hot heat. Fry fillets in oil in batches for 3-4 minutes on each side or until fish flakes easily with a fork. **Yield:** 6 servings.

cornmeal-crusted walleye

ALLEN PLUNGIS
HARTLAND, MICHIGAN

These moist, tender fillets are a terrific option when you want a meal that's not too heavy. The corn and roasted pepper side dish goes perfectly with the walleye.

  2 large sweet red peppers
  4 large ears sweet corn, husks removed
  3 tablespoons vegetable oil, divided
  1/2 cup yellow cornmeal
  1 3/4 teaspoons salt, divided
  1/2 teaspoon white pepper
Dash cayenne pepper
  4 walleye fillets (6 ounces each)
  1/2 pound sliced fresh mushrooms
  3 tablespoons butter

[1] Broil red peppers 4 in. from the heat until skins blister, about 15 minutes. With tongs, rotate peppers a quarter turn. Broil; rotate until all sides of pepper are blistered and blackened. Immediately place peppers in a large bowl; cover and let stand for 15-20 minutes.

[2] Meanwhile, brush corn with 1 tablespoon oil. Transfer to an ungreased 13-in. x 9-in. baking dish. Cover and bake at 350° for 30-40 minutes or until tender. Peel off and discard charred skin from peppers. Remove stems and seeds from peppers. Finely chop peppers. Cut corn from cobs.

[3] In a shallow bowl, combine the cornmeal, 1 teaspoon salt, pepper and cayenne. Coat walleye in cornmeal mixture.

[4] In a large skillet, saute mushrooms in butter until tender. Add peppers, corn and remaining salt; saute 2-3 minutes longer.

[5] In another large skillet, fry fillets in remaining oil for 2-3 minutes on each side or until fish flakes easily with a fork. Serve with corn salsa. **Yield:** 4 servings (about 4 cups corn salsa).

chunky crawfish spread

  1 package (16 ounces) frozen cooked crawfish tails, thawed
  1 package (8 ounces) cream cheese, softened
  1 medium green pepper, finely chopped
  1 medium sweet red pepper, finely chopped
  1 small onion, finely chopped
  6 garlic cloves, minced
  1/2 to 1 teaspoon Creole seasoning
  1/2 teaspoon salt
  6 to 12 drops hot pepper sauce
Assorted crackers

Chop crawfish; pat dry. In a small bowl, beat cream cheese until smooth. Add the peppers, onion, garlic, Creole seasoning, salt and hot pepper sauce; stir in the crawfish. Cover and refrigerate for at least 2 hours. Serve with crackers. **Yield:** 3 cups.

Editor's Note: The following spices may be substituted for 1 teaspoon Creole seasoning: 1/4 teaspoon each salt, garlic powder and paprika; and a pinch each of dried thyme, ground cumin and cayenne pepper.

SUNDRA HAUCK
BOGALUSA, LOUISIANA

Seafood is plentiful here, and crawfish is my favorite. I like to serve this tasty appetizer while the main course is finishing up in the oven. If you don't have crawfish, you might substitute store-bought fully cooked shrimp.

CHUNKY CRAWFISH SPREAD

SHAUNIECE FRAZIER
LOS ANGELES, CALIFORNIA

You won't miss the fat and calories in this lightened-up version of a restaurant-style sandwich. Serve it alongside your favorite vegetable side dish and enjoy.

cajun catfish sandwiches

3/4 teaspoon seasoned pepper
1/2 teaspoon chili powder
1/2 teaspoon cayenne pepper
1/4 teaspoon seasoned salt
4 catfish fillets (4 ounces each)
2 teaspoons olive oil, divided
2 green onions, chopped
3 garlic cloves, minced
1/2 cup fat-free mayonnaise
4 French or kaiser rolls, split and toasted
4 romaine leaves

[1] Combine the seasoned pepper, chili powder, cayenne and seasoned salt; sprinkle over fillets. In a large skillet, cook fillets in 1 teaspoon oil for 4-6 minutes on each side or until fish flakes easily with a fork. Remove and keep warm.

[2] In the same skillet, saute onions and garlic in remaining oil until tender. Remove from the heat; stir in mayonnaise. Spread over rolls; top each with a romaine leaf and fillet. Replace tops. **Yield:** 4 servings.

crawfish corn bread

ELOISE WALER
RAYVILLE, LOUISIANA

Moist and crusty, with tasty flecks of crawfish tail meat and zippy peppers, this is a distinctive corn bread. I like to serve it warm alongside soups and stews for a memorable lunch or supper.

1 medium onion, finely chopped
1/2 cup finely chopped green pepper
1/2 cup canola oil, divided
1 to 2 medium jalapeno peppers, minced
2 cups cornmeal
3 teaspoons baking powder
1 teaspoon salt
1/2 teaspoon baking soda
3 eggs
1 cup milk
1 can (14 3/4 ounces) cream-style corn
1 1/2 cups (6 ounces) shredded cheddar cheese
3/4 cup sliced green onions
1 cup crawfish tail meat, cooked

[1] In a skillet, saute onion and green pepper in 1 tablespoon oil until tender. Remove from the heat. Stir in jalapenos; set aside.

[2] In a bowl, combine cornmeal, baking powder, salt and baking soda. In another bowl, beat the eggs, milk and remaining oil; stir into the dry ingredients just until blended. Stir in the corn, cheese, green onions, crawfish and reserved jalapeno mixture. Pour into a greased 13-in. x 9-in. baking pan.

[3] Bake at 400° for 35-40 minutes or until a toothpick inserted near the center comes out clean. Cut into squares. Serve warm. Refrigerate leftovers. **Yield:** 15 servings.

Editor's Note: When cutting hot peppers, disposable gloves are recommended. Avoid touching your face.

CAJUN CATFISH SANDWICHES

HUNTING & FISHING tip

For a change of pace, I coat baked and deep-fried fish fillets with mashed potato flakes.
SANDRA, WISCONSIN

busy-day baked fish

BEVERLY KRUEGER
YAMHILL, OREGON

An onion soup and sour cream mixture really adds zip to this quick-to-make recipe. Your family would never guess that it's so easy to prepare.

- 1 cup (8 ounces) sour cream
- 2 tablespoons onion soup mix
- 1 1/2 cups seasoned bread crumbs
- 2 1/2 pounds fish fillets
- 1/4 cup butter, melted
- 1/3 cup shredded Parmesan cheese

[1] In a shallow bowl, combine sour cream and soup mix. Place bread crumbs in another shallow bowl. Cut fish into serving-size pieces; coat with sour cream mixture, then roll in crumbs.

[2] Place in two greased 13-in. x 9-in. baking dishes. Drizzle with butter. Bake, uncovered, at 425° for 12 minutes. Sprinkle with cheese; bake 2-6 minutes longer or until fish flakes easily with a fork. **Yield:** 6-8 servings.

taco fish

EVELYN EYERMANN
CUBA, MISSOURI

Since my husband is an avid angler, fish tops my list of mealtime ingredients. Kids and adults alike will go for the crunchy tortilla chip topping on this scrumptious fish. If you don't have fresh-caught fish, orange roughy from the store is excellent in this recipe.

- 4 orange roughy or bass fillets (6 ounces each)
- 1/2 teaspoon salt
- 1/4 teaspoon chili powder
- 1/2 cup taco sauce
- 1/3 cup tortilla chips, crushed
- 1/3 cup shredded reduced-fat cheddar cheese

[1] Place fish in a 13-in. x 9-in. baking dish coated with cooking spray; sprinkle with salt and chili powder.

[2] Cover and bake at 350° for 20 minutes. Pour taco sauce over fish. Bake, uncovered, for 5-8 minutes longer or until heated through. Immediately sprinkle with tortilla chips and cheese. **Yield:** 4 servings.

FISH WITH FENNEL

fish with fennel

- 1 medium lime
- 1 teaspoon fennel seeds
- 1 large fennel bulb, sliced
- 1/4 teaspoon salt
- 4 teaspoons olive oil, divided
- 2 garlic cloves, minced
- 4 striped bass or barramundi fillets (8 ounces each)
- 1 tablespoon chopped fennel fronds

[1] Cut lime in half; cut four slices from one half for garnish. Finely grate enough peel from the remaining half to measure 3/4 teaspoon; squeeze juice from lime half. Set aside.

[2] In a small dry skillet over medium heat, toast fennel seeds until aromatic, about 1-2 minutes. Cool. Crush seeds in a spice grinder or with a mortar and pestle.

[3] In a large saucepan, bring 1 in. of water to a boil. Add sliced fennel and salt; cover and boil for 6-10 minutes or until crisp-tender. Drain and pat dry.

[4] In a large nonstick skillet, saute fennel in 2 teaspoons oil for 3 minutes. Add garlic; cook 1-2 minutes longer or until fennel is lightly browned. Remove from the pan and set aside.

[5] In the same skillet over medium-high heat, cook fillets in remaining oil for 3-4 minutes on each side or until fish flakes easily with a fork. Drizzle with lime juice; sprinkle with lime peel and crushed fennel seeds. Serve with sauteed fennel. Garnish with fennel fronds and lime slices. **Yield:** 4 servings.

BARBARA STELLUTO
DEVON, PENNSYLVANIA

This brightly flavored fish is a great showcase for fennel. You'll use the seeds, bulb and fronds. This is an excellent springtime recipe, when fennel is at its peak.

Hunting & Fishing COOKBOOK

Prepping ingredients before you leave home makes all of these recipes quick and easy to fix at the hunting camp or cabin. In most cases, a skillet (and a bowl to scramble eggs) is all you need.

BREAKFAST SAUSAGE PATTIES, P. 156
CINNAMON SWIRL QUICK BREAD, P. 161
BREAKFAST EGGS IN FOIL BOWLS, P. 164

BACKCOUNTRY BREAKFASTS 4

COUNTRY-STYLE SCRAMBLED EGGS,
PAGE 155

**NANCY BLOC
KANSAS CITY,
MISSOURI**

Once when we had overnight guests, my husband, Ernie, made this easy, all-in-one breakfast. It was a success. Now these guests request this dish whenever they come to visit.

ONE-PAN BREAKFAST

one-pan breakfast

    1 pound bulk pork sausage
    4 large potatoes, peeled, cooked and cubed
    1 large onion, chopped
    6 eggs, beaten
    6 slices process American cheese

Salt and pepper to taste

In a large skillet, brown and crumble sausage; add potatoes and onion. Cook over medium-high heat for 18-20 minutes or until potatoes are browned. Gradually stir in eggs; cook and stir until set. Remove from the heat; top with cheese. Season with salt and pepper. **Yield:** 4-6 servings.

corny scrambled eggs

**MRS. JOHN PERSCHKE
MICHIGAN CITY, INDIANA**

Corn adds surprising sweetness to these effortless eggs. Try varying the flavor by adding some chopped onion and chopped green pepper.

    6 eggs
    1 can (14¾ ounces) cream-style corn
    ½ pound sliced bacon, cooked and crumbled
    2 tablespoons butter

In a bowl, beat eggs. Add corn and bacon. Melt butter in a skillet over medium heat; add egg mixture. Cook and stir until the eggs are completely set. **Yield:** 3 servings.

tip
HUNTING & FISHING

Bring along bottled water or other canned or bottled drinks. Always assume that streams and rivers are not safe for drinking. If camping in a remote area for an extended time, bring along water-purification tablets or equipment. These are available at camping supply stores.

TASTE OF HOME TEST KITCHEN

south-of-the-border scrambled eggs

FAY DEAR
GLENDIVE, MONTANA

When my family gathers at our cabin, these slightly spicy eggs are a must. And my kids insist I'm the only one who can make them. The crushed tortilla chips really add a unique and tasty texture.

 6 eggs
 1/4 cup milk
 3/4 cup crushed tortilla chips
 3/4 cup chopped fully cooked ham
 1/4 cup chopped onion
 1/4 cup chopped green pepper
 1 tablespoon butter
 3/4 cup shredded cheddar cheese
 1 small tomato, chopped
 1/2 cup sour cream

Taco sauce

[1] Lightly beat eggs with milk; add tortilla chips. Let stand for 15 minutes. In a large skillet, saute ham, onion and green pepper in butter. Add egg mixture and cook over medium heat, stirring occasionally, until eggs are set.

[2] Remove from heat; gently stir in cheese and tomato. Serve in skillet or transfer to a warm serving platter. Top with sour cream and taco sauce. **Yield:** 4 servings.

southern breakfast skillet

 1/4 pound sliced bacon, diced
 1/4 cup chopped onion
 1 can (15 1/2 ounces) hominy, drained
 4 eggs, beaten
 1/8 teaspoon pepper

In a skillet, cook bacon until almost crisp; drain. Add onion; continue cooking until the bacon is crisp and onion is tender. Stir in hominy, eggs and pepper. Cook and stir until eggs are completely set. **Yield:** 2 servings.

JAMES NEWTON
MINOCQUA,
WISCONSIN

This recipe has a long tradition in our family. It was a special meal at my mother's table, and I enjoyed cooking it for my seven children. Now they prepare it for their families. I'm glad this recipe was easy to adjust for just the two of us. My wife and I enjoy it two or three times a week.

SOUTHERN BREAKFAST SKILLET

HUNTING & FISHING COOKBOOK

NANCY MEEKS VERONA, VIRGINIA

For a fun way to present basic breakfast ingredients, try this family favorite. I inherited the recipe from my mother-in-law.

bacon potato omelet

3 bacon strips, diced

2 cups diced peeled potatoes

1 medium onion, chopped

3 eggs, lightly beaten

Salt and pepper to taste

1/2 cup shredded cheddar cheese

[1] In a 9-in. nonstick skillet, cook bacon until crisp. Drain, reserving drippings. Set bacon aside. Cook potatoes and onion in drippings until tender, stirring occasionally. Add eggs, salt and pepper; mix gently.

[2] Cover and cook over medium heat until the eggs are completely set. Sprinkle with cheese. Remove from the heat; cover and let stand until cheese is melted. Sprinkle with bacon. Carefully run a knife around edge of skillet to loosen; transfer to a serving plate. Cut into wedges. **Yield:** 3 servings.

farmer's country breakfast

JUNE SMITH BYRON CENTER, MICHIGAN

When my family has a busy day ahead of them, I prepare a hearty breakfast to get them through the morning. Packed with pork sausage and potatoes, this one-skillet dish surely fills the bill.

6 ounces bulk pork sausage

1 1/2 cups frozen hash brown potatoes

1/4 cup chopped onion

6 eggs

1/3 cup milk

2 tablespoons minced fresh parsley

1/4 teaspoon salt

1/2 cup shredded cheddar cheese

BACON POTATO OMELET

[1] In a skillet, crumble sausage and brown over medium heat until fully cooked. Remove sausage, reserving drippings. In the drippings, cook potatoes and onion until the potatoes are browned, stirring occasionally.

[2] In a bowl, beat eggs, milk, parsley and salt; pour over potato mixture. Add sausage; cook and stir gently over medium heat until eggs are set. Sprinkle with cheese. Cover for 1-2 minutes or until the cheese melts. **Yield:** 4 servings.

french-toasted muffins

AURORA DENNEY
SPENCER, WISCONSIN

Here's a way to dress up ordinary English muffins! I often serve these with maple syrup, seasonal fruit and pork sausage patties or links.

    4 eggs
    1/2 cup half-and-half cream
    2 tablespoons sugar
    1/2 teaspoon vanilla extract
    6 English muffins, split
    1/4 cup butter

Maple syrup

[1] In a small mixing bowl, beat eggs. Add cream, sugar and vanilla; mix well. Soak muffins, cut side down, in egg mixture for 1 minute; turn and dip the other side just until moistened.

[2] In a large skillet, melt butter. Fry muffins, cut side down, for 2-3 minutes or until golden brown. Turn and cook 2-3 minutes longer or until golden brown. Serve with syrup. **Yield:** 6 servings.

cajun corned beef hash

    6 cups frozen shredded hash
      brown potatoes, thawed
    1/4 cup butter
    1/2 cup each finely chopped green
      onions, sweet red pepper and
      green pepper
    1 teaspoon seasoned salt
    3/4 teaspoon Cajun seasoning
    3/4 teaspoon chili powder

CAJUN CORNED BEEF HASH

    1/2 teaspoon pepper
    1 1/2 cups chopped cooked corned beef
    1 tablespoon white vinegar
    8 eggs

Additional Cajun seasoning and hot pepper sauce, optional

[1] In a large skillet, cook hash browns in butter until almost tender. Stir in onions, peppers and seasonings. Cook until hash browns are lightly browned and peppers are tender. Add corned beef; heat through.

[2] Meanwhile, in a skillet with high sides, bring 2-3 in. of water and vinegar to a boil. Reduce heat; simmer gently. For each egg, break cold egg into a custard cup or saucer, then hold the cup close to the surface of the water and slip the egg into simmering water.

[3] Cook 4 eggs at a time, uncovered, until whites are completely set and yolks begin to thicken, about 3-5 minutes. With a slotted spoon, remove each egg. Repeat with remaining eggs.

[4] Serve over hash mixture. Sprinkle with additional Cajun seasoning and serve with hot pepper sauce if desired. **Yield:** 4 servings.

Editor's Note: If poaching using a metal poaching insert, increase poaching time to 6-7 minutes.

DEL MASON
MARTENSVILLE,
SASKATCHEWAN

Both the flavor and texture are delectable in this tongue-tingling hash. This skillet is an all-time favorite of mine. I created it after sampling a similar variation in Texas.

HUNTING & FISHING COOKBOOK

BREAKFAST MESS

[2] In another greased skillet, combine eggs, salt and pepper. Cook and stir gently until eggs are set. Stir into potato mixture. Top with cheese; cover for 3-5 minutes or until cheese is melted. **Yield:** 6-8 servings.

breakfast sausage fried rice

TAMI THOMAS
PALMDALE, CALIFORNIA

This is a great camp breakfast because it uses last night's leftover rice! The soy sauce and garlic make it interesting.

- 1/4 **pound bulk pork sausage**
- 1 **egg, lightly beaten**
- 3/4 **cup cold cooked long grain rice**
- 4 **teaspoons soy sauce**
- 1/4 **teaspoon minced garlic**

Pepper to taste

Crumble sausage into a skillet; cook over medium heat until no longer pink. Remove with a slotted spoon and set aside. In same skillet, cook and stir egg over medium heat until completely set. Stir in rice, sausage, soy sauce, garlic and pepper. Cook until heated through. **Yield:** 2 servings.

ham and cheese frittata

NANCY BROWN
JANESVILLE, WISCONSIN

This recipe is very flexible because it can be served around the clock. In summer, I frequently add a variety of fresh vegetables, including zucchini.

- 2 **tablespoons butter**
- 1/2 **cup sliced fresh mushrooms**
- 1/2 **cup chopped sweet red or green pepper**
- 1/4 **cup sliced green onions**
- 6 **eggs**
- 2 **tablespoons water**
- 1/2 **cup diced fully cooked ham**
- 1 **cup (4 ounces) shredded cheddar cheese**

[1] In a large skillet, melt the butter over medium heat. Saute mushrooms, pepper and onions in the pan until tender.

DEE ANDERSON
KENT,
WASHINGTON

Whenever my family goes camping (which is a lot!), this wonderful, filling breakfast really gets the day going. Everyone who's tried the "Anderson Family Special" agrees that it's the best.

breakfast mess

- 1 **package (26 ounces) frozen shredded hash brown potatoes**
- 1/4 **cup vegetable oil**
- 1 **large green pepper, chopped**
- 1 **large onion, chopped**
- 2 **garlic cloves, minced**
- 2 **cans (12 ounces each) Spam or 3 cups cubed fully cooked ham**
- 6 **eggs, lightly beaten**
- 1/2 **teaspoon salt**
- 1/4 **teaspoon pepper**
- 1 1/2 **cups (6 ounces) shredded cheddar cheese**

[1] In a large skillet, fry potatoes in oil for 10 minutes. Add green pepper, onion and garlic; continue to cook for 25 minutes or until potatoes are browned and vegetables are tender. Stir in Spam; heat through. Cover and remove from heat.

HUNTING & FISHING COOKBOOK

SAUSAGE EGG SUBS

DEE PASTERNAK
BRISTOL,
INDIANA
Spicy chunks of sausage give winning flavor to this scrambled egg mixture. Served in a bun, it's a satisfying all-in-one sandwich for breakfast or lunch.

[2] In a mixing bowl, beat eggs until foamy; stir in ham. Pour over the vegetables. Let eggs set on the bottom, then lift the edges to allow any uncooked egg to flow underneath. Cover and cook until the eggs are set, about 3 minutes. Sprinkle with cheese and cut into wedges to serve. **Yield:** 4 servings.

sausage egg subs

- 1¼ **pounds bulk pork sausage**
- ¼ **cup chopped onion**
- 12 **eggs, lightly beaten**
- ½ **cup chopped fresh mushrooms**
- 1 **to 2 tablespoons finely chopped green pepper**
- 1 **to 2 tablespoons finely chopped sweet red pepper**
- 6 **submarine sandwich buns (about 6 inches), split**

[1] In a large skillet over medium heat, cook sausage and onion until meat is no longer pink; drain. Remove with a slotted spoon and keep warm.

[2] In the same skillet, add eggs. Cook and stir eggs until eggs are nearly set, about 7 minutes. Add mushrooms, peppers and the sausage mixture. Cook until eggs are completely set and mixture is heated through. Serve on buns. **Yield:** 6 servings.

HUNTING & FISHING tip

When camping, take along only the amount of food that can be eaten. That way, you won't have leftovers.

TASTE OF HOME TEST KITCHEN

**GLENN POWELL
HAVANA, FLORIDA**

Omelets are one of my husband's specialties. The filling of fresh-tasting vegetables and cheese adds a one-of-a-kind taste the whole family enjoys.

daddy's omelet

¼ cup each diced green pepper, onion and mushrooms

1 to 2 tablespoons butter

2 eggs

⅛ teaspoon salt

Pinch pepper

¼ cup shredded cheddar cheese

[1] In an 8-in. skillet, saute green pepper, onion and mushrooms in butter until tender. Remove with a slotted spoon and set aside. In a small bowl, beat eggs, salt and pepper. Pour into the skillet.

[2] Cook over medium heat; as eggs set, lift edges, letting uncooked portion flow underneath. When the eggs are set, spoon vegetables and cheese over one side; fold omelet over filling. Cover and let stand for 1-2 minutes or until cheese is melted. **Yield:** 1 serving.

o'brien kielbasa skillet

**SHER KOCZKO
WINCHESTER, CALIFORNIA**

When serving this, be prepared to dish out second helpings—and even thirds! The quick combination of hash browns and sausage complements many different menus.

1 pound fully cooked kielbasa or Polish sausage, cut into ½-inch slices

1 package (24 ounces) frozen O'Brien hash brown potatoes

3 tablespoons vegetable oil

Pepper to taste

In a large skillet, brown sausage; remove with a slotted spoon and set aside. Add potatoes and oil to drippings. Cover and cook over medium heat for 10 minutes, stirring occasionally. Season with pepper. Return sausage to the pan; cover and cook until heated through. **Yield:** 6 servings.

cheddar hash brown omelet

**BETTY KLEBERGER
FLORISSANT, MISSOURI**

My husband loves it when I make crescent rolls to go with this easy family favorite.

2 cups frozen shredded hash brown potatoes, thawed

½ cup chopped onion

½ cup chopped green pepper

2 tablespoons butter

1 cup diced fully cooked ham or Polish sausage

6 eggs

¼ cup milk

¼ teaspoon pepper

⅛ teaspoon salt

½ cup shredded cheddar cheese

[1] In a 10-in. nonstick skillet, saute potatoes, onion and green pepper in butter until tender. Sprinkle with ham. In a bowl, beat eggs, milk, pepper and salt; add to skillet.

[2] As the eggs set, lift edges, letting uncooked portion flow underneath. When eggs are set, remove from the heat. Sprinkle with cheddar cheese; fold omelet in half. Cover; cook for 1-2 minutes or until cheese is melted. **Yield:** 4 servings.

DADDY'S OMELET

CHICKEN AND EGG HASH

chicken and egg hash

4 bacon strips, diced

1 medium onion, chopped

2 garlic cloves, minced

1 pound boneless skinless chicken breasts, cubed

2 large potatoes, peeled and diced

1 tablespoon vegetable oil

½ cup frozen peas, thawed

½ cup frozen corn, thawed

2 tablespoons minced fresh parsley

¾ teaspoon salt

⅛ teaspoon pepper

4 eggs

[1] In a skillet, cook bacon over medium heat until crisp. Remove with a slotted spoon to paper towels to drain. In the drippings, saute onion and garlic until tender. Stir in chicken, potatoes and oil. Cover and cook for 10 minutes or until potatoes are tender and chicken is cooked through.

[2] Stir in peas, corn, parsley, salt and pepper. Make four wells in the hash; break an egg into each well. Cover and cook over low heat for 8-10 minutes or until eggs are completely set. Sprinkle with bacon. **Yield:** 4 servings.

JOYCE PRICE WHITEFISH, ONTARIO

This recipe is one of my daughter's favorites. To reduce cooking time and clean out the fridge, dice up leftover potatoes and use cooked chicken or ham instead.

EDNA HOFFMAN
HEBRON,
INDIANA

Dill and a sprinkling of cheese give these scrambled eggs farm-fresh flavor. Dijon mustard really dresses up this simple dish that cooks up in a matter of minutes. Serve the eggs with dressed-up English muffins for a nice change from plain toast.

DILLY SCRAMBLED EGGS

ENGLISH MUFFINS WITH BACON BUTTER

dilly scrambled eggs

    6 eggs

    ¼ cup water

    ½ teaspoon salt

Dash pepper

    2 tablespoons butter

    ¼ cup shredded cheddar cheese

    1 teaspoon snipped fresh dill or ¼ teaspoon dill weed

In a bowl, beat eggs, water, salt and pepper. Melt butter in a skillet; add egg mixture. Cook and stir gently over medium heat until eggs are almost set. Sprinkle with cheese and dill; cook until eggs are completely set and cheese is melted. **Yield:** 4 servings.

english muffins with bacon butter

    ½ cup butter, softened

    ½ to ¾ teaspoon Dijon mustard

    4 bacon strips, cooked and crumbled

    4 to 6 English muffins, split

In a bowl, combine butter and mustard; stir in bacon. Toast English muffins; spread with bacon butter. Refrigerate any leftover butter. **Yield:** 4-6 servings.

steak hash

BARBARA NOWAKOWSKI
NORTH TONAWANDA, NEW YORK

Give leftover steak and baked potatoes a flavorful face-lift. Green pepper, onion and garlic powder lend just enough seasoning to this easy dish.

    1 medium green pepper, chopped

    1 small onion, chopped

    2 tablespoons vegetable oil

    3 medium potatoes (about 1 pound), peeled, cooked and diced

tip

HUNTING & FISHING

Cast iron cookware that has not been coated with porcelain enamel requires seasoning. Seasoning, which is a process of rubbing the inside of a pan with vegetable oil and heating it for an hour in a 350° oven, gives cast iron a natural, nonstick finish. Continued use and careful cleaning improves the seasoning. Wipe with a paper towel or soft cloth, and if necessary, gently scrub with a nylon pad. Cast iron cookware may need to be reseasoned periodically.

TASTE OF HOME TEST KITCHEN

1 cooked steak, diced (about 1 cup)

¼ to ½ teaspoon garlic powder

Salt and pepper to taste

¼ cup shredded Monterey Jack cheese

4 eggs

[1] In a skillet, saute green pepper and onion in oil until tender. Stir in potatoes. Reduce heat; cover and cook over low heat for 10 minutes or until potatoes are heated through, stirring occasionally. Add steak, garlic powder, salt and pepper. Sprinkle with cheese.

[2] Cover and cook on low 5 minutes longer or until heated through and cheese is melted; keep warm. Prepare eggs as desired. Divide hash between four plates and top with an egg. **Yield:** 4 servings.

denver omelet scramble

RON GARDNER
GRAND HAVEN, MICHIGAN

For breakfast, lunch or dinner, this savory scramble is a satisfying entree any time of the day.

1 cup sliced peeled uncooked potatoes

½ cup diced fully cooked ham

½ cup each chopped onion, green pepper and sweet red pepper

1 can (4 ounces) mushroom stems and pieces, drained

1 tablespoon butter

1 teaspoon salt

4 eggs, lightly beaten

½ cup shredded cheddar cheese

[1] Place potato slices in a saucepan; cover with water. Bring to a boil. Cook until tender; drain. In a skillet, saute potato, ham, onion, peppers and mushrooms in butter for 6-8 minutes or until vegetables are tender. Sprinkle with salt.

[2] Pour the eggs over top. Cook and stir until the eggs are completely set. Sprinkle with cheese. **Yield:** 2 servings.

camper's breakfast hash

¼ cup butter, cubed

2 packages (20 ounces each) refrigerated shredded hash brown potatoes

1 package (7 ounces) brown-and-serve sausage links, cut into ½-inch pieces

¼ cup chopped onion

¼ cup chopped green pepper

12 eggs, lightly beaten

Salt and pepper to taste

1 cup (4 ounces) shredded cheddar cheese

[1] In a large skillet, melt butter. Add potatoes, sausage, onion and green pepper. Cook, uncovered, over medium heat for 10-15 minutes or until potatoes are lightly browned, turning once.

[2] Push potato mixture to the sides of pan. Pour eggs into center of pan. Cook and stir over medium heat until eggs are completely set. Season with salt and pepper. Reduce heat; stir eggs into potato mixture. Top with cheese; cover and cook for 1-2 minutes or until cheese is melted. **Yield:** 8 servings.

LINDA KRIVANEK
OAK CREEK, WISCONSIN

When we go camping with family and friends, I'm always asked to make this hearty breakfast. But it's also a favorite at home!

CAMPER'S BREAKFAST HASH

HUNTING & FISHING COOKBOOK

CAROLYN MCMASTERS JACKSONVILLE, FLORIDA

One of my favorite pastimes is cooking. Friends and family have always encouraged me, mainly because they get to sample my creations. This recipe is a classic I've been making for years.

hash brown omelet

4 bacon strips

2 cups frozen shredded hash brown potatoes

1/4 cup chopped onion

1/4 cup chopped green pepper

4 eggs, lightly beaten

1/4 cup milk

1/2 teaspoon salt

Dash pepper

1 cup (4 ounces) shredded sharp cheddar cheese

[1] In a medium nonstick skillet, cook bacon until crisp. Remove bacon; crumble and set aside. Add potatoes, onion and green pepper to drippings. Cook and stir over medium heat for 7-10 minutes or until potatoes are lightly browned and vegetables are tender.

[2] In a bowl, beat eggs, milk, salt and pepper; pour over potatoes. Sprinkle with cheese and bacon. Cover and cook over medium-low heat for 10-15 minutes or until eggs are set. Do not stir. Fold in half. **Yield:** 2-3 servings.

hurry-up hoosier sandwiches

SUE CALL
BEECH GROVE, INDIANA

These simple egg sandwiches are delicious and quick to make. They are especially great when you're hurrying out the door!

1 tablespoon butter

4 eggs

Salt and pepper to taste

4 slices process American cheese

8 slices bread, toasted

Mayonnaise and/or mustard, optional

4 lettuce leaves

4 slices fully cooked deli ham

[1] In a large skillet, melt butter over medium-high heat. Break each egg into the pan. Season with salt and pepper. Reduce heat to medium-low; cover and cook until yolks are nearly set.

[2] Place a cheese slice on each egg. Cook 1 minute longer. Spread each toast slice with mayonnaise and/or mustard if desired. On four toast slices, place an egg with cheese, lettuce leaf and ham slice. Top with remaining toast. **Yield:** 4 sandwiches.

HASH BROWN OMELET

QUICK SAUSAGE GRAVY

sunrise skillet

MARY STICKNEY
CORTLAND, NEBRASKA

I learned to cook at an early age. Instead of relying on recipes, most of my dishes come about from trial and error, including this skillet. We always make it when we go camping.

- 1/2 **pound ground beef**
- 2 **medium potatoes, peeled, cubed and cooked**
- 1 **medium onion, chopped**
- 1 **celery rib, chopped**
- 4 **eggs**

Salt and pepper to taste

[1] In a skillet, cook beef over medium heat until no longer pink; drain. Add potatoes, onion and celery. Cook and stir for 10-15 minutes or until potatoes are browned and celery is tender.

[2] Make four wells in beef mixture; break an egg into each well. Cover and cook over medium heat until eggs are completely set, about 10 minutes. Sprinkle with salt and pepper. **Yield:** 4 servings.

Note: To make wells in the Sunrise Skillet beef mixture, use the back of a large serving spoon or the bottom of a measuring cup or small glass. To prevent eggshells from getting into the beef mixture, first break the eggs, one at a time, into a custard cup or saucer. Then gently slide into the well.

quick sausage gravy

- 1 **pound bulk pork sausage**
- 2 **tablespoons all-purpose flour**
- 1 3/4 **cups milk**
- 6 **warm biscuits, halved**

In a skillet, crumble and brown sausage over medium heat until fully cooked; drain. Sprinkle with flour and blend. Gradually add milk, stirring constantly. Bring to a boil; boil for 1 minute. Cook until thickened. Serve over biscuits. **Yield:** 6 servings.

JOAN DAUMEYER
BLANCHESTER, OHIO

I found out how much everyone loved sausage gravy when my husband, George, and I served it for a breakfast we hosted. It disappeared quickly, and everyone who tried it asked for the recipe.

HUNTING & FISHING COOKBOOK

SWISS CHEESE POTATO PANCAKES

**FERNE MOE
NORTHBROOK,
ILLINOIS**

Years ago, when I was searching for just the right side to perk up a meal, my neighbor suggested these pancakes. They did the trick! Golden brown, crisp and cheesy, they make a deliciously different dish any time of day.

swiss cheese potato pancakes

    1 package (3 ounces) cream cheese, softened

    2 eggs

    2 tablespoons all-purpose flour

    4 cups shredded peeled potatoes (about 1 pound)

  1/4 cup shredded Swiss cheese

    2 tablespoons grated onion

  1/4 teaspoon salt

  1/8 teaspoon pepper

Dash cayenne pepper

    3 tablespoons butter

    3 tablespoons vegetable oil

[1] In a mixing bowl, beat cream cheese until smooth. Add eggs, one at a time, beating well after each addition. Add flour; mix well. Stir in potatoes, Swiss cheese, onion, salt, pepper and cayenne pepper.

[2] In a large skillet, heat butter and oil over medium heat. Drop batter by 1/4 cupfuls; press lightly to flatten. Fry until golden and crisp, about 5 minutes on each side. Drain on paper towels. **Yield:** 16 pancakes.

ham 'n' egg skillet

**LUELLEN SPAULDING
CARO, MICHIGAN**

This is great for a weekend brunch or as a spur-of-the moment supper. The nicely seasoned skillet dish is hearty with ham, cheese and potatoes.

    3 medium uncooked potatoes, peeled and diced

    1 tablespoon butter

  1/4 cup chopped onion

  1/4 cup chopped green pepper

    1 cup cubed fully cooked ham

    3 eggs, beaten

    1 cup (4 ounces) shredded cheddar cheese

Salt and pepper to taste

In a skillet, saute potatoes in butter until tender and golden brown. Add onion and green pepper; saute until crisp-tender. Add ham, eggs, cheese, salt and pepper. Cook until eggs are completely set, stirring occasionally. **Yield:** 4 servings.

bacon-potato burritos

**REESA BYRD
ENTERPRISE, ALABAMA**

You'll enjoy the tasty, hearty flavor of these unique breakfast burritos.

    8 bacon strips

 1 1/2 cups frozen Southern-style hash brown potatoes

    2 teaspoons minced dried onion

    4 eggs

  1/4 cup milk

    1 teaspoon Worcestershire sauce

  1/4 teaspoon salt

  1/4 teaspoon pepper

    1 cup (4 ounces) shredded cheddar cheese

    6 flour tortillas (8 inches)

[1] In a large skillet, cook bacon over until crisp; drain on paper towels and set aside. Brown potatoes and onion in drippings.

[2] In a bowl, beat eggs; add milk, Worcestershire sauce, salt and pepper. Pour over potatoes; cook and stir until eggs are set. Crumble bacon and stir into eggs. Sprinkle with cheese.

[3] Meanwhile, warm tortillas according to package directions. Spoon egg mixture down center of tortillas; fold in sides of tortilla. Serve with salsa. **Yield:** 4-6 servings.

farmhouse omelets

- 4 bacon strips, diced
- ¼ cup chopped onion
- 6 eggs
- 1 tablespoon water
- ¼ teaspoon salt, optional
- ⅛ teaspoon pepper

Dash hot pepper sauce

- 3 teaspoons butter, divided
- ½ cup cubed fully cooked ham, divided
- ¼ cup thinly sliced fresh mushrooms, divided
- ¼ cup chopped green pepper, divided
- 1 cup (4 ounces) shredded cheddar cheese, divided

[1] In a skillet, cook bacon over medium heat until crisp. Remove with a slotted spoon to paper towels. Drain, reserving 2 teaspoons drippings. In drippings, saute onion until tender; set aside.

[2] In a bowl, beat the eggs, water, salt if desired, pepper and pepper sauce. Melt 1½ teaspoons butter in a 10-in. nonstick skillet over medium heat; add half of the egg mixture. As the eggs set, lift the edges, letting uncooked portion flow underneath.

[3] When eggs are set, sprinkle half of the bacon, onion, ham, mushrooms, green pepper and cheese on one side; fold over. Cover and let stand for 1-2 minutes or until cheese is melted. Repeat with remaining ingredients for second omelet. **Yield:** 2 omelets.

**ROBERTA WILLIAMS
POPLAR BLUFF, MISSOURI**

We really enjoy eating brunch after church on Sundays, so I make an effort to serve something special. This pretty omelet provides a pleasant blend of tastes and textures.

FARMHOUSE OMELETS

HUNTING & FISHING COOKBOOK

My family named this dish because I served it when we vacationed at our cabin on the Mississippi River. Now it's become such a favorite that I often make it when we're home.

cabin hash

12 medium potatoes (about 4 pounds), peeled, cooked and cubed

3 cups cubed fully cooked ham (about 1 pound)

1/2 cup chopped onion

1/2 cup butter

1 package (10 ounces) frozen chopped broccoli, thawed

Salt and pepper to taste

Sour cream, optional

In a large skillet, cook potatoes, ham and onion in butter, stirring frequently, until potatoes are lightly browned. Add broccoli; heat through. Season with salt and pepper. Serve with sour cream if desired. **Yield:** 8-10 servings.

farmer's breakfast

**JEANNETTE WESTPHAL
GETTYSBURG, SOUTH DAKOTA**

Start the day right with this breakfast mixture of bacon, potatoes and eggs. It's a surefire way to get the crowd moving!

6 bacon strips, diced

2 tablespoons diced onion

3 medium potatoes, cooked and cubed

6 eggs, beaten

Salt and pepper to taste

1/2 cup shredded cheddar cheese

[1] In a skillet, cook bacon until crisp. Remove to paper towel to drain. In drippings, saute onion and potatoes until the potatoes are browned, about 5 minutes.

CABIN HASH

HUNTING & FISHING COOKBOOK

[2] Pour eggs into skillet; cook and stir gently until eggs are set and cooked to desired doneness. Season with salt and pepper. Sprinkle with cheese and bacon; let stand for 2-3 minutes or until cheese melts. **Yield:** 4-6 servings.

toasty egg sandwiches

DENISE HELMS
GLENVIEW, ILLINOIS

When I'm running late, these sandwiches make an easy and tasty breakfast. Both my son and daughter request them often. I like to serve fruit alongside.

2 tablespoons butter, softened, divided

2 eggs

4 slices bread

2 teaspoons mayonnaise

2 slices American cheese

[1] In a small skillet, heat 1 tablespoon butter until melted. Break each egg into skillet; reduce heat to low. Cook until white is completely set and yolk begins to thicken but is not hard.

[2] Meanwhile, toast bread. Spread remaining butter over one side of each slice of bread. Spread mayonnaise over buttered side of two bread slices; top with cheese slices, eggs and remaining bread. **Yield:** 2 servings.

bacon 'n' egg tacos

WENDY MATEJEK
CORPUS CHRISTI, TEXAS

Salsa perks up the flavor of this twist on a classic breakfast combo. This recipe can easily be divided to serve a few or doubled to serve a crowd.

6 eggs

1/4 cup crumbled cooked bacon

2 tablespoons butter

3 slices process American cheese, diced

1/4 teaspoon salt

1/4 teaspoon pepper

6 flour tortillas (6 inches), warmed

Salsa, optional

In a bowl, beat the egg; add bacon. Melt butter in a skillet over medium heat. Add egg mixture; cook and stir until the eggs are completely set. Stir in the cheese, salt and pepper.

[2] Spoon 1/4 cup filling down the center of each tortilla; fold sides over filling. Serve with salsa if desired. **Yield:** 6 servings.

SMOKED SAUSAGE SCRAMBLE

smoked sausage scramble

1 medium potato, cubed

1 tablespoon chopped onion

1 tablespoon vegetable oil

1 cup torn fresh spinach

1 cup cubed smoked sausage

4 eggs

1 tablespoon water

2 slices American cheese, diced

In a large skillet, cook the potato and onion in oil until potato is tender. Add spinach and sausage. In a bowl, whisk eggs and water. Pour over sausage mixture. Cook over medium heat, stirring occasionally, until the eggs are completely set. Top with cheese. Serve immediately. **Yield:** 2 servings.

STEPHANIE LEVEN
WARSAW, MISSOURI

I came up with this recipe one morning when we had smoked sausage left over from the day before. My husband really loved it! The spicy sausage, spinach, egg, potato and cheese scramble makes a very hearty morning meal or a satisfying light supper.

HUNTING & FISHING COOKBOOK

KIM SCHOLTING
SPRINGFIELD,
NEBRASKA

This filling dish is perfect for breakfast or supper. It's one of my family's favorites and it's kid friendly! Eggs, cheese, hash browns and ham go well together.

morning mix-up

2 cups frozen shredded hash brown potatoes

1 cup chopped fully cooked ham

1/2 cup chopped onion

2 tablespoons vegetable oil

6 eggs

Salt and pepper to taste

1 cup (4 ounces) shredded cheddar cheese

Minced fresh chives

[1] In a large skillet, saute potatoes, ham and onion in oil for 10 minutes or until potatoes are tender. In a small bowl, beat eggs, salt and pepper.

[2] Add egg mixture to skillet; cook, stirring occasionally, until eggs are set. Remove from heat and gently stir in cheese. Spoon onto a serving platter; sprinkle with chives. **Yield:** 4 servings.

toad in the hole

RUTH LECHLEITER
BRECKENRIDGE, MINNESOTA

This is one of the first recipes I had my children prepare when they were learning to cook. My little ones are now grown (and have advanced to more difficult recipes!), but this continues to be a traditional standby in my home and theirs.

1 slice of bread

1 teaspoon butter

1 egg

Salt and pepper to taste

Cut a 3-in. hole in the middle of the bread and discard. In a small skillet, melt the butter; place the bread in the skillet. Place egg in the hole. Cook for about 2 minutes over medium heat until the bread is lightly browned. Turn and cook the other side until yolk is almost set, Season with salt and pepper. **Yield:** 1 serving.

spicy maple sausages

TASTE OF HOME TEST KITCHEN

Wake up your guests' taste buds with this easy treatment for breakfast sausages. Just five ingredients are needed for the sweet and spicy glaze.

    2 packages (7 ounces each) brown-and-serve sausage links
    1/4 cup maple syrup
    1/4 cup honey
    2 teaspoons Dijon mustard
    1/2 teaspoon ground cinnamon
    1/2 teaspoon cayenne pepper

In a large skillet, cook sausage links until browned; drain. Combine remaining ingredients; stir into skillet. Bring to a boil; cook and stir for 2-3 minutes or until sausages are glazed. **Yield:** 6-8 servings.

breakfast pizza skillet

    1 pound bulk Italian sausage
    5 cups frozen hash brown potatoes
    1/2 cup chopped onion
    1/2 cup chopped green pepper
    1/4 to 1/2 teaspoon salt
    Pepper to taste
    1/2 cup sliced mushrooms
    4 eggs
    1 medium tomato, thinly sliced
    1 cup (4 ounces) shredded cheddar cheese
    Sour cream and salsa, optional

[1] In a large skillet, cook sausage over medium heat until no longer pink. Add potatoes, onion, green pepper, salt and pepper. Cook over medium-high heat for 18-20 minutes or until potatoes are browned.

[2] Stir in mushrooms. Beat in eggs; pour over the potato mixture. Arrange tomato slices on top. Sprinkle with cheese. Cover and cook over medium-low heat for 10-15 minutes or until eggs are completely set (do not stir). Serve with sour cream and salsa if desired. **Yield:** 6 servings.

MARILYN HASH ENUMCLAW, WASHINGTON
I found the recipe for this hearty stovetop dish several years ago and it was an instant hit at a Christmas brunch. This would be an extra-special treat at a camp breakfast!

BREAKFAST PIZZA SKILLET

TASTE OF HOME TEST KITCHEN

Eggs in the morning just aren't the same without sausage and potatoes. These two favorite breakfast side dishes are conveniently cooked in the same skillet, so you only dirty one pan.

sausage potato skillet

- 1 package (8 ounces) brown-and-serve sausage links
- 2 tablespoons water
- 2 tablespoons vegetable oil
- 3 cups frozen shredded hash brown potatoes
- ½ cup chopped sweet red or green pepper
- ¼ cup chopped onion

Salt and pepper to taste

[1] Cut sausage links into bite-size pieces. In a covered skillet, cook sausage in water and oil over medium heat for 5 minutes. Remove sausage with a slotted spoon and keep warm.

[2] Carefully add potatoes, red pepper and onion to pan. Cover and cook for 5 minutes. Uncover; cook 5-6 minutes longer or until potatoes are tender. Return sausage to pan; heat through. **Yield:** 4 servings.

breakfast scramble

MARY LILL
ROCK CAVE, WEST VIRGINIA

One day for breakfast, I reached for the ground beef and tossed in other ingredients as I went. This recipe was the mouthwatering result.

- 1 pound ground beef
- 1 medium onion, chopped
- 3 cups diced peeled potatoes
- ½ cup water

Salt and pepper to taste

- 1 can (14½ ounces) diced tomatoes, undrained
- 4 eggs, beaten
- 4 slices process American cheese

[1] In a skillet, cook beef and onion over medium heat until meat is no longer pink; drain. Add potatoes, water, salt and pepper. Cover and simmer for 20 minutes or until potatoes are tender. Add tomatoes; cook for 5 minutes.

SAUSAGE POTATO SKILLET

[2] Pour eggs over mixture. Cook, stirring occasionally, until eggs are completely set. Top with cheese. Cover and cook for 1 minute or until cheese is melted. **Yield:** 4-6 servings.

german farmer's breakfast

**MARY LOU WELSH
HINSDALE, ILLINOIS**

This casserole can be quickly prepared so it's perfect for on-the-go hunters or fishermen.

- 6 bacon strips, diced
- 3 large potatoes, peeled, cooked and cubed
- 1 small green pepper, diced
- 2 tablespoons finely chopped onion

Salt and pepper to taste

- 1/2 cup shredded cheddar cheese
- 6 eggs
- 1/4 cup milk

[1] In a skillet, cook bacon over medium heat until crisp; remove to paper towel. Reserve 2 tablespoons drippings; add potatoes, green pepper, onion, salt and pepper. Cook and stir over medium heat for 6-8 minutes or until potatoes are golden brown. Stir in cheese and bacon; remove the mixture to a bowl and set aside.

[2] Beat eggs and milk; pour into same skillet. Cook and stir gently over medium heat until eggs are completely set, about 3-5 minutes. Add potato mixture; cook and stir gently until heated through. **Yield:** 4-6 servings.

POTATO HAM SKILLET

HUNTING & FISHING tip

Eggs must always be refrigerated. Fresh shell eggs can be kept refrigerated in their carton for 4 to 5 weeks beyond the pack date. Hard-cooked eggs can be kept in the refrigerator for up to 1 week. Shell color is determined by the breed of hen and is not related to quality, nutrients, flavor or cooking characteristics. Since birds that lay brown eggs are slightly larger and require more food, brown eggs are usually more expensive than white.

THE AMERICAN EGG BOARD

potato ham skillet

- 4 1/2 teaspoons butter
- 3 medium potatoes, peeled and thinly sliced
- 1/2 teaspoon salt
- 1/4 teaspoon pepper
- 7 green onions, chopped
- 1/2 cup chopped green pepper
- 2 cup diced fully cooked ham
- 3 eggs, lightly beaten
- 1/2 cup shredded cheddar cheese

Minced fresh parsley

[1] In a 10-in. skillet, melt butter over medium heat. In the skillet, layer half of the potatoes, salt, pepper, onions, green pepper and ham; repeat layers. Cover and cook over medium heat for 10-15 minutes or until the potatoes are tender.

[2] Pour eggs over the top. Cover and cook for 3-5 minutes or until eggs are nearly set. Sprinkle with cheese. Cover and cook 3-5 minutes longer or until cheese is melted and eggs are completely set. Cut into wedges. Sprinkle with parsley. **Yield:** 6 servings.

**SHARON CRIDER
LEBANON,
MISSOURI**

Use leftover ham to create this stovetop dish. The delicious combination is great to serve anytime.

 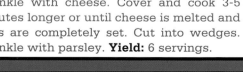

ELVIRA
BRUNNQUELL
PORT
WASHINGTON,
WISCONSIN

Frozen hash browns and packaged shredded cheese shave minutes off preparation of this skillet breakfast. Not only is it appealing, but it can be done in 30 minutes!

country brunch skillet

6 bacon strips

6 cups frozen cubed hash brown potatoes

3/4 cup chopped green pepper

1/2 cup chopped onion

1 teaspoon salt

1/4 teaspoon pepper

6 eggs

1/2 cup shredded cheddar cheese

[1] In a large skillet, cook bacon over medium heat until crisp. Remove bacon; crumble and set aside. Drain drippings, reserving 2 tablespoons. Add potatoes, green pepper, onion, salt and pepper to drippings; cover and cook, stirring occasionally, until potatoes are browned and tender, about 15 minutes.

[2] Make six wells in the potato mixture; break one egg into each well. Cover and cook on low heat for 8-10 minutes or until eggs are completely set. Sprinkle with cheese and bacon. **Yield:** 6 servings.

breakfast pitas

PEGGY BLATTEL
CAPE GIRARDEAU, MISSOURI

These pita pockets are great for a quick breakfast. But for a complete brunch, they are good with hash brown potatoes and fruit.

1 cup diced fully cooked ham

1/3 cup diced onion

1/3 cup diced green pepper

2 tablespoons butter

3 eggs, beaten

1/2 cup shredded cheddar cheese

1/2 teaspoon seasoned salt

1/4 teaspoon pepper

2 pita breads (6 inches), halved and warmed

In a large skillet, saute ham, onion and green pepper in butter until tender. Add eggs; cook and stir over medium heat until eggs are almost set. Add cheese, seasoned salt and pepper. Cook and stir until the eggs are completely set. Spoon into pita halves. **Yield:** 2 servings.

COUNTRY BRUNCH SKILLET

corned beef omelet

KITTY JONES
CHICAGO, ILLINOIS

I was raised on a farm, where we had chickens as well as other farm animals, so we ate a lot of egg dishes. We usually serve this simple omelet for breakfast with toast on the side.

    2 green onions, sliced
    2 tablespoons butter
    6 eggs
    1/4 cup milk
    1 cup cubed cooked corned beef
    1/2 cup shredded cheddar cheese

Dash pepper

[1] In a large skillet, saute onions in butter. In a bowl, lightly beat eggs and milk; pour over onions. Cook over medium heat; as the eggs set, lift the edges, letting uncooked portion flow underneath.

[2] When the eggs are nearly set, sprinkle with corned beef, cheese and pepper. Remove from the heat; cover and let stand for 1-2 minutes or until cheese is melted. Cut into wedges. **Yield:** 4 servings.

country-style scrambled eggs

(PICTURED ON PAGE 133)

JOYCE PLATFOOT
WAPAKONETA, OHIO

The colorful red potatoes and green peppers in this scrambled egg dish can help brighten the day before you head out for a long morning of hunting and fishing.

    8 bacon strips, diced
    2 cups diced red potatoes
    1/2 cup chopped onion
    1/2 cup chopped green pepper
    8 eggs
    1/4 cup milk
    1 teaspoon salt
    1/4 teaspoon pepper
    1 cup (4 ounces) shredded cheddar cheese

[1] In a skillet, cook bacon until crisp; remove with a slotted spoon. In the drippings, cook and stir potatoes over medium heat for

BREAKFAST PATTIES

12 minutes, or until tender. Add onion and green pepper; cook and stir for 3-4 minutes or until crisp-tender; drain. Stir in bacon.

[2] Beat eggs, milk, salt and pepper; pour into skillet. Cook and stir gently until eggs are set. Sprinkle with cheese and let stand until melted. **Yield:** 4 servings.

breakfast patties

    1/4 cup water
    2 teaspoons salt
    2 teaspoons rubbed sage
    1 teaspoon pepper
    1/2 teaspoon ground nutmeg
    1/4 teaspoon crushed red pepper flakes
    1/8 teaspoon ground ginger
    2 pounds ground pork

[1] In a large bowl, combine water and seasonings. Crumble pork over mixture and blend well. Shape into eight 4-in. patties.

[2] In a large skillet, cook patties over medium heat for 5-6 minutes on each side or until no longer pink in the center and a meat thermometer reads 160°. **Yield:** 8 patties.

JEANNINE STALLINGS
EAST HELENA, MONTANA

This homemade sausage is terrific because it is lean, holds together well and shrinks very little when cooked. It's incredibly easy to mix up a batch and make any breakfast special.

HUNTING & FISHING COOKBOOK

BREAKFAST SAUSAGE PATTIES

2 cups frozen shredded hash brown potatoes

2 eggs

2 tablespoons milk

Salt and pepper to taste

½ cup shredded cheddar cheese

2 to 3 tablespoons salsa or picante sauce

[1] In a skillet, saute ham and onion in 1 tablespoon oil until ham is lightly browned and onion is tender; remove and keep warm. Add remaining oil to skillet; cook potatoes over medium heat until tender, turning to brown.

[2] In a small bowl, beat eggs, milk, salt and pepper; add to skillet. As eggs set, lift edges, letting uncooked portion flow underneath. When the eggs are set, spoon ham mixture over top; heat through. Sprinkle with cheese; top with the salsa. Cut into wedges. **Yield:** 2 servings.

corny eggs

PAMELYN HOOLEY
GOSHEN, INDIANA

Adding hominy to the morning eggs makes this camp breakfast a filling meal! It's simple to prepare using convenient ingredients that you're likely to find in your kitchen pantry. Your family will thank you for this "egg-cellent" breakfast!

½ pound sliced bacon, diced

¼ cup chopped onion

¼ cup chopped green pepper

12 eggs, beaten

1 can (15½ ounces) hominy, drained

½ cup sour cream

¼ teaspoon pepper

1 cup (4 ounces) shredded cheddar cheese

[1] In a large skillet, cook bacon over medium heat until crisp; remove to paper towels. Drain, reserving 1 tablespoon drippings. In the drippings, saute onion and green pepper for 2-3 minutes or until tender. Add bacon.

[2] In a large bowl, combine eggs, hominy, sour cream and pepper; stir until blended. Pour over bacon mixture; cook and stir over medium heat until eggs are set. Sprinkle with cheese. **Yield:** 6-8 servings.

CAROLYN SYKORA
BLOOMER, WISCONSIN

Using ground turkey in these sausage patties gives breakfast a whole new twist!

breakfast sausage patties

1 pound ground turkey

¾ teaspoon salt

½ teaspoon rubbed sage

½ teaspoon dried thyme

½ teaspoon ground nutmeg

⅛ teaspoon cayenne pepper

2 teaspoons vegetable oil

In a large bowl, combine turkey, salt, sage, thyme, nutmeg and cayenne. Shape into eight patties. In a large skillet, cook patties in oil over medium heat for 5 minutes on each side or until juices run clear. Drain on paper towels. **Yield:** 4 servings.

tex-mex ham 'n' eggs

PAGE ALEXANDER
BALDWIN CITY, KANSAS

For a satisfying combo, you can't beat ham, eggs, potatoes and cheese, plus salsa for zip.

1 cup cubed fully cooked ham

½ cup chopped onion

2 tablespoons olive oil, divided

hash 'n' eggs

**DOROTHY SMITH
EL DORADO, ARKANSAS**

Turn last night's leftover corned beef and cooked potatoes into a hearty morning meal!

- 2 tablespoons butter
- 4 cups cubed cooked potatoes
- 1 can (10³/₄ ounces) condensed cream of celery soup, undiluted
- ¼ cup milk
- 1 teaspoon prepared mustard
- ¼ teaspoon hot pepper sauce
- 1½ cups cubed cooked corned beef (8 ounces)

Pepper to taste

[1] In a skillet, melt butter over medium heat. Add potatoes and cook for 2 minutes, stirring often. Stir in the soup, milk, mustard and hot pepper sauce; cook until heated through. Stir in corned beef. Reduce heat to low.

[2] Make four wells in potato mixture; break an egg into each well. Cover and cook for 10-15 minutes or until eggs are completely set. Add pepper to taste. **Yield:** 4 servings.

hearty scrambled eggs

- 8 eggs
- 1¼ cups diced fully cooked ham
- ¾ cup diced cheddar cheese
- ½ cup chopped fresh mushrooms
- ¼ cup chopped onion
- 2 to 3 tablespoons butter

In a bowl, beat eggs. Add the ham, cheese, mushrooms and onion. Melt the butter in a skillet; add egg mixture. Cook and stir over medium heat until eggs are completely set and cheese is melted. **Yield:** 4 servings.

**CAROLE ANHALT
MANITOWOC,
WISCONSIN**

This breakfast dish includes classic omelet ingredients in a fun egg scramble that's so quick to whip up! The eggs pick up plenty of flavor from the mushrooms, onion and cheese. To save time, I keep diced ham in the freezer.

HEARTY SCRAMBLED EGGS

HUNTING & FISHING COOKBOOK

MARILYN IPSON ROGERS, ARKANSAS

These colorful eggs are a delicious and hearty way to start the day. They're very quick and easy to make.

vegetable scrambled eggs

    4 eggs
    1/2 cup chopped green pepper
    1/4 cup milk
    1/4 cup sliced green onions
    1/2 teaspoon salt
    1/8 teaspoon pepper
    1 small tomato, seeded and chopped

In a small bowl, beat the eggs. Add the green pepper, milk, onions, salt and pepper. Pour into a lightly greased skillet. Cook and stir over medium heat until eggs are nearly set. Add the tomato; cook and stir until heated through. **Yield:** 2 servings.

curried scrambled egg

**LORRAINE WIECH
SAN LUIS OBISPO, CALIFORNIA**

This flavorful egg dish, which is easily adjusted to feed any number, is perfect for those who want a good breakfast without added salt.

    1 egg
    1 teaspoon water
    1 teaspoon finely chopped chives
    1/8 to 1/4 teaspoon curry powder
    1 teaspoon olive oil

In a small bowl, beat the egg, water, chives and curry powder. Pour oil into a small skillet: add egg mixture. Cook and stir gently over medium heat until egg is set. **Yield:** 1 serving.

wake-up breakfast omelet

**MARY RAYUNEC
HOMOSASSA, FLORIDA**

The hot pepper sauce adds the right amount of zip to this delicious omelet. And because it's so easy to prepare, it's perfect when you want to enjoy breakfast and then get on with the day.

    2 to 4 bacon strips, diced
    2 eggs
    2 tablespoons water
    2 teaspoons fresh or dried chives
    3 to 5 drops hot pepper sauce
Salt and pepper to taste

In an 8-in. nonstick skillet, cook bacon until crisp. Remove bacon to paper towel to drain; discard drippings. In a small bowl, beat eggs; add the water, chives, hot pepper sauce,

VEGETABLE SCRAMBLED EGGS

ZESTY BREAKFAST
BURRITOS

ANGIE IBARRA STILLWATER, MINNESOTA

My husband grew up in Mexico and prefers his food spicy. Special seasonings added to ordinary ground pork give a little life to standard sausage and eggs. Making the pork mixture the night before really adds flavor and speeds things up in the morning.

salt, pepper and bacon. Pour into the same skillet; cook over medium heat. As eggs set, lift edges, letting uncooked portion flow underneath. When eggs are set, fold omelet in thirds. **Yield:** 1 serving.

egg and sausage pockets

**RITA ADDICKS
WEIMAR, TEXAS**

When I want to spice up my breakfast, I make these finger-licking sausage sandwiches. They can be prepared quickly when I'm short on time. And it's a great portable breakfast when you're on the go.

- ¼ **pound bulk pork sausage**
- 4 **large or 8 small pita breads**
- 3 **green onions, sliced**
- ½ **teaspoon chili powder**
- 6 **eggs, lightly beaten**

In a skillet, brown and crumble sausage until fully cooked. Meanwhile, cut pita breads in half crosswise; wrap in foil and warm in the oven. Drain fat from skillet; to sausage add onions, chili powder and eggs. Cook and stir gently over medium heat until eggs are set. Spoon into pita halves. **Yield:** 4 servings.

zesty breakfast burritos

- 1 **pound ground pork**
- 2 **tablespoons white vinegar**
- 1 **tablespoon chili powder**
- 1 **teaspoon dried oregano**
- 1 **teaspoon salt**
- 1 **garlic clove, minced**
- 6 **eggs**
- ¼ **cup milk**
- 1 **tablespoon vegetable oil**
- 6 **flour tortillas (8 inches), warmed**

Taco sauce or salsa

[1] Combine the pork, vinegar, chili powder, oregano, salt and garlic; mix well. Cover and chill overnight.

[2] In a skillet, cook pork mixture over medium heat until no longer pink. Drain; keep warm. Beat eggs and milk. In another skillet, heat oil. Cook eggs over low heat until set, stirring occasionally.

[3] Spoon about ¼ cup pork mixture and ¼ cup eggs down the center of each tortilla. Top with taco sauce and roll up. **Yield:** 6 servings.

HUNTING & FISHING COOKBOOK

JOYCE MUMMAU, MT. AIRY, MARYLAND

Although it requires only a few basic ingredients and little preparation, this drink always draws raves from overnight guests about its "wake-up" taste.

MORNING ORANGE DRINK

morning orange drink

    1 can (6 ounces) frozen orange
      juice concentrate
    1 cup cold water
    1 cup milk
    $1/3$ cup sugar
    1 teaspoon vanilla extract
    10 ice cubes

Combine the first five ingredients in a blender; process at high speed. Add ice cubes, a few at a time, blending until smooth. Serve immediately. **Yield:** 4-6 servings.

mushroom omelet

**CHRISTINE WALKER
OKLAWAHA, FLORIDA**

This tasty version of a basic omelet reminds me of my childhood when I'd help my father search for mushrooms in the forest near our home. The caraway seed really enhances the subtle flavor of the mushrooms.

    1 tablespoon butter
    4 medium fresh mushrooms, sliced
    $1/8$ teaspoon caraway seed
    $1/8$ teaspoon lemon-pepper
      seasoning
    3 eggs
    2 tablespoons milk
    $1/8$ teaspoon salt

Dash pepper

[1] In an 8-in. skillet, heat butter until it sizzles. Saute the mushrooms, caraway seed and lemon-pepper for 3-5 minutes.

[2] In a small bowl, beat eggs, milk, salt and pepper. Pour over the mushrooms. Cook over medium heat. As the eggs set, lift the edges, letting uncooked portion flow underneath. When the eggs are set, fold the omelet in half. **Yield:** 1-2 servings.

salmon scramble

JANINE BAKER
KANSAS CITY, MISSOURI

One morning, years ago, my husband, Todd, and I whipped up this dish as a way to use leftover smoked salmon. It caught on! Now we always make extra portions of this tasty fish at dinner so we can have our family favorite in the morning. For convenience, you can also used canned salmon.

- 8 eggs
- 3/4 cup milk
- 1/2 teaspoon salt
- 1/8 teaspoon pepper
- 1 can (7 1/2 ounces) pink salmon, drained or 1 cup smoked salmon, flaked and cartilage removed
- 1/2 cup shredded Monterey Jack cheese
- 1/4 cup minced fresh parsley

[1] In a bowl, beat the eggs, milk, salt and pepper. Stir in salmon, cheese and parsley.

[2] In a greased skillet, cook and stir gently over medium heat until eggs are set, about 3-5 minutes. **Yield:** 4-6 servings

cinnamon swirl quick bread

- 1 1/2 cups sugar, divided
- 1 tablespoon ground cinnamon
- 2 cups all-purpose flour
- 1 teaspoon baking soda
- 1/2 teaspoon salt
- 1 cup buttermilk
- 1 egg
- 1/4 cup vegetable oil

GLAZE:
- 1/4 cup confectioners' sugar
- 1 1/2 to 2 teaspoons milk

[1] Combine 1/2 cup sugar and cinnamon; set aside. Combine flour, baking soda, salt and remaining sugar. Combine buttermilk, egg and oil; stir into dry ingredients just until combined. Grease the bottom only of a 9-in. x 5-in. x 3-in. loaf pan. Pour half of the batter into pan; sprinkle with half of the cinnamon-sugar.

[2] Carefully spread with the remaining batter and sprinkle with remaining cinnamon-sugar; swirl knife through batter.

[3] Bake at 350° for 45-50 minutes or until a toothpick inserted near the center comes out clean. Cool the bread in pan 10 minutes before removing to a wire rack to cool completely. Combine the glaze ingredients; drizzle over bread. **Yield:** 1 loaf.

HELEN RICHARDSON, SHELBYVILLE, MICHIGAN

I take this bread—which I've been making for over 20 years—to potlucks and parties. Plus, my family's always loved it.

CINNAMON SWIRL QUICK BREAD

HUNTING & FISHING COOKBOOK

KAY KROPFF
CANYON, TEXAS

I love to fix this spicy scrambled egg dish for friends and family. It's a meal in itself, but I serve it with muffins or biscuits, fresh fruit juice and coffee.

fiesta scrambled eggs

1/2 cup chopped onion

1/4 cup chopped sweet red pepper

1 jalapeno pepper, seeded and chopped

8 bacon strips, cooked and crumbled

8 eggs, lightly beaten

1 cup (4 ounces) shredded cheddar cheese, divided

1/2 teaspoon salt

1/8 teaspoon pepper

Salsa

In a nonstick skillet coated with nonstick cooking spray, saute the onion and peppers until tender. Sprinkle with bacon. Pour the eggs over the top; sprinkle with 1/2 cup cheese, salt and pepper. Cook over medium heat, stirring occasionally, until eggs are completely set. Sprinkle with remaining cheese. Serve with salsa. **Yield:** 6 servings.

Editor's Note: When cutting or seeding hot peppers, use rubber or plastic gloves to protect your hands. Avoid touching your face.

fast and flavorful eggs

MICHELE CHRISTMAN
SIDNEY, ILLINOIS

If you chop the green pepper and cook the bacon ahead, this recipe takes very little time to prepare.

1/4 cup chopped green pepper

1 tablespoon butter

6 eggs, lightly beaten

1 can (10 3/4 ounces) condensed cream of chicken soup, undiluted, divided

3/4 teaspoon salt

1/2 teaspoon pepper

6 bacon strips, cooked and crumbled

1/2 cup milk

FIESTA SCRAMBLED EGGS

In a skillet, saute the green pepper in butter until tender. Combine the eggs, 1/2 cup soup, salt and pepper. Add to skillet; cook and stir gently until the eggs are set. Stir in bacon. For sauce, heat milk and remaining soup; stir until smooth. Serve over eggs. **Yield:** 3-4 servings.

tater surprise

PAULA WEST
ST. LOUIS, MISSOURI

We enjoy this with ham, but you can use any breakfast meat. I often use chicken to make a nice dinner.

- 2 1/2 cups frozen Tater Tots or cubed hash brown potatoes
- 1 cup chopped fully cooked ham
- 1/4 cup chopped onion
- 1/4 cup chopped green pepper
- 2 tablespoons vegetable oil
- 4 eggs, beaten

Salt and pepper to taste

In a large skillet, cook potatoes, ham, onion and green pepper in oil over medium heat for 8-10 minutes or until browned, stirring constantly. (If using Tater Tots, break apart with a spatula; mix well.) Add eggs; cook and stir until eggs are completely set. Season with salt and pepper. **Yield:** 4 servings.

southwest skillet dish

VIRGINIA VARNER
TUCSON, ARIZONA

My family loves this variation of plain fried potatoes because they add some zing to our breakfast.

- 4 tablespoons butter
- 5 to 6 cups thinly sliced peeled raw potatoes
- 6 slices fully cooked ham, cubed
- 1 can (4 ounces) chopped green chilies
- 1 cup (4 ounces) shredded Colby cheese

Salsa

In a 10-in. cast-iron skillet, melt the butter over medium heat. Fry the potatoes until lightly browned and tender. Add ham and cook until heated through. Sprinkle with green chilies and cheese. Remove from the heat and

VEGETABLE FRITTATA

cover until the cheese is melted. Serve in the skillet. Top with salsa. **Yield:** 4-6 servings.

vegetable frittata

- 1/2 cup chopped onion
- 1/2 cup chopped green pepper
- 1/2 cup chopped sweet red pepper
- 1 garlic clove, minced
- 3 tablespoons olive oil, divided
- 2 medium red potatoes, cooked and cubed
- 1 small zucchini, cubed
- 6 eggs
- 1/2 teaspoon salt

Pinch pepper

[1] In a 10-in. ovenproof skillet, saute the onion, peppers and garlic in 2 tablespoons of oil until the vegetables are tender. Remove vegetables with a slotted spoon; set aside.

[2] In same skillet over medium heat, lightly brown the potatoes in remaining oil. Add the vegetable mixture and zucchini; simmer for 4 minutes.

[3] In a bowl, beat eggs, salt and pepper; pour over vegetables. Cover and cook for 8-10 minutes or until eggs are nearly set. Broil 6 in. from the heat for 2 minutes or until eggs are set on top. Cut into wedges. **Yield:** 4-6 servings.

JANET ECKHOFF
WOODLAND, CALIFORNIA

This tasty egg dish is easy and inexpensive. I love that it's loaded with hearty and nutritious vegetables.

JENNIFER MEADOWS MATTOON, ILLINOIS

Breakfast around the campfire couldn't be easier with these single-serving bowls. Filled with savory bacon, eggs, cheese and more, they'll give your family a great start to a day outdoors!

BREAKFAST EGGS IN FOIL BOWLS

breakfast eggs in foil bowls

    6 eggs
 1/3 cup milk
 1/8 teaspoon salt
 1/8 teaspoon garlic powder
 1/8 teaspoon pepper
 1/2 cup shredded cheddar cheese
 1/4 cup chopped green pepper
    4 brown-and-serve sausage links, chopped
    4 bacon strips, cooked and crumbled
    2 green onions, chopped

[1] Prepare grill for indirect medium heat.

[2] In a small bowl, whisk together the first five ingredients. Pour into three 4 1/2-in. disposable foil tart pans coated with nonstick cooking spray. Sprinkle with the cheese, green pepper, sausage, bacon and onions.

[3] Cover each pan with foil. Grill, covered, for 20-22 minutes or until the eggs are completely set. **Yield:** 3 servings.

maple oatmeal with dried fruit

CARRIE SANDBLOM CONCORD, NEW HAMPSHIRE

This thick, hearty oatmeal is the perfect chill-chaser on cold mornings. The cinnamon nicely spices this yummy cereal, lightly sweetened with fruit and a kiss of maple syrup.

    3 cups milk or water
 1/4 teaspoon salt
 1 1/2 cups quick-cooking oats
 1/3 cup dried cranberries
 1/3 cup golden raisins
    3 tablespoons maple syrup
 1 1/2 teaspoons ground cinnamon

In a large saucepan, bring milk and salt to a boil. Stir in oats; cook for 1-2 minutes or until thickened, stirring occasionally. Remove from the heat. Stir in the cranberries, raisins, syrup and cinnamon. **Yield:** 4 servings.

andouille egg burritos

FRANK MILLARD
JANESVILLE, WISCONSIN

Give yourself a morning wake-up call with these spicy burritos. They make a great on-the-go breakfast, but try them weeknights for a delicious and different dinner.

- 1/4 cup chopped onion
- 1 tablespoon butter
- 3/4 pound fully cooked andouille sausage links, sliced
- 1 tablespoon chopped green chilies
- 1 jalapeno pepper, seeded and chopped
- 8 eggs, lightly beaten
- 1/8 teaspoon salt
- 1/8 teaspoon pepper

Dash cayenne pepper

- 6 flour tortillas (8 inches), warmed
- 3/4 cup shredded pepper Jack cheese

Taco sauce, optional

[1] In a large skillet over medium heat, cook onion in butter until tender. Add the sausage, chilies and jalapeno; cook 4-5 minutes longer or until heated through. Add the eggs, salt, pepper and cayenne; cook and stir until the eggs are completely set.

[2] Spoon filling off center on each tortilla. Sprinkle each with 2 tablespoons cheese. Fold sides and ends over filling and roll up. Serve with taco sauce if desired. **Yield:** 6 servings.

Editor's Note: When cutting or seeding hot peppers, use rubber or plastic gloves to protect your hands. Avoid touching your face.

apple-cinnamon oatmeal mix

- 6 cups quick-cooking oats
- 1 1/3 cups nonfat dry milk powder
- 1 cup dried apples, diced
- 1/4 cup sugar
- 1/4 cup packed brown sugar
- 1 tablespoon ground cinnamon
- 1 teaspoon salt
- 1/4 teaspoon ground cloves

ADDITIONAL INGREDIENT (for each serving):
- 1/2 cup water

[1] In a large bowl, combine the first eight ingredients. Store in an airtight container in a cool dry place for up to 6 months. **Yield:** 8 cups total.

[2] To prepare oatmeal: Shake mix well. In a saucepan, bring water to a boil; slowly stir in 1/2 cup mix. Cook and stir over medium heat for 1 minute. Remove from heat. Cover and let stand 1 minute or until oatmeal reaches desired consistency. **Yield:** 1 serving.

LYNNE VAN WAGENEN SALT LAKE CITY, UTAH

Oatmeal is a breakfast staple at our house. It's a warm, nutritious start to the day that keeps us going all morning. We used to buy the oatmeal mixes, but we think our homemade version is better! Feel free to substitute raisins or other dried fruit for the apples.

HUNTING & FISHING  tip

Oatmeal not only fills you up, but warms you up, too. Here are some ways to jazz up this classic breakfast: Stir in a few drops of vanilla, almond, strawberry or cherry extract to freshly cooked oatmeal. Or, top your bowl with dried or fresh fruit, such as bananas, apricots, raisins, blueberries or raspberries.

TASTE OF HOME TEST KITCHEN

APPLE-CINNAMON OATMEAL MIX

4

LIANE DAVENPORT GREENSBORO, NORTH CAROLINA

I add plenty of cheese and chopped tomato to my take on this morning classic. Because I make the eggs quesadilla-style, they're easy and fun to eat.

huevos rancheros

1 tablespoon butter

4 eggs, lightly beaten

1 cup (4 ounces) shredded cheddar cheese

1 small tomato, seeded and chopped (about 1/2 cup)

1/4 cup picante sauce

2 flour tortillas (8 inches)

3 tablespoons sour cream

Additional picante sauce

[1] In a large skillet, heat butter until hot. Add eggs; cook and stir over medium heat until eggs are completely set. Remove from the heat; stir in the cheese, tomato and picante sauce.

[2] Spray one side of a tortilla with nonstick cooking spray. Place tortilla greased side down on a griddle. Spoon half the egg mixture on half of the tortilla.

[3] Fold tortilla over and cook over low heat for 1-2 minutes on each side or until cheese is melted and tortilla is golden brown. Repeat with remaining tortilla and egg mixture. Cut tortillas into wedges and serve with sour cream and picante sauce. **Yield:** 2 servings.

cranberry tea

KATHY TRAETOW WAVERLY, IOWA

This colorful tea with its sweet-spicy flavor provides a great cold-weather warm-up. The aroma will make people want to gather around!

1 bottle (32 ounces) cranberry juice

2 cups sugar

1 can (6 ounces) frozen orange juice concentrate

3/4 cup thawed lemonade concentrate

1/3 cup red-hot candies

1 cinnamon stick

2 whole cloves

[1] In a 3-qt. saucepan, combine all the ingredients; bring to a boil over medium heat. Boil for 7 minutes, stirring occasionally. Remove cinnamon and cloves. Store concentrate in a covered container in the refrigerator. **Yield:** (1-1/2 quarts concentrate).

[2] **To prepare tea:** Mix 1/3 cup concentrate and 2/3 cup water; heat through. **Yield:** 1 cup.

HUEVOS RANCHEROS

southern scrapple

RUSTY LOVIN
GREENSBORO, NORTH CAROLINA

When it comes to regional recipes, this certainly fits the bill. Scrapple is a breakfast staple in this area.

- 1/2 pound bulk pork sausage
- 4 cups water
- 1 cup grits
- 1 teaspoon salt
- 1 teaspoon pepper
- Dash cayenne pepper
- 1/4 cup butter, cubed
- 1 cup (4 ounces) shredded cheddar cheese
- Additional butter
- Maple syrup

[1] In a large skillet, cook the sausage over medium heat until no longer pink; drain and set aside. In a large saucepan, bring water to a boil. Gradually add grits, salt, pepper and cayenne, stirring constantly until thickened. Stir in the butter and cheese until melted. Stir in the sausage.

[2] Press the mixture into a greased 9-in. x 5-in. loaf pan. Cover and refrigerate for 1 hour or until cool.

[3] Remove scrapple from the pan; cut into 1/2-in. slices. In a skillet, cook the scrapple in butter until browned on both sides, adding more butter as needed. Serve warm with syrup. **Yield:** 8-10 servings.

homemade pancake mix

- 4 cups all-purpose flour
- 2 cups whole wheat flour
- 2/3 cup sugar
- 2 tablespoons baking powder
- 1 tablespoon baking soda

ADDITIONAL INGREDIENTS FOR PANCAKES:
- 1 egg
- 3/4 cup whole milk

ADDITIONAL INGREDIENTS FOR BLUEBERRY BANANA PANCAKES:
- 1 egg

HOMEMADE PANCAKE MIX

- 3/4 cup whole milk
- 1 medium ripe banana, mashed
- 3/4 cup blueberries

[1] In a bowl, combine first five ingredients. Store in an airtight container in a cool dry place for up to 6 months. **Yield:** 6-7 batches of pancakes (about 6 3/4 cups total).

[2] To prepare pancakes: Contents of mix may settle during storage. When preparing recipe, spoon mix into measuring cup. In a small bowl, whisk egg and milk. Whisk in 1 cup mix.

[3] Pour batter by 1/4 cupfuls onto a lightly greased hot griddle; turn when bubbles form on top of pancakes. Cook until second side is golden brown. **Yield:** about 6 pancakes per batch.

[4] For blueberry banana pancakes: Contents of mix may settle during storage. When preparing recipe, spoon mix into measuring cup. In a large bowl, combine egg, milk and banana. Whisk in 1 cup of mix. Fold in berries. Cook pancakes as directed above. **Yield:** about 8 pancakes per batch.

WENDY MINK
HUNTINGTON, INDIANA

I use whole wheat flour to bring extra flavor to the flapjacks at my breakfast table. My family particularly likes the blueberry-banana variation.

HUNTING & FISHING COOKBOOK

Hunting & Fishing
COOKBOOK

For days when you're not cooking up a fresh catch, plan to bring along some of these satisfying favorites. You'll even want to save room for a tasty campfire dessert!

CHICKEN CAESAR BURGERS, P. 172
SAUSAGE VEGETABLE PACKETS, P. 171
GRILLED CHICKEN WRAPS, P. 182

BRIQUETTE SCALLOPED POTATOES,
PAGE 180

**ROSALIE USRY
FLAXTON,
NORTH DAKOTA**

We have these tempting steaks weekly. If neighbors happen to drop by when I'm preparing steaks, I cut the meat into cubes and grill it on skewers with onions and mushrooms as appetizers.

HUNTING & FISHING COOKBOOK

marinated ribeyes

- 2 **beef ribeye steaks (about 1 inch thick and 12 ounces each)**
- 1/3 **cup hot water**
- 3 **tablespoons finely chopped onion**
- 2 **tablespoons red wine vinegar**
- 2 **tablespoons olive oil**
- 2 **tablespoons soy sauce**
- 1 **teaspoon beef bouillon granules**
- 1 **garlic clove, minced**
- 1/2 **teaspoon paprika**
- 1/2 **teaspoon coarsely ground pepper**

[1] Pierce both sides of steaks several times with a fork. In a small bowl, combine the remaining ingredients. Remove 1/2 cup marinade to another bowl; cover and refrigerate until serving. Pour remaining marinade into a large resealable plastic bag; add the steaks. Seal bag and turn to coat; cover and refrigerate overnight.

[2] Drain and discard marinade. Grill steaks, covered, over medium heat for 5-7 minutes on each side or until meat reaches desired done-ness (for medium-rare, a meat thermometer should read 145°; medium, 160°; well-done, 170°). Warm reserved marinade; serve with steaks. **Yield:** 2 servings.

grilled cajun green beans

**SHANNON LEWIS
ANDOVER, MINNESOTA**

This is a perfect way to use up your garden's green beans. The Cajun flavor makes it different from your regular green bean recipe.

- 1 **pound fresh green beans, trimmed**
- 1/2 **teaspoon Cajun seasoning**
- 1 **tablespoon butter**

[1] Place green beans on a double thickness of heavy-duty foil (about 18 in. square). Sprinkle with Cajun seasoning and dot with butter. Fold foil around beans and seal tightly.

[2] Grill, covered, over medium heat for 10 minutes. Turn packet over; grill 8-12 minutes longer or until beans are tender. Carefully open foil to allow steam to escape. **Yield:** 4 servings.

tailgate sausages

**TASTE OF HOME TEST KITCHEN
GREENDALE, WISCONSIN**

You will need only a handful of ingredients to fix these tasty sandwiches. Fully cooked sausages are stuffed with cheese and a homemade relish, then wrapped in foil so they are easy to transport and a breeze to grill.

- ¹⁄₂ cup giardiniera
- ¹⁄₂ teaspoon sugar
- 4 cooked Italian sausage links
- 4 slices provolone cheese, cut into strips
- 4 brat buns or hot dog buns, split

[1] In a small food processor, combine giardiniera and sugar; cover and process until blended. Make a lengthwise slit three-fourths of the way through each sausage to within ¹⁄₂ in. of each end. Fill with giardiniera mixture and cheese.

[2] Place sausages in buns; wrap individually in a double thickness of heavy-duty foil (about 12 in. x 10 in.). Grill, uncovered, over medium-hot heat for 8-10 minutes or until heated through. **Yield:** 4 servings.

hot dogs with the works

**MARIA REGAKIS
SOMERVILLE, MASSACHUSETTS**

I place hot dogs in buns before topping them with a zesty cheese sauce and grilling them in a double layer of foil.

- 1-¹⁄₂ cups (6 ounces) shredded pepper Jack cheese
- ³⁄₄ cup chopped seeded tomato
- 3 tablespoons chopped onion
- 2 tablespoons sweet pickle relish
- 8 hot dogs
- 8 hot dog buns

[1] In a small bowl, combine the cheese, tomato, onion and relish. Place hot dogs in buns; top with cheese mixture.

[2] Wrap each hot dog in a double thickness of heavy-duty foil (about 12 in. x 10 in.). Grill, covered, over medium-hot heat for 8-10 minutes or until heated through. Open foil carefully to allow steam to escape. **Yield:** 8 servings.

sausage vegetable packets

- ¹⁄₂ pound smoked sausage, cut into ¹⁄₂-inch pieces
- 3 medium zucchini, sliced
- 3 medium tomatoes, sliced
- 1 medium green pepper, julienned
- ¹⁄₄ cup butter, melted
- 1 envelope onion soup mix
- 1 tablespoon brown sugar
- ¹⁄₄ teaspoon salt
- ¹⁄₄ teaspoon pepper

[1] In a large bowl, combine all ingredients. Divide between two pieces of double-layered heavy-duty foil (about 12-in. square). Fold foil around sausage mixture and seal tightly.

[2] Grill, covered, over medium heat for 25-30 minutes or until the vegetables are tender. Open foil carefully to allow steam to escape. **Yield:** 4 servings.

**KAY BISH
THOMPSONVILLE,
ILLINOIS**

We have so much squash in the summer, but we never tire of this recipe. We often leave the sausage out of the foil packets and just serve the veggies as a side dish. Even people who don't usually like zucchini enjoy it.

SAUSAGE VEGETABLE PACKETS

HUNTING & FISHING COOKBOOK

5

RACHEL RICCOMINI SAINT MARYS, KANSAS

This is a great no-guilt recipe. I sometimes substitute ground turkey for the chicken. To make your dinner even lighter, omit the rolls and use the burgers to top a salad!

chicken caesar burgers

1/4 cup finely chopped onion

2 tablespoons shredded Parmesan cheese, divided

1 tablespoon lemon juice

1-1/2 teaspoons dried parsley flakes

1 garlic clove, minced

1 teaspoon Worcestershire sauce

1/4 teaspoon salt

1/4 teaspoon pepper

1/2 pound ground chicken

2 hamburger buns, split

1/4 cup torn romaine

4 teaspoons fat-free creamy Caesar salad dressing

[1] In a small bowl, combine the onion, 1 tablespoon cheese, lemon juice, parsley, garlic, Worcestershire sauce, salt and pepper. Crumble chicken over mixture and mix well. Shape into two patties.

[2] Grill burgers, covered, over medium heat for 5-7 minutes on each side or until a meat thermometer reads 165° and juices run clear. Sprinkle with remaining cheese.

[3] Serve on buns with romaine and salad dressing. **Yield:** 2 servings.

brats with onions

GUNNARD STARK ROTUNDA WEST, FLORIDA

After years of eating plain old brats, I came up with this great-tasting version slathered in zippy onions. Best of all, this makes enough to feed a hungry crowd.

3 cans (12 ounces each) beer or 4 1/2 cups water

3 large onions, thinly sliced and separated into rings

6 garlic cloves, minced

1 tablespoon hot pepper sauce

2 to 3 teaspoons celery salt

2 to 3 teaspoons pepper

CHICKEN CAESAR BURGERS

1 teaspoon chili powder

15 fresh bratwurst links
   (3½ to 4 pounds)

15 hot dog or brat buns, split

[1] In a Dutch oven, combine the beer or water, onion, garlic, pepper sauce, celery salt, pepper and chili powder. Bring to a boil. Add bratwurst. Reduce heat; simmer, uncovered, for 20-25 minutes or until bratwurst is firm and cooked. Drain, reserving onions.

[2] Broil brats 4 in. from heat or grill over medium heat for 4-5 minutes or until browned, turning once. Serve on buns with reserved onions. **Yield:** 15 servings.

zesty t-bone steaks

BETH WENGER
DAYTON, VIRGINIA

Grilling brings out the robust flavor of this steak marinade. Enjoy it while camping or at home.

½ cup water

½ cup soy sauce

2 tablespoons brown sugar

2 tablespoons lemon juice

2 tablespoons red wine vinegar

2 tablespoons canola oil

1 tablespoon Montreal steak seasoning

½ teaspoon garlic powder

½ teaspoon hot pepper sauce

¼ teaspoon pepper

4 beef T-bone steaks (1-inch thick and ¾ pound each)

[1] In a large resealable plastic bag, combine the first 10 ingredients. Add steaks; seal bag and turn to coat. Refrigerate overnight.

[2] Drain and discard marinade. Grill steaks, covered, over medium heat for 8-12 minutes on each side or until meat reaches desired doneness (for medium-rare, a meat thermometer should read 145°; medium, 160°; well-done, 170°). **Yield:** 4 servings.

Editor's Note: This steak recipe was tested with McCormick's Montreal Steak Seasoning. Look for it in the spice aisle.

CAMPFIRE COBBLER

campfire cobbler

1¼ cups biscuit/baking mix

1 envelope instant maple and brown sugar oatmeal

¼ cup cold butter, cubed

⅓ cup milk

2 cans (21 ounces each) blueberry pie filling

¾ cup unsweetened apple juice

Vanilla ice cream, optional

[1] Prepare grill or campfire for low heat, using 12-16 charcoal briquettes or large wood chips.

[2] In a large resealable plastic bag, combine biscuit mix and oatmeal. Add butter; squeeze bag until mixture resembles coarse crumbs. Gradually add milk; knead to form a soft dough. Spread into a greased ovenproof Dutch oven. Combine pie filling and apple juice; pour over dough.

[3] Cover Dutch oven. When briquettes or wood chips are covered with white ash, place Dutch oven directly on top of 6-8 of them. Using long-handled tongs, place 6-8 briquettes on pan cover. Cook for 15 minutes or until filling is bubbly.

[4] To check for doneness, use the tongs to carefully lift cover. If necessary, cook 5 minutes longer. Serve with ice cream if desired. **Yield:** 6 servings.

TASTE OF HOME TEST KITCHEN
GREENDALE, WISCONSIN

At your next campfire, try preparing this wonderful dish for dessert. It is so quick and simple.

HUNTING & FISHING COOKBOOK

LINDA EMILY DOW PRINCETON JUNCTION, NEW JERSEY

I like to spend a lot of time with our family and friends on weekends. That's when this meat-and-potatoes recipe comes in handy. We marinate the meat in the fridge overnight, then grill it quickly for a fast, filling meal.

STEAK AND POTATO SALAD

steak and potato salad

1/2 cup red wine vinegar
1/4 cup olive oil
1/4 cup soy sauce
1 beef top sirloin steak (2 pounds)
6 cups cubed cooked potatoes
1 cup diced green pepper
1/3 cup chopped green onions
1/4 cup minced fresh parsley
1/2 cup creamy Caesar salad dressing

Lettuce leaves, optional

[1] In a large resealable plastic bag, combine the vinegar, oil and soy sauce; add steak. Seal bag and turn to coat. Refrigerate for 1 hour or overnight.

[2] Drain and discard marinade. Grill steak over medium heat or broil 3-4 in. from the heat for 8-10 minutes on each side or until meat reaches desired doneness (for medium-rare, a meat thermometer should read 145°; medium, 160°; well-done, 170°).

[3] Slice the steak into thin strips across the grain and place in a large bowl. Add the potatoes, green pepper, onions, parsley and dressing; toss to coat. Serve on lettuce if desired. **Yield:** 8-10 servings.

broccoli & cauliflower foil pack

TARA DELGADO WAUSEON, OHIO

This is a great side to just about any meat. For a variation, add one chopped large baking potato, or mix in asparagus for a veggie extravaganza!

1 cup fresh broccoli florets
1 cup fresh cauliflowerets
1 small onion, cut into wedges

Refrigerated butter-flavored spray

1/4 teaspoon garlic salt
1/8 teaspoon paprika
1/8 teaspoon pepper

[1] In a large bowl, combine the broccoli, cauliflower and onion; spritz with butter-flavored spray. Sprinkle with the garlic salt, paprika and

pepper; toss to coat. Place on a double thickness of heavy-duty foil (about 18 in. x 12 in.); fold foil around vegetables and seal tightly.

[2] Grill, covered, over medium heat for 10-15 minutes or until tender. Open foil carefully to allow steam to escape. **Yield:** 2 servings.

teriyaki turkey burgers

TASTE OF HOME TEST KITCHEN GREENDALE, WISCONSIN

Teriyaki sauce and pineapple give these turkey burgers a special treatment. One bite and you may never go back to an ordinary burger again.

- 1 egg
- $\frac{1}{2}$ cup dry bread crumbs
- 3 green onions, chopped
- 4 tablespoons teriyaki sauce, divided
- $\frac{1}{4}$ teaspoon onion powder
- 1 pound ground turkey
- 1 can (8 ounces) sliced pineapple, drained
- 4 hamburger buns, split and toasted

[1] In a bowl, combine egg, bread crumbs, onions, 2 tablespoons teriyaki sauce and onion powder. Crumble turkey over mixture; mix well. Shape into four $\frac{3}{4}$-in.-thick patties.

[2] Moisten a paper towel with cooking oil; using long-handled tongs, lightly coat the grill rack. Grill patties, covered, over medium heat for 6-8 minutes on each side or until a meat thermometer reads 165° and juices run clear. Brush with remaining teriyaki sauce during the last 5 minutes.

[3] Grill pineapple slices for 3-4 minutes on each side or until heated through. Serve burgers and pineapple on buns. **Yield:** 4 servings.

HUNTING & FISHING tip

Before a camping trip, I open cans of fruit, pour them into separate resealable bags and lay them flat in my kitchen freezer. I can store several of these bags in my cooler, and I don't have to deal with canned goods. This also works with homemade stews and other dishes.

JAN, NEW MEXICO

tuscan pork wraps

- $\frac{1}{2}$ teaspoon garlic powder
- $\frac{1}{2}$ teaspoon dried oregano
- $\frac{1}{2}$ teaspoon ground coriander
- $\frac{1}{2}$ teaspoon pepper, divided
- $\frac{1}{4}$ teaspoon salt
- $\frac{1}{2}$ pound pork tenderloin
- $\frac{1}{2}$ cup balsamic vinegar
- 1 tablespoon brown sugar
- 2 flour tortillas (8 inches)
- 4 teaspoons Dijon mustard
- 2 romaine leaves
- 1 small red onion, sliced

[1] In a small bowl, combine the garlic powder, oregano, coriander, $\frac{1}{4}$ teaspoon pepper and salt; rub over pork. Grill pork, covered, over medium heat for 8-10 minutes on each side or until a meat thermometer reads 160°.

[2] Meanwhile, in a small saucepan, combine the vinegar, brown sugar and remaining pepper. Bring to a boil; cook until liquid is reduced by half. Brush 2 tablespoons sauce mixture over pork; cut into thin strips.

[3] Spread tortillas with mustard. Layer with the lettuce, pork and onion. Drizzle with remaining sauce. Fold in edges of tortilla and roll up. **Yield:** 2 servings.

ROBYN CAVALLARO EASTON, PENNSYLVANIA

Though these roll-ups have an easy feel, you'll think you were dining in a fancy corner bistro. These wraps look as good as they taste!

TUSCAN PORK WRAPS

HUNTING & FISHING COOKBOOK

TASTE OF HOME
TEST KITCHEN
GREENDALE,
WISCONSIN

Grilled pineapple gives these fajitas a different, fun twist people will love. If you have time, allow the pork to marinate for up to an hour.

pork tenderloin fajitas

- 1 can (8 ounces) sliced pineapple
- 1 envelope fajita seasoning mix
- 1 pork tenderloin (1 pound)
- 1 medium sweet red pepper, sliced
- 1 medium onion, sliced
- 4 flour tortillas (8 inches), warmed
- 1 cup (4 ounces) shredded Monterey Jack cheese
- 1 medium ripe avocado, peeled and sliced

[1] Drain pineapple, reserving juice; set pineapple aside. In a large resealable plastic bag, combine seasoning mix and reserved juice; add the pork. Seal bag and turn to coat; refrigerate for 15 minutes.

[2] Meanwhile, place the red pepper, onion and pineapple on a double thickness of heavy-duty foil (about 12 in. square). Fold foil around mixture and seal tightly.

[3] Prepare grill for indirect heat. Drain and discard marinade from pork. Grill pork and foil packet, covered, over indirect medium heat for 25-40 minutes or until a meat thermometer inserted in the pork reads 160° and vegetables are tender. Remove from the grill. Cover pork and let stand for 5 minutes.

[4] Cut tenderloin into strips; place on tortillas. Top with vegetable mixture, cheese and avocado; fold in sides. **Yield:** 4 servings.

cajun burgers

JULIE CULBERTSON
BANSALEM, PENNSYLVANIA

My family likes spicy food. I found the original recipe for these burgers in a cookbook, then added and subtracted ingredients until they suited our taste. These nicely seasoned burgers are always on the menu whenever we have company over for a backyard cookout.

CAJUN SEASONING BLEND:

- 3 tablespoons ground cumin
- 3 tablespoons dried oregano
- 1 tablespoon garlic powder
- 1 tablespoon paprika
- 2 teaspoons salt
- 1 teaspoon cayenne pepper

BURGERS:

- 1 pound ground beef
- 1/4 cup finely chopped onion
- 1 teaspoon salt
- 1 teaspoon Cajun Seasoning Blend (recipe above)
- 1/2 to 1 teaspoon hot pepper sauce
- 1/2 teaspoon dried thyme
- 1/4 teaspoon dried basil
- 1 garlic clove, minced
- 4 hamburger buns

Sauteed onions, optional

[1] Combine all seasoning blend ingredients in a small bowl or resealable plastic bag; mix well.

[2] In a bowl, combine the first eight burger ingredients; shape into four patties. Cook in a skillet or on a grill over medium-hot heat for 4-5 minutes per side or until burgers reach desired doneness.

[3] Serve on buns; top with sauteed onions if desired. Store remaining seasoning blend in an airtight container. **Yield:** 4 servings.

PORK TENDERLOIN FAJITAS

UE CHEESE FLANK STEAK

**LAURIE NUDO
THE WOODLANDS,
TEXAS**

While building a house, we lived with my parents for a few months. During that time, I browsed through my mother's recipe file. One of the many treasures I found was this steak recipe.

blue cheese flank steak

- 1 medium onion, sliced
- 1 garlic clove, peeled and sliced
- 1/3 cup water
- 1/3 cup white wine vinegar
- 2 tablespoons reduced-sodium soy sauce
- 1/2 teaspoon coarsely ground pepper
- 1 beef flank steak (1 pound)
- 1/2 cup crumbled blue cheese

[1] In a large resealable plastic bag, combine the first six ingredients. Add the steak; seal bag and turn to coat. Refrigerate overnight, turning occasionally.

[2] Drain and discard marinade. Moisten a paper towel with cooking oil; using long-handled tongs, lightly coat the grill rack.

[3] Grill beef, covered, over medium-hot heat for 5-7 minutes on each side or until meat reaches desired doneness (for medium-rare, a meat thermometer should read 145°; medium, 160°; well-done, 170°).

[4] Let stand for 5 minutes; thinly slice across the grain. Sprinkle with blue cheese. **Yield:** 4 servings.

HUNTING & FISHING **tip**

Instead of using ice cubes in your cooler when you go camping, fill clean milk jugs with water and freeze. The blocks of ice don't melt as quickly, and when they do melt, the water stays in the container and doesn't get your food wet.

KIM, OHIO

FIESTA RIBEYE STEAKS

grilled corn pasta salad

TASTE OF HOME TEST KITCHEN
GREENDALE, WISCONSIN

A perfect warm-weather salad, this colorful dish is especially tasty when sweet corn, tomatoes and zucchini are in season. The garden-fresh ingredients are lightly dressed in a mild basil vinaigrette.

4 large ears sweet corn in husks
1-1/2 cups uncooked penne pasta
2 cups cherry tomatoes
1 medium zucchini, thinly sliced
1 can (2-1/4 ounces) sliced ripe olives, drained
1/3 cup white wine vinegar
2 tablespoons olive oil
1 tablespoon minced fresh basil or 1 teaspoon dried basil
1 teaspoon sugar
1 teaspoon salt
1/2 teaspoon ground mustard
1/4 teaspoon garlic powder
1/4 teaspoon pepper

[1] Carefully peel back corn husks to within 1 in. of bottom; remove silk. Rewrap corn in husks and secure with string. Place in a kettle; cover with water. Soak for 20 minutes; drain. Grill corn, covered, over medium heat for 25-30 minutes or until tender, turning often.

[2] Meanwhile, cook pasta according to package directions; drain and rinse in cold water. When corn is cool enough to handle, remove kernels from cobs and place in a large bowl. Add the pasta, tomatoes, zucchini and olives.

[3] Whisk remaining ingredients; pour over salad and gently toss to coat. Refrigerate until serving. **Yield:** 8 servings.

JODEE HARDING
GRANVILLE,
OHIO

This is a great recipe for grilling out or for camping trips. Adapt it for indoors by cooking the steaks in a skillet and heating the tortillas in a warm oven.

fiesta ribeye steaks

8 flour tortillas (6 inches)
8 beef ribeye steaks (3/4 inch thick and 8 ounces each)
1/4 cup lime juice
1 cup (4 ounces) shredded Colby-Monterey Jack cheese
2 cups salsa

[1] Place tortillas on a sheet of heavy-duty foil (about 18 in. x 12 in.). Fold foil around tortillas and seal tightly; set aside.

[2] Drizzle both sides of steaks with lime juice. Grill, covered, over medium-hot heat for 7-9 minutes on each side or until meat reaches desired doneness (for medium-rare, a meat thermometer should read 145°; medium, 160°; well-done, 170°).

[3] Place tortillas on outer edge of grill; heat for 5-6 minutes, turning once. Sprinkle cheese over steaks; serve with salsa and warmed tortillas. **Yield:** 8 servings.

tip   **HUNTING & FISHING**

Be a good camper and never leave a campfire unattended. Extinguish a fire by dousing the entire fire pit with plenty of water (not just the red embers) until there is no hissing sound. Stir the embers to ensure that everything is wet and cold to the touch.

TASTE OF HOME TEST KITCHEN

swiss steak burgers

GREG DALENBERG
PEORIA, ARIZONA

If you're hungry for steak, but only have ground beef, these hearty burgers will hit the spot. Who would believe you could have a restaurant-quality burger in just 20 minutes and with only five ingredients?

- 4 tablespoons A.1. steak sauce, divided
- 2 tablespoons Dijon mustard, divided
- 1 pound ground beef
- 4 slices Swiss cheese
- 4 hamburger buns, split and toasted

[1] In a small bowl, combine 2 tablespoons steak sauce and 1 tablespoon mustard. Crumble beef over mixture and mix well. Shape into four patties.

[2] Grill burgers, covered, over medium heat or broil 4 in. from the heat for 5-7 minutes on each side or until a meat thermometer reads 160° and juices run clear. Top with cheese. Grill 1 minute longer or until cheese is melted.

[3] Spread buns with the remaining steak sauce and mustard; top with burgers. **Yield:** 4 servings.

chicken bundles

CHERYL LANDIS
HONEY BROOK, PENNSYLVANIA

I season chicken and vegetables with sage and fresh dill, then wrap them in foil so everything grills together. Cleanup is a snap!

- 2 boneless skinless chicken breast halves
- 2 medium red potatoes, quartered and cut into $1/2$-inch slices
- $1/4$ cup chopped onion
- 1 medium carrot, cut into $1/4$-inch slices
- 1 celery rib, cut into $1/4$-inch slices
- $1/2$ teaspoon rubbed sage

Salt and pepper to taste

Fresh dill sprigs

[1] Divide chicken and vegetables between two pieces of double-layered heavy-duty foil (about 18 in. square). Sprinkle with the sage, salt and pepper; top with dill sprigs. Fold foil around the mixture and seal tightly.

[2] Grill, covered, over medium heat for 30 minutes or until a meat thermometer reaches 170°. **Yield:** 2 servings.

chocolate dessert wraps

- $1/2$ cup creamy peanut butter
- 4 flour tortillas (8 inches)
- 1 cup miniature marshmallows
- $1/2$ cup miniature semisweet chocolate chips

Vanilla ice cream

Chocolate shavings, optional

[1] Spread 2 tablespoons of peanut butter on each tortilla. Sprinkle $1/4$ cup marshmallows and 2 tablespoons chocolate chips on half of each tortilla.

[2] Roll up, beginning with the topping side. Wrap each tortilla in heavy-duty foil; seal the foil tightly.

[3] Grill, covered, over low heat for 5-10 minutes or until heated through.

[4] Unwrap tortillas and place on dessert plates. Serve with ice cream. Garnish with chocolate shavings if desired. **Yield:** 4 servings.

LAURIE GWALTNEY
INDIANAPOLIS, INDIANA

I came up with this chocolate and peanut butter treat when I needed a unique dessert for an outdoor dinner. These wraps take just minutes on the grill and get a chewy consistency from the warm marshmallows.

HUNTING & FISHING COOKBOOK

CHOCOLATE DESSERT WRAPS

**JUNE DRESS
BOISE,
IDAHO**

Creamy and cheesy with a touch of garlic, these delicious potatoes make a great side dish for anything! Don't worry about leftovers—there won't be any!

briquette scalloped potatoes

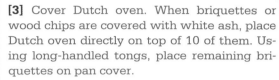

- 5 pounds potatoes (about 6 large), peeled and thinly sliced
- 3 cups (12 ounces) shredded cheddar cheese
- 1 large onion, chopped
- 1/4 cup butter, cubed
- 6 garlic cloves, minced
- 2 teaspoons onion salt
- 1/2 teaspoon salt
- 1/2 teaspoon pepper
- 1 cup milk

[1] Prepare grill or campfire for low heat, using 20-24 charcoal briquettes or large wood chips.

[2] Line a Dutch oven with heavy-duty aluminum foil; add half of the potatoes. Top with 1 1/2 cups cheese, onion, butter, garlic, onion salt, salt and pepper. Top with remaining potatoes and cheese. Pour milk over the top.

[3] Cover Dutch oven. When briquettes or wood chips are covered with white ash, place Dutch oven directly on top of 10 of them. Using long-handled tongs, place remaining briquettes on pan cover.

[4] Cook for 70-80 minutes or until bubbly and potatoes are tender. To check for doneness, use the tongs to carefully lift the cover. **Yield:** 16 servings (3/4 cup each).

barbecued beans

**MILLIE VICKERY
LENA, ILLINOIS**

Cooking this classic on the grill introduces a subtle flavor. Preparation time is minimal with this nice combination of canned beans.

- 1 can (16 ounces) kidney beans, rinsed and drained
- 1 can (15-1/2 ounces) great northern beans, rinsed and drained
- 1 can (15 ounces) pork and beans
- 1/2 cup barbecue sauce
- 2 tablespoons brown sugar
- 2 teaspoons prepared mustard

[1] In an ungreased 8-in. x 8-in. disposable foil pan, combine all ingredients.

[2] Grill, covered, over medium heat for 15-20 minutes or until heated through, stirring occasionally. **Yield:** 5 servings.

snappy peas 'n' mushrooms

**LAURA MAHAFFEY
ANNAPOLIS, MARYLAND**

Seasoned with dill, this versatile side dish can be on the table in mere minutes. Just wrap the fresh vegetables in foil, seal tightly and grill until tender. It's that easy!

- 1 pound fresh sugar snap or snow peas
- 1/2 cup sliced fresh mushrooms
- 2 tablespoons sliced green onions
- 1 tablespoon snipped fresh dill or 1 teaspoon dill weed
- 2 tablespoons butter

Salt and pepper to taste

BRIQUETTE SCALLOPED POTATOES

[1] Place peas and mushrooms on a double thickness of heavy-duty foil (18 in. square). Sprinkle with onions and dill; dot with butter. Fold foil around the mixture and seal tightly.

[2] Grill, covered, over medium-hot heat for 5 minutes. Turn; grill 5-8 minutes longer or until the vegetables are tender. Season with salt and pepper. **Yield:** 8-10 servings.

grilled corn in husks

NANCY ZIMMERMAN

CAPE MAY COURT HOUSE, NEW JERSEY

Seasoned with butter, Parmesan cheese and parsley, this corn is especially good. Be sure to give the ears a long soak before putting them on the grill. Hot off the grate, the kernels are moist and tender with a wonderfully sweet flavor.

   4 large ears sweet corn in husks

 1/4 cup butter, softened

   2 tablespoons minced fresh parsley

 1/4 cup grated Parmesan cheese

[1] Carefully peel back the husks from corn to within 1 in. of bottom; remove silk. Combine the butter and parsley; spread over the corn. Rewrap corn in husks and secure with string. Soak in cold water for 20 minutes; drain.

[2] Grill corn, covered, over medium heat for 20-25 minutes or until tender, turning often. Serve with Parmesan cheese. **Yield:** 4 servings.

barbecue italian sausages

   4 uncooked Italian sausage links

 1/2 cup chopped green pepper

 1/4 cup chopped onion

   1 tablespoon olive oil

 1/3 cup dry red wine or beef broth

 1/2 cup ketchup

   1 tablespoon cider vinegar

   1 tablespoon soy sauce

   1 teaspoon brown sugar

 1/4 teaspoon ground cumin

 1/4 teaspoon chili powder

 1/8 teaspoon Liquid Smoke, optional

   4 hot dog buns, split

BARBECUE ITALIAN SAUSAGES

[1] Grill sausages, covered, over medium heat for 5-8 minutes on each side or until no longer pink. Meanwhile, in a large skillet, saute green pepper and onion in oil for 3-4 minutes or until tender. Stir in wine. Bring to a boil; cook for 2 minutes or until liquid is evaporated.

[2] Stir in the ketchup, vinegar, soy sauce, brown sugar, cumin, chili powder and Liquid Smoke if desired. Bring to a boil. Reduce heat; simmer for 2-3 minutes or until thickened. Place sausages in buns; serve with sauce. **Yield:** 4 servings.

TASTE OF HOME TEST KITCHEN GREENDALE, WISCONSIN

The tangy barbecue sauce in this recipe is fast, flavorful and extremely versatile. It's fantastic on sausages, but don't stop there; give it a try on ribs or with pulled pork.

HUNTING & FISHING tip

To make a camper's taco salad, I chop vegetables and cook the ground beef at home. On site, I simmer the meat with canned chili beans, taco seasoning and water. Come time to eat, we top tortilla chips with the meat, veggies and shredded cheese.

SUSAN, NORTH DAKOTA

GRILLED CHICKEN WRAPS

sirloin sandwiches

JUDI MESSINA
COEUR D'ALENE, IDAHO

Mom is always happy to share her cooking, and these tender, delicious beef sandwiches are a real crowd-pleaser. A simple three-ingredient marinade flavors the grilled beef wonderfully.

> 1 cup soy sauce
> 1/2 cup canola oil
> 1/2 cup cranberry or apple juice
> 1 beef sirloin tip roast (3 to 4 pounds)
> 1 envelope beef au jus gravy mix
> 1 dozen French rolls, split

[1] In a large resealable plastic bag, combine the soy sauce, oil and juice. Remove 1/2 cup for basting. Add the roast to remaining marinade; seal bag and turn to coat. Refrigerate for 8 hours or overnight, turning occasionally. Cover and refrigerate reserved marinade.

[2] Drain and discard marinade. Grill roast, covered, over indirect heat, for 1 hour, turning every 15 minutes or until meat reaches desired doneness (for medium-rare, a meat thermometer should read 145°; medium, 160°; well-done, 170°), basting frequently with reserved marinate. Remove from the grill; let stand for 1 hour. Cover and refrigerate overnight.

[3] Just before serving, prepare gravy mix according to package directions. Thinly slice roast; add to the gravy and heat through. Serve on rolls. **Yield:** 12 servings.

campfire potatoes

MICHELLE ISENHOFF
WAYLAND, MICHIGAN

Nothing beats these buttery potatoes grilled in a no-mess foil pack. Try them with your favorite grilled chicken or steak.

> 5 medium potatoes, peeled and sliced
> 1/4 cup grated Parmesan cheese
> 2 teaspoons minced fresh parsley
> 3/4 teaspoon garlic powder
> 1/2 teaspoon salt
> 1/8 teaspoon pepper
> 1/4 cup butter, cubed

CHERYL ZELINGER SCHWENKSVILLE, PENNSYLVANIA

My husband and I love Mexican food and are always looking for new ways to prepare burritos. This recipe is one we came up with together. Everyone who has tried it loves it!

grilled chicken wraps

> 1/4 cup olive oil
> 3 tablespoons lime juice
> 2 garlic cloves, minced
> 1/4 teaspoon ground cumin
> 1/4 teaspoon cayenne pepper
> 1/2 pound boneless skinless chicken breast
> 2 flour tortillas (8 inches), warmed

Optional toppings: chopped green onions, sliced ripe olives, chopped tomatoes, shredded cheddar cheese, sour cream and/or shredded lettuce

[1] In a large resealable plastic bag, combine the first five ingredients; add the chicken. Seal bag and turn to coat; refrigerate for up to 2 hours.

[2] Drain and discard marinade. Grill chicken, uncovered, over medium heat for 4-5 minutes on each side or until juices run clear. Slice chicken into strips.

[3] Serve in tortillas with toppings of your choice. **Yield:** 2 servings.

[1] Place half of the potatoes on a large piece of heavy-duty foil. Sprinkle with Parmesan cheese, parsley, garlic powder, salt and pepper; dot with butter. Top with the remaining potatoes. Fold foil over and seal tightly.

[2] Grill, covered, over medium heat for 30-35 minutes or until the potatoes are tender. **Yield:** 4 servings.

sugar cookie s'mores

TASTE OF HOME TEST KITCHEN
GREENDALE, WISCONSIN

Change up traditional s'mores with the use of sugar cookies and candy bars. The fun can't be beat!

- 8 fun-size Milky Way candy bars
- 8 sugar cookies (3 inches)
- 4 large marshmallows

[1] Place two candy bars on each of four cookies; place on grill rack. Grill, uncovered, over medium-hot heat for 1 to 1-1/2 minutes or until bottoms of cookies are browned.

[2] Meanwhile, using a long-handled fork, toast marshmallows 6 in. from the heat until golden brown, turning occasionally. Remove marshmallows from fork and place over candy bars; top with remaining cookies. Serve immediately. **Yield:** 4 servings.

stuffed bacon burgers

JOHNNIE MCLEOD
BASTROP, LOUISIANA

Everyone comes running when they hear the sizzle of these juicy burgers on the grill!

- 1½ pounds ground beef
- 1 envelope onion soup mix
- ¼ cup water
- 6 slices (1 ounce each) process American cheese
- 6 bacon strips
- 6 hamburger buns, toasted

[1] In a bowl, combine ground beef, soup mix and water. Shape into 12 thin patties. Place a cheese slice on six patties. Cover each with another patty. Pinch edges to seal. Wrap a strip of bacon around each; fasten the bacon with wooden toothpicks.

[2] Grill, covered, over medium heat for 5-7 minutes on each side or until a meat thermometer reads 160° and juices run clear. Discard toothpicks. Serve on buns. **Yield:** 6 servings.

grilled steak and mushroom salad

- 6 tablespoons olive oil, divided
- 2 tablespoons Dijon mustard, divided
- ½ teaspoon salt
- ¼ teaspoon pepper
- 1½ pounds beef top sirloin steak (¾ inch thick)
- 1 pound fresh mushrooms, sliced
- ¼ cup red wine vinegar
- 1 medium bunch romaine, torn

[1] In a small bowl, whisk 1 tablespoon oil, 1 tablespoon mustard, salt and pepper; set aside.

[2] Grill steak, covered, over medium-hot heat for 4 minutes. Turn; spread with mustard mixture. Grill 4 minutes longer or until meat reaches desired doneness (for medium-rare, a meat thermometer should read 145°; medium, 160°; well-done, 170°).

[3] Meanwhile, in a large skillet, cook mushrooms in 1 tablespoon oil until tender. Stir in the vinegar, remaining oil and mustard; mix well.

[4] Thinly slice steak across the grain; add to mushroom mixture. Serve over romaine. **Yield:** 6 servings.

JULIE CASHION
SANFORD, FLORIDA

My husband loves this salad, especially during summertime. He says he feels like he's eating a healthy salad and getting his steak, too! I always serve it with delicious homemade bread.

HUNTING & FISHING COOKBOOK

GRILLED STEAK AND MUSHROOM SALAD

Hunting & Fishing COOKBOOK

Whether you prefer a sweet or a savory snack, you're sure to find a new favorite (or two) in this section. These recipes make wonderful portable munchies that are sure to satisfy.

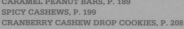
CARAMEL PEANUT BARS, P. 189
SPICY CASHEWS, P. 199
CRANBERRY CASHEW DROP COOKIES, P. 208

PORTABLE SNACKS

ZESTY SNACK MIX,
PAGE 190

BUTTERSCOTCH CASHEW BARS

big chocolate cookies

MARIE MACY
FORT COLLINS, COLORADO

The combination of different kinds of chocolate makes these cookies irresistible. Friends and family are delighted to have a big cookie to enjoy.

- 6 tablespoons butter
- 6 squares (1 ounce each) semisweet chocolate
- 2 squares (1 ounce each) unsweetened chocolate
- 2 eggs
- 3/4 cup sugar
- 2 teaspoons instant coffee granules
- 1 tablespoon boiling water
- 2 teaspoons vanilla extract
- 1/4 cup all-purpose flour
- 1/2 teaspoon salt
- 1/4 teaspoon baking powder
- 1 cup (6 ounces) semisweet chocolate chips
- 1 cup coarsely chopped walnuts
- 1 cup coarsely chopped pecans

[1] In a microwave or double boiler, melt butter and the chocolate squares; cool. In a mixing bowl, beat eggs until foamy; gradually add sugar. Dissolve coffee granules in water. Add coffee, vanilla and cooled chocolate mixture to egg mixture. Combine flour, salt and baking powder; gradually add to the egg mixture. Stir in chocolate chips and nuts.

[2] Drop by 1/3 cupfuls 4 in. apart onto ungreased baking sheets. Bake at 350° for 15-17 minutes or until firm. Cool for 4 minutes before removing to wire racks. **Yield:** 1 dozen.

Editor's Note: 1/4 cup flour is the correct amount called for in the recipe.

LORI BERG
WENTZVILLE, MISSOURI

I knew these nutty bars were a success when I took them on our annual vacation. My husband couldn't stop eating them… and my sister-in-law, who is a great cook, asked for the recipe. It makes a big batch, which is good, because they go quickly!

butterscotch cashew bars

- 1 cup plus 2 tablespoons butter, softened
- 3/4 cup plus 2 tablespoons packed brown sugar
- 2 1/2 cups all-purpose flour
- 1 3/4 teaspoons salt

TOPPING:
- 1 package (10 to 11 ounces) butterscotch chips
- 1/2 cup plus 2 tablespoons light corn syrup
- 3 tablespoons butter
- 2 teaspoons water
- 2 1/2 cups salted cashew halves

[1] In a large mixing bowl, cream butter and brown sugar. Combine flour and salt; add to creamed mixture just until combined. Press into a greased 15-in. x 10-in. x 1-in. baking pan. Bake at 350° for 10-12 minutes or until lightly browned.

[2] Meanwhile, combine butterscotch chips, corn syrup, butter and water in a saucepan. Cook and stir over medium heat until chips and butter are melted. Spread over crust. Sprinkle with cashews; press down lightly. Bake for 11-13 minutes or until topping is bubbly and lightly browned. Cool on a wire rack. Cut into bars. **Yield:** 3 1/2 dozen.

 **HUNTING & FISHING tip**

String cheese or cheese cubes bagels (pre-spread with cream cheese or peanut butter), or carrots and celery sticks make great portable snacks.

TASTE OF HOME TEST KITCHEN

candied cereal mix

1 cup packed brown sugar
$1/2$ cup butter
$1/4$ cup corn syrup
1 teaspoon vanilla extract
$1/2$ teaspoon baking soda
6 cups rice Chex
6 cups corn Chex

[1] In a microwave-safe bowl, combine brown sugar, butter and corn syrup. Microwave, uncovered, on high for $3^{1/2}$ minutes or until sugar is dissolved and corn syrup is bubbly, stirring frequently. Stir in vanilla and baking soda; microwave 30 seconds longer or until the mixture begins to foam.

[2] In a large bowl, combine cereals. Add syrup mixture and toss to coat. Transfer to two greased 15-in. x 10-in. x 1-in. baking pans. Bake, uncovered, at 300° for 30 minutes, stirring every 10 minutes. Remove to waxed paper to cool. Store in an airtight container. **Yield:** about 3 quarts.

Editor's Note: This recipe was tested in an 850-watt microwave.

LISA ELLIOTT WEST PLAINS, MISSOURI

This is a favorite treat at our house. It's easy to make and is convenient for on-the-go snacking.

CANDIED CEREAL MIX

HUNTING & FISHING COOKBOOK

LISA HESS
BOUNTIFUL,
UTAH

Sliced almonds and almond extract set this crunchy Chex mix apart. Be forewarned, however: Once you start eating it, you can't stop!

almond snack mix

1 package (17.6 ounces) Rice Chex
2³⁄₄ cups sliced almonds
1 cup sugar
1 cup light corn syrup
³⁄₄ cup butter
1 teaspoon almond extract

[1] Place cereal and almonds in a large bowl; set aside. In a heavy saucepan, combine the sugar, corn syrup and butter. Slowly bring to a boil over medium heat, stirring occasionally, until a candy thermometer reads 250° (hard-ball stage).

[2] Remove from heat; stir in extract. Pour over cereal mixture; mix well. Spread onto waxed paper-lined baking sheets; cool. Toss to break apart. Store in an airtight container. **Yield:** 5 quarts.

Editor's Note: We recommend that you test your candy thermometer before each use by bringing water to a boil; the thermometer should read 212°. Adjust your recipe temperature up or down based on your test.

chocolate almond crumble bars

MARTY ROSE
WOODWARD, IOWA

This is my own recipe, one I created in a hurry when guests were coming and chocolate chips and condensed milk were just about all I had in my baking cupboard!

2¹⁄₂ cups all-purpose flour
¹⁄₂ cup confectioners' sugar
¹⁄₈ teaspoon salt
1 cup cold butter
1 cup (6 ounces) chocolate chips
1 can (14 ounces) sweetened condensed milk

ALMOND SNACK MIX

TOPPING:

1½ cups all-purpose flour

½ cup sugar

1 cup chopped almonds

½ cup cold butter

[1] Combine flour, sugar and salt in a mixing bowl; cut in butter until mixture is crumbly. Press firmly into a 13-in. x 9-in. x 2-in. baking pan. Sprinkle chocolate chips evenly over crust. Drizzle milk over chips.

[2] For topping, combine flour, sugar and almonds in a bowl; cut in butter until crumbly. Sprinkle over top. Bake at 350° for 35-40 minutes or until golden. **Yield:** 2-3 dozen.

oyster cracker snack

VERONA KOEHLMOOS
PILGER, NEBRASKA

Everyone will be eating these crackers by the handful…they're that good!

2 packages (10 ounces each) oyster crackers

¾ cup vegetable oil

1 envelope ranch salad dressing mix

1 teaspoon dill weed

½ teaspoon onion powder

½ teaspoon garlic powder

½ teaspoon lemon-pepper seasoning

Place crackers in a large bowl. In a small bowl, combine remaining ingredients; pour over crackers and mix well. Let stand for 2 hours. Store in an airtight container. **Yield:** 12 cups.

caramel peanut bars

1½ cups quick-cooking oats

1½ cups all-purpose flour

1¼ cups packed brown sugar

¾ teaspoon baking soda

¼ teaspoon salt

¾ cup butter, melted

1 package (14 ounces) caramels

½ cup heavy whipping cream

CARAMEL PEANUT BARS

1½ cups (9 ounces) semisweet chocolate chips

¾ cup chopped peanuts

[1] In a bowl, combine the first five ingredients; stir in butter. Set aside 1 cup for topping. Press remaining mixture into a greased 13-in. x 9-in. x 2-in. baking pan. Bake at 350° for 10 minutes or until lightly browned.

[2] Meanwhile, combine caramels and cream in a heavy saucepan or microwave-safe bowl. Cook over low heat or microwave until melted, stirring often. Sprinkle chocolate chips and peanuts over the crust; top with caramel mixture. Sprinkle with reserved oat mixture.

[3] Bake for 15-20 minutes or until topping is golden brown. Cool completely before cutting. **Yield:** 3 dozen.

ARDYCE PIEHL
WISCONSIN DELLS, WISCONSIN

With goodies like chocolate, peanuts and caramel peeking out from between golden oat and crumb layers, these bars are very popular. They taste like candy bars but have irresistible, homemade goodness.

HUNTING & FISHING tip

If you're bringing a batch of granola or trail mix to munch on as a snack, consider bringing containers of yogurt as well. Yogurt topped with granola makes a quick breakfast or snack to tide you over while you're waiting for the campfire to get going. ELLEN, CONNECTICUT

HUNTING & FISHING COOKBOOK

**PAT HABIGER
SPEARVILLE,
KANSAS**

This snack recipe has a good mix of fruit and nuts. The mild cinnamon flavor adds a tasty touch.

fruit 'n' nut trail mix

- 1/4 cup sunflower kernels
- 2 tablespoons butter
- 4 cups old-fashioned oats
- 1/2 cup vegetable oil
- 3/4 cup cashew halves
- 2/3 cup slivered almonds, toasted
- 1/2 cup sesame seeds, toasted
- 1/2 cup packed brown sugar
- 1/2 cup honey
- 1 teaspoon ground cinnamon
- 1 1/4 cups assorted bite-size dried fruit (raisins, apricots, dates, apples, bananas)

[1] In a large skillet over medium heat, lightly toast sunflower kernels in butter; remove and set aside. In the same skillet, lightly toast the oats in oil. Add the sunflower kernels, cashews, almonds and sesame seeds. Combine the brown sugar, honey and cinnamon; add to oat mixture. Cook and stir for 5 minutes.

[2] Spread in two ungreased 15-in. x 10-in. x 1-in. baking pans. Bake at 350° for 15-20 minutes or until golden brown, stirring every 5 minutes. Cool, stirring occasionally. Stir in dried fruit. Store in an airtight container. **Yield:** 10 cups.

zesty snack mix

(PICTURED ON PAGE 185)

**JEANETTE GRANTSTEIN
WICHITA, KANSAS**

This crisp snack mix is a mouthwatering combination of sweet and spicy. I've taken it to numerous gatherings. Make a bowlful when the munchies hit.

- 4 cups square oat or Chex cereal
- 4 cups corn chips
- 1 cup salted peanuts
- 1 cup quick-cooking oats
- 1/3 cup butter, melted
- 3 tablespoons honey
- 4 teaspoons chili powder
- 1 teaspoon dried oregano
- 1 teaspoon onion salt

[1] In a large bowl, combine cereal, corn chips, peanuts and oats. Combine butter and honey; drizzle over cereal mixture. Sprinkle with chili powder, oregano and onion salt; toss to coat. Spread evenly on an ungreased 15-in. x 10-in. x 1-in. baking pan.

[2] Bake at 350° for 25 minutes, stirring once. Cool. Store in an airtight container. **Yield:** about 10 cups.

chewy peanut butter bars

BEVERLY SWIHART
MARION, OHIO
These yummy bars are extra special for lunches, car trips and bake sales, yet use only ordinary kitchen staples.

- 1/2 cup butter, softened
- 2/3 cup packed brown sugar
- 2 egg yolks
- 1 teaspoon vanilla extract
- 1 1/2 cups all-purpose flour
- 1/2 teaspoon baking powder
- 1/2 teaspoon salt
- 1/4 teaspoon baking soda
- 3 cups miniature marshmallows

TOPPING:
- 2/3 cup light corn syrup
- 1/4 cup butter
- 1 package (10 ounces) peanut butter chips
- 2 teaspoons vanilla extract
- 2 cups crisp rice cereal
- 2 cups salted peanuts

[1] In a mixing bowl, cream butter and sugar. Add egg yolks and vanilla; mix well. Combine flour, baking powder, salt and baking soda; add to creamed mixture and mix well. Press into a greased 13-in. x 9-in. x 2-in. baking pan. Bake at 350° for 12-15 minutes or until golden. Sprinkle with marshmallows; return to oven just until marshmallows begin to puff, about 2 minutes. Cool.

[2] Meanwhile, combine corn syrup, butter, chips and vanilla in a large saucepan; cook and stir over low heat until chips are melted and mixture is smooth. Remove from the heat; stir in cereal and peanuts. Evenly spread warm topping over marshmallow layer. Refrigerate until set. **Yield:** 24-30 servings.

crunchy italian mix

- 1/2 cup butter
- 1 tablespoon Worcestershire sauce
- 1 teaspoon Italian seasoning
- 1/2 teaspoon garlic powder
- 5 cups Crispix
- 2 cups Cheerios
- 2 1/2 cups miniature pretzels
- 1 can (10 ounces) mixed nuts
- 1/4 cup grated Parmesan cheese

[1] In a saucepan or microwave-safe bowl, heat the first four ingredients until butter is melted; mix well. In a large bowl, combine the cereals, pretzels, nuts and Parmesan cheese. Drizzle with butter mixture and mix well.

[2] Place in an ungreased 15-in. x 10-in. x 1-in. baking pan. Bake, uncovered, at 250° for 45 minutes, stirring every 15 minutes. **Yield:** 10 cups.

SHARON EVANS
ROCKWELL,
IOWA
We love this savory mix when we get the munchies in the evening. I started out fixing it for the friends in our bridge group, and now I make it for my family, too.

CRUNCHY ITALIAN MIX

HUNTING & FISHING COOKBOOK

SUSAN MARIE TACCONE
ERIE, PENNSYLVANIA

These crunchy almonds make a great portable snack because they're filling, satisfying and they aren't sticky.

iced almonds

¼ cup butter
2½ cups whole unblanched almonds
1 cup sugar
1 teaspoon vanilla extract

In a heavy saucepan, melt butter over medium-high heat. Add almonds and sugar. Cook and stir constantly for 7-8 minutes or until syrup is golden brown. Remove from the heat; stir in vanilla. Immediately drop by clusters or separate almonds on a greased baking pan. Cool. Store in an airtight container. **Yield:** 4 cups.

italian pretzels

CARRIE ROGERS
NORTH WILKESBORO, NORTH CAROLINA

It's fun to have the savory flavor of spaghetti in a crispy pretzel snack. It's a great way to satisfy appetites until the next meal.

2 cups miniature pretzel twists
1 tablespoon butter, melted
1½ teaspoons spaghetti sauce mix
1½ teaspoons grated Parmesan cheese

Place pretzels in a microwave-safe bowl. Combine butter and spaghetti sauce mix; pour over pretzels and toss to coat evenly. Microwave on high for 2-3 minutes or until pretzels are toasted, stirring every 30 seconds. Immediately sprinkle with cheese; toss to coat. Cool. **Yield:** 2 cups.

corn chip crunch

NANCY SCHREUR
ZEELAND, MICHIGAN

Folks can't seem to stop eating this sweet and salty treat when I serve it. A nice twist on popcorn or cereal snack mix, it's great for munching during movies and at parades or football games.

6 cups corn chips
1½ cups dry roasted peanuts
½ cup packed brown sugar
½ cup dark corn syrup
¼ cup butter

ICED ALMONDS

CANDIED POPCORN SNACK

[1] In a large heatproof bowl, combine the corn chips and peanuts. In a small saucepan, combine the brown sugar, corn syrup and butter. Bring to a boil over medium heat, stirring constantly. Pour over corn chip mixture; toss to coat.

[2] Transfer to a greased 15-in. x 10-in. x 1-in. baking pan. Bake at 250° for 30-40 minutes, stirring every 15 minutes. Spread onto waxed paper; cool. Break apart and store in airtight containers. **Yield:** 8 cups.

candied popcorn snack

  6 quarts plain popped popcorn

¾ cup light corn syrup

¼ cup butter

  2 tablespoon water

  4 cups (1 pound) confectioners' sugar

  1 cup miniature marshmallows

Place popcorn in a large roasting pan. In a 3-qt. saucepan, combine remaining ingredients; cook and stir over low heat just until mixture comes to a boil. Pour over popcorn and toss to coat. Cool. Store in an airtight container. **Yield:** 6 quarts.

HUNTING & FISHING tip

If you take store-bought chips or cookies camping, put the store-bought package inside a resealable plastic bag. Once the store packaging has been opened, the bag can be resealed to keep the snacks fresh and contained.

SUSAN, WISCONSIN

VICTORIA WALZER LAKEPORT, CALIFORNIA

I got this family-favorite recipe long ago. It makes a big, chewy batch that you can't put down until it's gone.

harvest snack mix

MARLENE HARGUTH
MAYNARD, MINNESOTA

Candy corn makes this a natural snack for fall gatherings. The sweet and salty flavors are irresistible.

- 2 cups pretzel sticks
- 1 cup mixed nuts
- 1/2 cup sunflower kernels
- 6 tablespoons butter, melted
- 1/2 teaspoon ground cinnamon
- 1/8 teaspoon ground cloves
- 8 cups popped popcorn
- 1 cup candy corn
- 1 cup chocolate bridge mix

[1] In a large bowl, combine pretzels, nuts and sunflower kernels. Combine butter, cinnamon and cloves. Drizzle a third of butter mixture over pretzel mixture; toss to coat. Transfer to a greased 15-in. x 10-in. x 1-in. baking pan. Bake at 300° for 15 minutes.

[2] Place popcorn in a large bowl; drizzle with remaining butter mixture and toss to coat. Stir into pretzel mixture. Bake 15 minutes longer or until heated through. Cool; transfer to a large bowl. Add the candy corn and bridge mix; toss to combine. **Yield:** 3 quarts.

nacho snack mix

ELIZABETH LODER
FOX POINT, WISCONSIN

This colorful mixture of bite-size snack foods, cereal and crackers gets its south-of-the-border accent from taco seasoning. The recipe makes a big batch, but it always goes fast.

- 4 cups Crispix
- 1 can (4 1/2 ounces) crisp cheese ball snacks
- 3 cups corn chips

MARY DETWEILER
WEST FARMINGTON, OHIO

Folks love the zippy burst of flavor in every bite of this snack mix.

cheese ball snack mix

- 1 1/2 cups salted cashews
- 1 cup crisp cheese ball snacks
- 1 cup corn Chex
- 1 cup rice Chex
- 1 cup miniature pretzels
- 1 cup chow mein noodles
- 1/2 cup butter, melted
- 1 tablespoon soy sauce
- 1 teaspoon Worcestershire sauce
- 1/2 teaspoon seasoned salt
- 1/4 teaspoon chili powder
- 1/4 teaspoon hot pepper sauce

[1] In a bowl, combine cashews, cheese balls, cereal, pretzels and chow mein noodles. In another bowl, combine remaining ingredients. Pour over the cereal mixture and toss to coat.

[2] Transfer to an ungreased 15-in. x 10-in. x 1-in. baking pan. Bake at 250° for 1 hour, stirring every 15 minutes. **Yield:** about 6 cups.

Editor's Note: This recipe was prepared with Planters' Cheeze Balls.

tip HUNTING & FISHING

When you return to camp, remove any food bags from your pack, and don't leave pieces of crumbled snacks inside. The smell of tasty tidbits may attract hungry animals. MEGAN, ARIZONA

   2 cups pretzel sticks

   1 cup cheese-flavored snack
     crackers

   2 tablespoons taco seasoning

   $1/2$ cup vegetable oil

   $1/2$ cup butter, melted

[1] In a bowl, combine the first five ingredients. Spread in two ungreased 15-in. x 10-in. x 1-in. baking pans. Combine the taco seasoning, oil and butter; pour over cereal mixture and toss to coat.

[2] Bake at 200° for 2 hours, stirring every 30 minutes. Cool. Store in airtight containers. **Yield:** 4 quarts.

Editor's Note: This recipe was prepared with Planters' Cheeze Balls.

coconut granola bars

MARIA CADE
FORT ROCK, OREGON

These quick-to-fix bars are wholesome and delicious. I sometimes make them for bake sales.

   $3/4$ cup packed brown sugar

   $2/3$ cup peanut butter

   $1/2$ cup corn syrup

   $1/2$ cup butter, melted

   2 teaspoons vanilla extract

   3 cups old-fashioned oats

   1 cup (6 ounces) semisweet
     chocolate chips

   $1/2$ cup flaked coconut

   $1/2$ cup sunflower kernels

   $1/3$ cup wheat germ

   2 teaspoons sesame seeds

[1] In a large bowl, combine brown sugar, peanut butter, corn syrup, butter and vanilla. Combine remaining ingredients; add to peanut butter mixture and stir to coat.

[2] Press into two greased 13-in. x 9-in. x 2-in. baking pans. Bake at 350° for 25-30 minutes or until golden brown. Cool on wire racks. Cut into bars. **Yield:** 3 dozen.

barbecued peanuts

   $1/3$ cup barbecue sauce

   2 tablespoons butter, melted

   1 teaspoon garlic powder

   $1/4$ to $1/2$ teaspoon cayenne pepper

   1 jar (16 ounces) dry roasted
     peanuts

[1] In a large bowl, combine barbecue sauce, butter, garlic powder and cayenne. Add peanuts; stir until evenly coated. Transfer to a greased 13-in. x 9-in. x 2-in. baking pan. Bake, uncovered, at 325° for 25-30 minutes, stirring every 10 minutes.

[2] Spread on waxed paper; cool completely. Store in an airtight container. **Yield:** 3 cups.

ABBEY BOYLE
TAMPA, FLORIDA

These peanuts are great for football parties, as after-school snacks or on movie nights. I especially like preparing them at the holidays to give as gifts.

BARBECUED PEANUTS

HUNTING & FISHING COOKBOOK

CAROL ALLEN
MCLEANSBORO,
ILLINOIS

For a great change of pace from the usual mix, try this recipe. It's almost impossible to stop eating this treat.

favorite snack mix

    6 cups Crispix
    1 can (10 ounces) mixed nuts
    1 package (10 ounces) pretzel sticks
 3/4 cup butter
 3/4 cup packed brown sugar

[1] In a large bowl, combine the cereal, nuts and pretzels. In a small saucepan over low heat, melt butter. Add brown sugar; cook and stir until dissolved. Pour over cereal mixture; stir to coat.

[2] Place a third on a greased 15-in. x 10-in. x 1-in. baking pan. Bake at 325° for 8 minutes; stir and bake for 6 minutes more. Spread on waxed paper to cool. Repeat with remaining mixture. Store in an airtight container. **Yield:** about 14 cups.

kookie cookies

**HELEN BACHMAN
CHAMPAIGN, ILLINOIS**

You won't be able to stop eating this sweet, salty, crunchy and chewy snack. It's a quick way to dress up plain corn chips.

    1 package (10 1/2 ounces) corn chips
    1 cup light corn syrup
    1 cup sugar
    1 cup creamy peanut butter

Spread corn chips in a greased 15-in. x 10-in. x 2-in. baking pan. In a saucepan over medium heat, bring corn syrup and sugar to a boil. Remove from heat; stir in peanut butter until smooth. Pour over corn chips. Cool. Break into pieces. **Yield:** about 3 dozen.

really good snack mix

**LORI GENSKE
WALDO, WISCONSIN**

I grew tired of my family picking through a snack mix for their favorite items and leaving the rest. So I experimented using only their favorite ingredients and came up with this recipe.

    2 cups bite-size Shredded Wheat
    2 cups Corn Chex
    2 cups Crispix
 1 1/2 cups salted cashew halves
    3 tablespoons butter, melted

FAVORITE SNACK MIX

HUNTING & FISHING COOKBOOK

1 tablespoon canola oil

4 teaspoons Worcestershire sauce

1 teaspoon seasoned salt

$1/2$ teaspoon garlic powder

[1] In a large bowl, combine cereals and cashews. In a small bowl, combine butter, oil, Worcestershire sauce, seasoned salt and garlic powder. Pour over cereal mixture and toss to evenly coat.

[2] Transfer to a 15-in. x 10-in. x 1-in. baking pan coated with nonstick cooking spray. Bake at 250° for 45 minutes, stirring every 15 minutes. Store in airtight containers. **Yield:** $7^1/2$ cups.

jerky party mix

LISA COFFELL
SWARTZ CREEK, MICHIGAN

Talk about a popular gift! Our friends get such a kick out of this spicy twist on an old party-mix favorite, they ask for it at Christmas, New Year's and even the Fourth of July.

4 cups each Corn Chex, Rice Chex and Wheat Chex

2 packages (3 ounces each) Beer Nuts

$1/2$ cup butter, melted

1 envelope taco seasoning

1 package (4 ounces) beef jerky

[1] In a large bowl, combine cereal and nuts. In a small bowl, combine butter and taco seasoning; mix well. Pour over cereal mixture and toss to evenly coat.

[2] Transfer to two greased 15-in. x 10-in. x 1-in. baking pans. Bake, uncovered, at 250° for 1 hour, stirring every 15 minutes. Stir in beef jerky. Cool completely, stirring several times. Store in an airtight container. **Yield:** about 13 cups.

oatmeal chip cookies

$1/2$ cup shortening

1 cup sugar

1 tablespoon molasses

1 egg

1 teaspoon vanilla extract

1 cup all-purpose flour

OATMEAL CHIP COOKIES

1 cup quick-cooking oats

1 teaspoon baking soda

1 teaspoon ground cinnamon

$1/2$ teaspoon salt

1 cup (6 ounces) semisweet chocolate chips

[1] In a large mixing bowl, cream shortening and sugar. Beat in the molasses, egg and vanilla. Combine flour, oats, baking soda, cinnamon and salt; gradually add to creamed mixture. Stir in chocolate chips.

[2] Roll into $1^1/2$-in. balls. Place 2 in. apart on greased baking sheets. Bake at 350° for 8-10 minutes or until golden brown. Cool for 5 minutes before removing from pans to wire racks. **Yield:** about $1^1/2$ dozen.

**SUSAN HENRY
BULLHEAD CITY,
ARIZONA**

These cookies are a fun way to end a meal or to grab as a take-along treat. My mom liked to add different spices to traditional recipes and create unexpected tastes. Molasses and cinnamon make these cookies stand out.

HUNTING & FISHING tip

My husband, Jim, and I have had a lake cottage for over 40 years. When we go out fishing or hiking in the woods, I usually pack snacks that won't spoil quickly, like peanut butter sandwiches or peanut butter between crackers and dried apricots, granola bars and bottles of water.

GEORGIE, WISCONSIN

HUNTING & FISHING COOKBOOK

MICHAEL VYSKOCIL GLEN ROCK, PENNSYLVANIA

Hit the great outdoors with this tasty snack. Make a big bunch and package individual portions in small resealable plastic bags.

TRAIL MIX

trail mix

½ cup unblanched whole almonds
½ cup coarsely chopped walnuts
½ cup golden raisins
½ cup chopped dates
½ cup dried apple slices, chopped
½ cup dried apricots, chopped
½ cup semisweet chocolate chips
½ cup Honey Nut Cheerios

In a large bowl, combine all ingredients. Store in an airtight container. **Yield:** 4 cups.

taco pickup sticks

KATHY HUNT DALLAS, TEXAS

Looking for something a bit different to munch on? We enjoy the extra kick our taste buds get from this zesty treat. But watch out! One batch is never enough to satisfy my crew!

3 cans (7 ounces each) potato sticks
2 cans (6 ounces each) french-fried onions
1 can (12 ounces) salted peanuts

⅓ cup butter, melted
1 envelope taco seasoning

[1] In a large bowl, combine potato sticks, onions and peanuts. Combine butter and taco seasoning; mix well. Pour over potato stick mixture and toss to coat. Place in three ungreased 15-in. x 10-in. x 1-in. baking pans.

[2] Bake, uncovered, at 250° for 45 minutes, stirring every 15 minutes. Store in airtight containers. **Yield:** 24 cups.

tumbleweeds

VICTORIA JOHNSON VENICE, FLORIDA

I sure like making these crisp and creamy treats because they require only four ingredients. It's hard to stop eating them—they're irresistible!

1 can (12 ounces) salted peanuts
1 can (7 ounces) potato sticks
3 cups butterscotch chips
3 tablespoons peanut butter

Combine peanuts and potato sticks in a bowl; set aside. In a microwave, heat butterscotch chips and peanut butter at 70% powder for 1-2 minutes or until melted, stirring every 30 seconds. Add to peanut mixture; stir to coat

evenly. Drop by rounded tablespoonfuls onto waxed paper-lined baking sheets. Refrigerate until set, about 5 minutes. Store in an airtight container. **Yield:** about 4¹⁄₂ dozen.

sweet cereal clusters

SUE YOUNT
MCBAIN, MICHIGAN

You'll enjoy this crunchy combination of peanuts, pretzels and cereal covered with a white candy coating. I often fill small resealable storage bags with these clusters for bake sales. They always disappear fast!

    6 cups Corn Chex

    3 cups miniature pretzels

    1 jar (16 ounces) dry roasted peanuts

    1 package (14 ounces) milk chocolate M&M's

    1 cup raisins, optional

 1¹⁄₂ pounds white candy coating, melted

In a large bowl, combine the first five ingredients. Pour candy coating over cereal mixture; stir until coated. Spread onto waxed paper-lined baking sheets. Refrigerate for 15 minutes or until set. Break into pieces. Store in an airtight container. **Yield:** about 4¹⁄₂ pounds.

buttery onion pretzels

BETTY CLAYCOMB
ALVERTON, PENNSYLVANIA

Make a good snack even better by turning store-bought big pretzels into buttery, onion-flavored munchies. If you like spicy flavor, add a dash or two of hot pepper sauce to the butter.

 1¹⁄₄ cups butter

    1 package (1¹⁄₂ ounces) onion soup mix

    1 package (16-ounce) chunky pretzels, broken into pieces

In a skillet, melt butter. Stir in soup mix. Heat and stir until well mixed. Add pretzels; toss to coat. Spread pretzel mixture in a baking pan. Bake at 250° for 1¹⁄₂ hours, stirring

every 15 minutes. Cool. Store in an airtight container. **Yield:** 6 cups.

spicy cashews

    2 cans (10 ounces each) salted cashews

    3 tablespoons butter

    1 tablespoon vegetable oil

 ¹⁄₂ teaspoon salt

 ¹⁄₂ teaspoon chili powder

 ¹⁄₄ to ¹⁄₂ teaspoon crushed red pepper flakes

[1] In a large skillet, saute cashews in butter and oil for 4-5 minutes or until golden brown. Spread on a paper towel-lined baking sheet; let stand for 2-3 minutes.

[2] Transfer to a large bowl. Sprinkle with the salt, chili powder and pepper flakes; toss to coat. Store in an airtight container. **Yield:** 2²⁄₃ cups.

JEAN VOAN SHEPHERD, TEXAS

These seasoned nuts are so good. Packaged in a festive tin, they are perfect as a hostess gift.

SPICY CASHEWS

HUNTING & FISHING COOKBOOK

DONNA SCULLY
NEWARK,
DELAWARE

The pleasant sweetness of this crisp, munchable mixture will surprise you. I've taken it to my childrens' schools for parties or as a special treat. I've also packaged it in bow-topped tins for special gifts.

cinnamon snack mix

1 package (17.9 ounces) Crispix cereal

11 whole cinnamon graham crackers, broken into bite-size pieces

1 cup miniature pretzels

1 cup pecan halves

2/3 cup butter, melted

1/2 cup honey

1 cup vanilla or butterscotch baking chips

[1] In a bowl, combine cereal, crackers, pretzels and pecans. Combine butter and honey; drizzle over cereal mixture and mix well.

[2] Transfer to two greased 15-in. x 10-in. x 1-in. baking pans. Bake at 350° for 12-15 minutes, stirring once. Cool completely. Stir in chips. Store in an airtight container **Yield:** 6 quarts.

spiced pecans

MIRIAM HERSCHBERGER
HOLMESVILLE, OHIO

Toasting nuts intensifies their flavor, and the sweet coating on these pecans is absolutely delicious.

1 egg white

1 teaspoon cold water

4 cups (about 1 pound) pecan halves

1/2 cup sugar

1/2 teaspoon ground cinnamon

1/4 teaspoon salt

[1] In a small mixing bowl, lightly beat the egg white. Add water; beat until frothy but not stiff. Add pecans; stir until well coated. Combine the sugar, cinnamon and salt. Sprinkle over pecans; toss to mix.

[2] Spread in a greased 15-in. x 10-in. x 1-in. baking pan. Bake at 250° for 1 hour, stirring occasionally. Store in an airtight container. **Yield:** 4 cups.

CINNAMON SNACK MIX

HUNTING & FISHING COOKBOOK

healthy snack mix

CINDY GIOVANETTI
ARGYLE, TEXAS

For a crunchy, tasty snack mix that's perfect for parties or to take along to satisfy the munchies, give this nutty, whole grain version a try.

- 6 tablespoons egg substitute
- 3 tablespoons sesame seeds, toasted
- 2 tablespoons Worcestershire sauce
- 1 tablespoon seasoned salt
- 1 tablespoon fat-free cheese-flavored sprinkles
- 1 1/2 teaspoons onion powder
- 1 1/2 teaspoons garlic powder
- 1 teaspoon prepared mustard
- 1 package (16 ounces) Wheat Chex
- 1/3 cup each toasted almonds, salted cashews and dry-roasted peanuts

[1] In a large bowl, whisk the first eight ingredients. Add the cereal and nuts; toss gently until coated. Spread onto two 15-in. x 10-in. x 1-in. baking pans coated with nonstick cooking spray. Bake at 250° for 20 minutes. Stir to break apart large pieces.

[2] Bake 30 minutes longer or until dried, stirring every 15 minutes. Spread on waxed paper-lined baking sheets to cool. Store in an airtight container. **Yield:** 9 cups.

Editor's Note: This recipe was tested with Molly McButter fat-free natural cheese flavor sprinkles.

roasted mixed nuts

CAROLYN ZIMMERMAN
FAIRBURY, ILLINOIS

It's impossible to stop eating these savory mixed nuts once you start. We often enjoy them as an evening snack.

- 1 pound mixed nuts
- 1/4 cup maple syrup
- 2 tablespoons brown sugar
- 1 envelope ranch salad dressing mix

[1] In a bowl, combine the nuts and maple syrup; mix well. Sprinkle with brown sugar

DOUBLE PEANUT BARS

and salad dressing mix; stir gently to coat. Spread in a greased 15-in. x 10-in. x 1-in. baking pan.

[2] Bake at 300° for 20-25 minutes or until lightly browned. Cool. Store in an airtight container. **Yield:** 3 cups.

double peanut bars

- 1 1/2 cups Wheaties
- 1 cup Multi Grain Cheerios
- 1/2 cup unsalted dry roasted peanuts
- 1/2 cup chopped dried mixed fruit
- 1/3 cup packed brown sugar
- 1/3 cup honey
- 3 tablespoons peanut butter

[1] In a bowl, combine cereals, peanuts and mixed fruit.

[2] In a small saucepan, combine brown sugar, honey and peanut butter. Cook and stir until brown sugar and peanut butter are melted and mixture is smooth. Pour over cereal mixture; gently stir to coat evenly.

[3] Transfer to an 8-in. square dish coated with nonstick cooking spray; gently press down. Cool and cut into bars. Store in the refrigerator. **Yield:** 9 servings.

KIM ROCKER
LAGRANGE,
GEORGIA

These sweet, no-bake snacks are great energy bars. Any dried fruit works well, but I prefer cranberries. Grain cereals, plus honey, peanuts and peanut butter, make the bars popular at my house.

HUNTING & FISHING COOKBOOK

KAREN
BUCHHOLZ
SITKA, ALASKA

Almonds add a nice nutty flavor to this tasty snack. This mix is perfect for taking anywhere. It's hearty and filling but not too sweet.

nutty o's snack

- 1 cup packed brown sugar
- 1 cup dark corn syrup
- 1/2 cup butter
- 12 cups Cheerios
- 2 cups pecan halves
- 1 cup whole almonds

In a large saucepan, heat brown sugar, corn syrup and butter until sugar is dissolved. Stir in cereal and nuts; mix well. Spread onto greased 15-in. x 10-in. x 1-in. baking pans. Cool for 10 minutes; stir to loosen from pan. Cool completely. Store in airtight containers. **Yield:** 16 cups.

oatmeal raisin bars

ANNIE BEILER
LEOLA, PENNSYLVANIA

These bars are satisfying as well as wonderfully light and chewy.

- 9 1/2 cups crisp rice cereal
- 5 cups quick-cooking oats

NUTTY O'S SNACK

- 2 cups (12 ounces) semisweet chocolate chips
- 1 1/2 cups raisins
- 1 cup chopped peanuts
- 1 1/2 pounds marshmallows
- 1/4 cup butter
- 1/2 cup honey
- 1/4 cup vegetable oil
- 1/4 cup peanut butter

[1] In a large bowl, combine the first five ingredients; set aside. In a large saucepan over low heat, cook and stir marshmallow and butter until smooth. Add honey, oil and peanut butter; mix well.

[2] Pour over cereal mixture; toss to coat. Pour into two greased 13-in. x 9-in. x 2-in. baking pans; press firmly and evenly. Cool. **Yield:** 3 dozen.

munchable snack mix

LISA KEYLOR
LOUISVILLE, KENTUCKY

My family loves to take along individual bags of this colorful, fast-to-fix mixture when we go on long car trips. The sweet and salty flavors really taste great together.

- 1 package (16 ounces) M&M's
- 1 can (12 ounces) salted peanuts
- 1 package (11 ounces) butterscotch chips
- 2 cups raisins
- 1 cup cashews

In a large bowl, combine all ingredients; mix well. Place in resealable plastic bags. **Yield:** about 10 cups.

cinnamon-glazed almonds

TASTE OF HOME TEST KITCHEN

This snack is so yummy for any occasion or to take along anywhere. It's hard to stop eating these almonds once you start.

- 1/3 cup butter
- 2 egg whites

Pinch salt

CRACKER SNACK MIX

1 cup sugar

4 teaspoons ground cinnamon

3 cups whole almonds

[1] Place butter in a 15-in. x 10-in. x 1-in. baking pan. Bake at 325° until melted, about 5-7 minutes.

[2] Meanwhile, in a mixing bowl, beat egg whites with salt until soft peaks form. Gradually add sugar, beating until stiff peaks form. Fold in cinnamon and almonds; pour over butter and toss to coat.

[3] Bake at 325° for 40 minutes, turning every 10 minutes, or until almonds are crisp. Cool. Store in an airtight container. **Yield:** 3 cups.

cracker snack mix

12 cups original flavor Bugles

6 cups miniature pretzels

1 package (11 ounces) miniature butter-flavored crackers

1 package (10 ounces) Wheat Thins

1 package (9¼ ounces) Cheese Nips

1 package (7½ ounces) nacho cheese Bugles

1 package (6 ounces) miniature Parmesan fish-shaped crackers

1 cup mixed nuts or peanuts

1 bottle (10 or 12 ounces) butter-flavored popcorn oil

2 envelopes ranch salad dressing mix

[1] In a very large bowl, combine the first eight ingredients. In a small bowl, combine oil and salad dressing mix. Pour over cracker mixture; toss to coat evenly.

[2] Transfer to four ungreased 15-in. x 10-in. x 1-in. baking pans. Bake at 250° for 45 minutes, stirring every 15 minutes. Cool completely, stirring several times. **Yield:** about 8 quarts.

HUNTING & FISHING tip

Hunting and fishing can require a good amount of exercise. Frequent snacks can help keep your energy up between meals. If you'll be carrying your snacks in a backpack, stick to sturdy snacks (nuts and granola, for example) that will hold up to the rigors of travel.

TASTE OF HOME TEST KITCHEN

SHARON NICHOLS
BROOKINGS, SOUTH DAKOTA

Family and friends will munch this fun mix of crackers, nuts and ranch dressing by the handful! Everyone is sure to find something they like. If not, substitute other snack packages to vary the flavors.

FRUIT 'N' NUT SNACK MIX

DONNA BROCKETT
KINGFISHER, OKLAHOMA

You can't beat this medley of nuts, dried fruit and sweet chips to make a great take-along snack. The recipe makes a big batch.

HUNTING & FISHING COOKBOOK

fruit 'n' nut snack mix

- 1 cup sunflower kernels
- 1 cup pecan halves
- 1 cup whole salted cashews
- 1 cup salted peanuts
- 1 cup raisins
- 1 cup (6 ounces) semisweet chocolate chips
- 1 cup butterscotch chips
- 1 cup coarsely chopped dried apricots
- $3/4$ cup coarsely chopped dried peaches or apples
- $1/2$ cup dried cranberries

In a large bowl, combine all of the ingredients; mix well. Store in an airtight container. **Yield:** 8 cups.

peanut butter squares

MARSHA MURRAY
NIVERVILLE, MANITOBA

This recipe is so quick and easy to make and uses ingredients usually found in ample supply in my cupboard. The chocolate-topped bars are great for potlucks, showers and camping. They always disappear fast.

- $3/4$ cup peanut butter
- $1/2$ cup packed brown sugar
- $1/2$ cup corn syrup
- 1 tablespoon butter
- 1 teaspoon vanilla extract
- 2 cups cornflakes
- 1 cup crisp rice cereal
- $1^{1/2}$ cups semisweet chocolate chips

[1] In a microwave-safe bowl, combine the peanut butter, brown sugar, corn syrup and butter. Microwave, uncovered, on high for 1 minute or until butter is melted. Stir in vanilla until combined. Add cereal; mix well. Spread into a greased 8-in. square pan.

[2] In a microwave-safe bowl, melt the chocolate chips; stir until smooth. Spread over cereal mixture. Refrigerate until chocolate is set. Cut into squares. **Yield:** 16 squares.

taco tidbits

SHARON MENSING
GREENFIELD, IOWA

This four-ingredient combination is a great change of pace from typical snack mixes. And it's a good thing the crispy treat is so simple to throw together. Your family will empty the bowl in no time.

    6 tablespoons butter
    2 to 3 tablespoons taco seasoning
    8 cups Corn Chex
    1/4 cup grated Parmesan cheese

[1] Place butter in an 11-in. x 7-in. x 2-in. microwave-safe dish. Cover and microwave on high for 60-70 seconds or until melted. Add taco seasoning. Stir in cereal until evenly coated.

[2] Microwave on high for 1 minute; stir. Heat 1 to 1½ minutes longer; stir. Sprinkle with Parmesan cheese; microwave for 1 minute. Stir; heat 1 minute longer. **Yield:** 8 cups.

cereal trail mix

HOLLY YOUNGERS
CUNNINGHAM, KANSAS

All ages are sure to enjoy this easy-to-assemble snack. We spend a lot of time camping, canoeing and attending softball games. This crunchy mix is good for all of those occasions.

    5 cups cookie-flavored crisp cereal
    5 cups Honey-Nut Cheerios
    5 cups miniature pretzel twists
    2 cups dried banana chips
    2 cups salted mixed nuts

In a large bowl, combine all ingredients; mix well. Store in an airtight container. **Yield:** about 4¾ quarts.

candied pumpkin seeds

TASTE OF HOME TEST KITCHEN

Fall's fresh pumpkin seeds taste great prepared this way. They're a real treat.

    1 cup fresh pumpkin seeds
    1/4 cup packed brown sugar
    1/2 teaspoon pumpkin pie spice
    1/4 teaspoon salt

[1] In a small bowl, combine all ingredients. Spread into a greased foil-lined 15-in. x 10-in. x 1-in. baking pan.

[2] Bake, uncovered, at 250° for 45-50 minutes or until seeds are well-glazed, stirring occasionally. Cool completely; break into pieces. Store in an airtight container. **Yield:** 1 cup.

crunchy trail mix

    1 package (16 ounces) milk
      chocolate M&M's
    1 package (10 ounces) peanut
      butter chips
    1 can (3 ounces) chow mein
      noodles
    1½ cups raisins
    1¼ cups peanuts

In a large bowl, combine all of the ingredients; mix well. Store in an airtight container. **Yield:** 8 cups.

THERESA GINGERY HOLMESVILLE, NEBRASKA

This mix was the perfect item for my daughter to take to high school track meets. Five ingredients make up this colorful crowd-pleaser that's crunchy, chewy and not too sweet.

CRUNCHY TRAIL MIX

HUNTING & FISHING COOKBOOK

KAREN ANN BLAND
GOVE, KANSAS

Kansas is called the Sunflower State because of the wild sunflowers that grow abundantly. Cultivated varieties of sunflowers are now becoming an important crop for many Kansas farmers.

sunflower popcorn bars

- 1 cup sugar
- 1/2 cup light corn syrup
- 1/2 cup honey
- 1/2 cup peanut butter
- 1/4 cup butter, softened
- 1 teaspoon vanilla extract
- 1 cup salted sunflower kernels
- 4 quarts popped popcorn

[1] In a saucepan over medium heat, bring the sugar, corn syrup and honey to a boil, stirring often. Boil for 2 minutes. Remove from heat; stir in peanut butter, butter and vanilla until smooth. Add sunflower kernels.

[2] Place popcorn in a large bowl. Add syrup and stir to coat. Press into two greased 13-in. x 9-in. x 2-in. baking pans. Cut into bars. Store in an airtight container. **Yield:** 4 dozen.

Editor's Note: Reduced-fat or generic brands of peanut butter are not recommended for this recipe.

SUNFLOWER POPCORN BARS

peanut butter cookies

JESSIE MACLEOD
ST. STEPHEN, NEW BRUNSWICK

The old-fashioned taste of these crisp, peanut buttery cookies is irresistible. And they're as quick to make as they are to disappear. I often double the recipe.

- 1/2 cup butter, softened
- 1/2 cup sugar
- 1/2 cup packed brown sugar
- 1/2 cup peanut butter
- 1 egg
- 1/2 teaspoon vanilla extract
- 1 1/4 cups all-purpose flour
- 1/2 teaspoon baking soda
- 1/2 teaspoon baking powder

Additional sugar

[1] In a mixing bowl, cream butter and sugars. Add peanut butter, egg and vanilla; beat until smooth. Combine the flour, baking soda and baking powder; add to creamed mixture and mix well. For easier shaping, chill the dough for 1 hour.

[2] Shape into 1-in. balls; place 2 in. apart on ungreased baking sheets. Flatten each ball by crisscrossing with the tines of a fork dipped in sugar. Bake at 375° for 10-12 minutes or until bottoms are lightly browned and cookies are set. **Yield:** about 4 dozen.

Editor's Note: Reduced-fat or generic brands of peanut butter are not recommended for this recipe.

trail mix snack

CHRIS KOHLER
NELSON, WISCONSIN

The salty peanuts and sweet raisins work well together in this tasty treat.

- 1 jar (12 ounces) dry roasted peanuts
- 2 cups (12 ounces) semisweet chocolate chips
- 1 box (9 ounces) raisins
- 1 3/4 cups salted sunflower kernels

Combine ingredients in a large bowl; mix gently. Store in an airtight container. **Yield:** 8 cups.

GRANOLA TRAIL MIX

oatmeal raisin cookies

**GERALDINE LARKIN
SAN ANTONIO, TEXAS**

A friend gave me this recipe many years ago, and it's since become a family favorite. I love the aroma of these cookies baking!

- 1 cup shortening
- 1 cup sugar
- 1 cup packed brown sugar
- 2 eggs
- 1 teaspoon vanilla extract
- 3 cups old-fashioned oats
- 1½ cups all-purpose flour
- 1 teaspoon baking soda
- 1 teaspoon salt
- ½ cup chopped walnuts
- ½ cup golden raisins

[1] In a large mixing bowl, cream shortening and sugars. Beat in eggs and vanilla. Combine oats, flour, baking soda and salt; gradually add to creamed mixture. Stir in walnuts and raisins.

[2] Drop by tablespoonfuls 2 in. apart onto ungreased baking sheets. Bake at 375° for 10-12 minutes or until golden brown. Remove to wire racks to cool. **Yield:** 5 dozen.

granola trail mix

- 1 package (16 ounces) banana-nut granola
- 1 package (15 ounces) raisins
- 1 package (14 ounces) milk chocolate M&M's
- 1 can (12 ounces) honey roasted peanuts

In a large bowl, combine all of the ingredients. Store in an airtight container. **Yield:** 11 cups.

**SHELLEY RIDDLESPURGER
AMARILLO,
TEXAS**

My family has always enjoyed this crunchy four-ingredient snack. When we go camping, each person includes one additional ingredient like mini marshmallows, corn chips or cookie pieces. The taste is never the same, and we're often surprised by the combinations.

MONICA
MCGILVRAY
MUKWONAGO,
WISCONSIN

This exceptional cookie features a wonderful chunky combination of cashews, dried cranberries and white chips. Make plenty—they will disappear quickly.

cranberry-cashew drop cookies

1 cup butter, softened
1 cup packed brown sugar
1/2 cup sugar
2 eggs
1 teaspoon vanilla extract
2 1/4 cups all-purpose flour
1 teaspoon baking soda
1 teaspoon salt
1 package (10 to 12 ounces) white baking chips
1 cup chopped cashews
1 cup dried cranberries

[1] In a large bowl, cream butter and sugars until light and fluffy. Beat in eggs and vanilla.

[2] Combine the flour, baking soda and salt; gradually add to creamed mixture and mix well. Stir in the chips, cashews and cranberries.

[3] Drop by rounded tablespoonfuls 2 in. apart onto ungreased baking sheets. Bake at 350° for 9-11 minutes or until golden brown. Remove to wire racks to cool. **Yield:** 4-1/2 dozen.

sugar 'n' spice nuts

DEBBI BAKER
GREEN SPRINGS, OHIO

To tell the truth, I can't recall where this recipe came from. It's been a regular in my holiday baking for many years. Between Thanksgiving and New Year's, I hand these out to almost everybody

3 cups lightly salted mixed nuts
1 egg white
1 tablespoon orange juice
2/3 cup sugar
1 tablespoon grated orange peel
1 teaspoon ground cinnamon
1/2 teaspoon ground ginger
1/2 teaspoon ground allspice

CRANBERRY-CASHEW DROP COOKIES

[1] Place nuts in a large bowl. In a small bowl, beat egg white and orange juice with a fork until foamy. Add sugar, orange peel, cinnamon, ginger and allspice; mix well. Pour over nuts and stir to coat.

[2] Gently spread into an ungreased 15-in. x 10-in. x 1-in. baking pan. Bake at 275° for 45-50 minutes or until nuts are crisp and lightly browned, stirring every 15 minutes.

[3] Cool completely. Store in an airtight container. **Yield:** 4 cups.

hook, line 'n' sinker mix

**TASTE OF HOME TEST KITCHEN
GREENDALE, WISCONSIN**

As the name implies, people will fall hook, line and sinker for this munchable mix that features pretzel stick "fishing rods" and cheddar cheese goldfish crackers. It only takes minutes to toss this mix together and zap it in the microwave.

    3 tablespoons butter, melted
    1 tablespoon dried parsley flakes
  3/4 teaspoon dried tarragon
  1/2 teaspoon onion powder
  1/4 to 1/2 teaspoon celery salt
    1 cup goldfish crackers
    1 cup pretzel sticks
  1/2 cup Cheerios
  1/2 cup dry roasted peanuts

[1] In a 2-qt. microwave-safe bowl, combine the first five ingredients. Add the crackers, pretzels, Cheerios and peanuts; toss to coat.

[2] Microwave, uncovered, on high for 1 minute, stirring once. Cool completely. Store in an airtight container. **Yield:** 3 cups.

Editor's Note: This recipe was tested in a 1,100-watt microwave.

sunflower cookies

**DONNA CLINE
PENSACOLA, FLORIDA**

These cookies were a popular tradition in my Kansas hometown. Sometimes I add chopped nuts, raisins or dates. This recipe makes a wholesome, satisfying cookie.

HAM CHEDDAR BISCUITS

  1/2 cup vegetable oil
  1/2 cup honey
    2 eggs
    1 teaspoon vanilla extract
  1 1/2 cups whole wheat flour
  1/4 teaspoon salt
    1 cup sunflower kernels

[1] In a bowl, combine the oil, honey, eggs and vanilla. Combine the flour and salt; gradually add to honey mixture and mix well (dough will be very soft). Stir in sunflower kernels.

[2] Drop by heaping teaspoonfuls 2 in. apart onto greased baking sheets. Bake at 350° for 10-12 minutes or until golden brown. Remove to wire racks to cool. **Yield:** 4 dozen.

ham cheddar biscuits

  2 1/4 cups biscuit/baking mix
  3/4 cup milk
  3/4 cup shredded cheddar cheese
  1/2 cup chopped fully cooked ham

[1] In a bowl, combine the biscuit mix and milk just until moistened. Stir in the cheese and ham. Drop by rounded tablespoonfuls onto greased baking sheets.

[2] Bake at 450° for 8-10 minutes or until golden brown. **Yield:** 20 biscuits.

**SARAH MARSHALL
BROKEN ARROW, OKLAHOMA**

My husband often skipped breakfast until I created these savory biscuits that have become his favorite. I keep a batch in the freezer, and he reheats a few in the microwave on busy mornings.

HUNTING & FISHING COOKBOOK

**JEAN BOYCE
NEW ULM,
MINNESOTA**

My husband and I enjoy these bars every day. It's a basic recipe to which you can add any of your favorite flavors...coconut or different kinds of chips, nuts and dried fruits.

honey-oat granola bars

4 cups quick-cooking oats

1 cup packed brown sugar

1 cup chopped salted peanuts

1 cup (6 ounces) semisweet chocolate chips

1/2 cup sunflower kernels

3/4 cup butter, melted

2/3 cup honey

1 teaspoon vanilla extract

[1] In a large bowl, combine the oats, brown sugar, peanuts, chocolate chips and sunflower kernels. Stir in the butter, honey and vanilla until combined (mixture will be crumbly). Press into a greased parchment paper-lined 15-in. x 10-in. x 1-in. baking pan.

[2] Bake at 350° for 15-20 minutes or until browned and bubbly. Cool for 15 minutes on a wire rack; cut into squares. Cool completely before removing from pan. **Yield:** 3 dozen.

homemade crisp crackers

**TASTE OF HOME TEST KITCHEN
GREENDALE, WISCONSIN**

Store-bought crackers have nothing on these cheesy crisps. Make them in advance and keep them handy in an airtight container for anytime snacking.

1 3/4 cups all-purpose flour

1/2 cup cornmeal

1/2 teaspoon baking soda

1/2 teaspoon sugar

1/2 teaspoon salt

1/2 teaspoon garlic powder

1/4 teaspoon Italian seasoning

1/2 cup cold butter, cubed

1 1/2 cups (6 ounces) shredded Colby-Monterey Jack cheese

1/2 cup plus 2 tablespoons cold water

2 tablespoons cider vinegar

[1] In a large bowl, combine the first seven ingredients; cut in butter until crumbly. Stir in cheese. Gradually add water and vinegar, tossing with a fork until dough forms a ball. Wrap in plastic wrap and refrigerate for 1 hour or until firm.

[2] Divide into six portions. On a lightly floured surface, roll each portion into an 8-in. circle. Cut into eight wedges and place on greased baking sheets.

[3] Bake at 375° for 17-20 minutes or until edges are lightly browned. Cool on wire racks. Store in an airtight container. **Yield:** 4 dozen.

sausage cheese puffs

**DELLA MOORE
TROY, NEW YORK**

People are always surprised when I tell them there are only four ingredients in these tasty bite-size puffs.

1 pound bulk Italian sausage

3 cups biscuit/baking mix

HONEY-OAT GRANOLA BARS

4 cups (16 ounces) shredded
   cheddar cheese

¾ cup water

[1] In a skillet, cook and crumble sausage until no longer pink; drain.

[2] In a bowl, combine biscuit mix and cheese; stir in sausage. Add water and toss with a fork until moistened. Shape into 1½-in. balls. Place 2 in. apart on ungreased baking sheets.

[3] Bake at 400° for 12-15 minutes or until puffed and golden brown. Cool on wire racks. **Yield:** about 4 dozen.

turtle pretzels

BARBARA LOUDENSLAGER
O'FALLON, MISSOURI

Who doesn't love the classic combination of chocolate, caramel and pecans? These sweet and crunchy treats will be devoured in no time!

1 package (14 ounces) caramels

1 tablespoon water

1 package (10 ounces) pretzel rods

8 ounces German sweet chocolate or semisweet chocolate

2 teaspoons shortening

1 cup finely chopped pecans

[1] In a double boiler, melt caramels in water. Dip half of each pretzel into the hot caramel. Place on a greased sheet of foil to cool.

[2] In a microwave, melt chocolate and shortening; stir until smooth. Dip caramel-coated end of pretzels into the chocolate, allowing excess to drip off; sprinkle with nuts. Return to foil to cool. **Yield:** about 2½ dozen.

cornish pasties

FILLING:

1 pound beef top round steak, cut into ½-inch pieces

2 to 3 medium potatoes, peeled and cut into ½-inch cubes

1 cup chopped carrots

½ cup finely chopped onion

2 tablespoons minced fresh parsley

1 teaspoon salt

CORNISH PASTIES

½ teaspoon pepper

¼ cup butter, melted

PASTRY:

3 cups all-purpose flour

1 teaspoon salt

1 cup shortening

8 to 9 tablespoons ice water

1 egg, beaten, optional

[1] In a bowl, combine round steak, potatoes, carrots, onion, parsley, salt and pepper. Add butter and toss to coat; set aside.

[2] For pastry, combine flour and salt in a bowl. Cut in shortening until mixture forms pea-size crumbs. Sprinkle with water, 1 tablespoon at a time. Toss lightly with a fork until dough forms a ball. Do not overmix.

[3] Divide dough into fourths. Roll out one portion into a 9-in. circle; transfer to a greased baking sheet. Mound about 1-¼ cups of meat filling on half of circle. Moisten edges with water; fold dough over mixture and press edges with fork to seal. Repeat with remaining pastry and filling.

[4] Cut slits in top of each pasty. Brush with beaten egg if desired. Bake at 375° for 50-60 minutes or until pasties are golden brown. **Yield:** 4 servings.

GAYLE LEWIS
YUCAIPA,
CALIFORNIA

Years ago, when bakeries in my Midwestern hometown made pasties, people scrambled to get there before they were all gone. Now I make my own. Filled with meat, potatoes and vegetables, they make a complete handheld meal.

Hunting & Fishing COOKBOOK

Cooking with wild ingredients can be a fun and rewarding experience. When harvesting wild ingredients, like those used in the recipes in this chapter, be certain you've properly identified what you're picking and that it's edible. Don't pick from areas treated with chemicals. If you're unsure of what you're picking, check with your county Extension agent before cooking with those ingredients.

FLOWER GARDEN SALAD, P. 220
WILD ASPARAGUS QUICHE, P. 224
BLUEBERRY BREAKFAST SAUCE, P. 225

BLACK WALNUT BROWNIES,
PAGE 214

BRAND X PICTURES/PUNCHSTOCK

STEPHANIE MULLEN WHITEHORSE, YUKON

Mossberries, also called crowberries, are small, shiny, black berries found all over Alaska, in northern areas of the Lower 48 states and in some parts of Canada. They grow on a creeping evergreen plant and ripen in August. Mossberries have a mild flavor, so they're best cooked. They combine nicely with other berries.

berry tarts

 2 **cups all-purpose flour**
 3/4 **cup sugar**
 1 **teaspoon grated lemon peel**
 1/4 **teaspoon salt**
 2/3 **cup cold butter**
 2 **eggs**
 1 **tablespoon ice water**
 1 **teaspoon lemon juice**
FILLING:
 2 **cups wild blueberries or mossberries**
 3/4 **cup sugar**
 1/4 **cup all-purpose flour**
 1 **teaspoon grated lemon peel**
 1 1/2 **cups (12 ounces) sour cream**
 1 **egg yolk**

[1] In a bowl, combine flour, sugar, lemon peel and salt; cut in butter until crumbly. Combine eggs, water and lemon juice until smooth; drizzle over flour mixture. Toss with a fork until mixture is moist enough to shape into a ball (dough will be sticky). Divide in half; shape into balls and wrap in plastic wrap. Refrigerate for at least 30 minutes.

[2] Remove from the refrigerator; let stand for 15 minutes before rolling. On a floured sur-face, roll the dough to 1/8 -in. thickness. Cut into 3-in. circles. Ease into 2-in. tart pans, pressing pastry onto the bottom and sides of the pan. Bake at 400° for 10 minutes. Cool.

[3] Place three to four berries in each shell. In a bowl, combine sugar, flour and lemon peel. Stir in sour cream and egg yolk. Spoon 1 tablespoon of filling over berries. Place pans on a baking sheet. Bake at 350° for 15-20 minutes or until the pastry is golden and filling is set. Cool in pans for 1 minute before removing to wire racks. **Yield:** 32 tarts.

black walnut brownies

(PICTURED ON PAGE 213)
CATHERINE BERRA BLEEM WALSH, ILLINOIS

The distinctive flavor of black walnuts stands out in this yummy brownie recipe. Every fall, we gather the slightly bitter-tasting nuts and use them to make these brownies. My father used to tell me to plant black walnut trees—he said it is something that will be enjoyed by future generations. I followed his advice and have planted more than 1,000 black walnut trees over the years.

 1 **cup sugar**
 1/4 **cup vegetable oil**
 2 **eggs**

  1 teaspoon vanilla extract
  1/2 cup all-purpose flour
  2 tablespoons baking cocoa
  1/2 teaspoon salt
  1/2 cup chopped black walnuts

[1] In a small mixing bowl, combine sugar and oil. Add eggs and vanilla; mix well. Combine the flour, cocoa and salt; add to sugar mixture and mix well. Stir in walnuts.

[2] Pour into a greased 8-in. square baking pan. Bake at 350° for 30-35 minutes or until a toothpick comes out clean. Cool on wire rack. **Yield:** 16 servings.

black walnut cookies

DOUG BLACK
CONOVER, NORTH CAROLINA

Black walnuts have a more distinctive flavor than the traditional English walnuts you would find in a store. They have a short shelf life, so it is best to store them in the freezer. Black walnut trees thrive in the rich soil of the eastern United States and in the Great Plains west to Texas.

  1 cup butter, softened
  2 cups packed brown sugar
  2 eggs
  1 teaspoon vanilla extract
  3 1/2 cups all-purpose flour
  1 teaspoon baking soda
  1/4 teaspoon salt
  2 cups chopped black walnuts, divided

[1] In a mixing bowl, cream butter and brown sugar. Beat in eggs and vanilla. Combine flour, baking soda and salt; gradually add to the creamed mixture. Stir in 1 1/4 cups of walnuts. Finely chop the remaining nuts. Shape dough into two 15-in. logs. Roll logs in chopped nuts, pressing gently. Wrap each log in plastic wrap.

[2] Refrigerate for 2 hours or until firm. Unwrap and cut into 1/4-in. slices. Place 2 in. apart on greased baking sheets. Bake at 350° for 8-11 minutes. Cool on wire racks. **Yield:** 10 dozen.

buttery black walnut brittle candy

ANNE MEDLIN
BOLIVAR, MISSOURI

We begin harvesting black walnuts in October so I can use them to make candy at Christmas. It's no easy task. Removing husks releases a permanent brown dye that stains clothes, skin and even cement. Machines can remove husks, but rolling the nut under your foot also works. After the husks are removed, you must crack the shells to get to the nut meat. I use a hammer! This recipe is my favorite holiday candy—your family is sure to be as wild about it as mine!

  1 cup sugar
  1/2 cup corn syrup
  1/4 cup water
  1/2 cup butter
  1 to 1 1/2 cups black walnuts
  1/2 teaspoon baking soda

[1] In a saucepan, cook sugar, corn syrup and water until sugar dissolves and mixture comes to a boil. Add butter; cook until mixture reaches 280° on a candy thermometer. Stir in walnuts; cook until 300° (hard-crack stage).

[2] Remove from the heat and stir in baking soda. Spread immediately into a greased 15-in. x 10-in. x 1-in. baking pan. When cool, break into pieces. **Yield:** 1 1/4 pounds.

Editor's Note: We recommend that you test your candy thermometer before each use by bringing water to a boil; the thermometer should read 212°. Adjust your recipe temperature up or down based on your test.

HUNTING & FISHING COOKBOOK

TASTE OF HOME TEST KITCHEN

Downy gray-green leaves and sky-blue star-shaped flowers make this annual herb a delightful attraction in a garden. It gives a cucumber-like flavor to this spread.

borage party spread

1 package (8 ounces) cream cheese, softened

1 tablespoon milk

1/2 teaspoon garlic salt

1/4 cup finely chopped sweet red pepper

2 tablespoons shredded carrot

Snack bread, toasted English muffins or miniature bagels

Young borage leaves (2 to 3 inches)

Borage flowers, sepals removed, optional

In a mixing bowl, beat the cream cheese, milk and garlic salt until smooth. Stir in the red pepper and carrot. Spread over bread. Garnish with borage leaves and flowers if desired. **Yield:** 1 cup.

Editor's Note: Make sure to properly identify flowers before picking. Double-check that they're edible and have not been treated with chemicals.

candied violets

**JEANNE CONTE
COLUMBUS, OHIO**

You don't have to go far to find wild ingredients—in some cases, they are right in your backyard. Also known as Johnny-jump-ups or pansy violets, these petite purple and blue flowers flourish in fields, open woods and even residential lawns from the Canadian border to Texas. Children especially like to help make these candied flowers, which make a lovely garnish for salads or desserts.

2 egg whites

Sugar

1 large bunch wild violets (including stems), washed

[1] In a bowl, beat egg whites with a wire whisk just until frothy. Place sugar in another bowl. Taking one violet at a time, pick it up by the stem and dip into egg whites, covering all surfaces. Gently dip into the sugar, again being sure all of the petals, top and bottom, are covered. Place on waxed paper-lined baking sheets; snip off stems.

BORAGE PARTY SPREAD

HUNTING & FISHING COOKBOOK

BRAND X PICTURES/PUNCHSTOCK

[2] Using a toothpick, open petals to original shape. Sprinkle sugar on any uncoated areas. Dry in a 200° oven for 30-40 minutes or until sugar crystallizes.

[3] Gently remove the violets to wire racks with a spatula or two-tined fork. Sprinkle again with sugar if violets appear syrupy. Cool. Store in airtight containers with waxed paper between the layers. **Yield:** 12 servings.

Editor's Note: Be sure to use the common wild purple violet, not the African violet (often grown as a houseplant) and make sure to properly identify flowers before picking.

fried cactus strips

    4 to 6 large cactus pads (about 8
      inches x 4 inches)
    1 cup all-purpose flour
 1 1/2 teaspoons salt, divided
  1/4 teaspoon pepper
    3 eggs
  1/2 cup milk
    1 cup soft bread crumbs
  3/4 cup saltine crumbs
 1 1/2 teaspoons chili powder
 1 1/2 teaspoons cayenne pepper

Oil for deep-fat frying

Picante sauce

[1] Remove all needles and spines from cactus pads. Slice into 1/2-in.-wide strips. Wash thoroughly; drain and pat dry. Set aside. In a shallow bowl, combine flour, 1/2 teaspoon salt and pepper.

[2] In another bowl, lightly beat the eggs and milk. Combine bread and saltine crumbs, chili powder, cayenne pepper and remaining salt; set aside. Dredge the cactus strips in the flour mix-ture; shake off excess.

[3] Dip in egg mixture, then coat with the crumb mixture. In a deep-fat fryer, heat oil to 375°. Fry strips until golden brown, about 1-2 minutes. Drain on paper towels. Serve with the picante sauce. **Yield:** 8 servings.

NEMA LU PARKER EASTLAND, TEXAS

Ever eat a cactus? It's not such a wild idea! Folks in the West and Southwest have done so for decades. The prickly pear cactus—called nopales—has green pads that are jointed and often found in large, low clumps. Some grocery stores also carry cactus pads in their produce section. Look for plump, fresh-looking pads. Before cooking, be sure to carefully remove the clumps of tiny spines from the pads, using the end of a potato peeler or a sharp knife to dig them out. Or scrape them off with a blunt knife.

HUNTING & FISHING COOKBOOK

dandelion soup

MARY ELLEN DYCUS
LELAND, MISSISSIPPI

This soup is a great way to celebrate the end of winter. I've found that dandelion greens are less bitter if picked early in the day from plants that have yet to produce buds or blooms. Light-colored leaves are better than darker ones. Serve this dish and you'll have compliments to your cooking cropping up like weeds!

- 1 package (6.9 ounces) chicken-flavored rice mix
- 3 cans (10³/4 ounces each) condensed cream of chicken soup, undiluted
- 5 cups water
- 2 cups cubed cooked chicken
- 4 cups dandelion greens, torn

Prepare the rice mix according to the package directions; set aside. In a large saucepan or Dutch oven over medium heat, combine the soup and water. Add the rice and chicken; heat through. Add dandelion greens; cook until tender, about 6-8 minutes. **Yield:** 10-12 servings.

chilled sorrel soup

SARAH SELTZER
SACRAMENTO, CALIFORNIA

Fresh sorrel is a tempting spring treat I enjoy. If you don't have juicy sorrel leaves growing wild in your area, you can cultivate a patch in your own backyard by ordering seeds through catalogs that carry herbs and more uncommon plants. This distinctive soup is tart and refreshing, with a lovely spring-green color. I especially like serving sorrel this way.

- ¹/2 pound fresh sorrel
- 4 cups water
- 1 tablespoon lemon juice
- 2 egg yolks
- 1 teaspoon salt
- ¹/4 teaspoon pepper

Sour cream

Additional chopped fresh sorrel, optional

[1] Remove center ribs and stems from sorrel; tie the ribs and stems in a bundle and wrap in cheesecloth. Chop the leaves into strips. In a 2-qt. saucepan, combine water, lemon juice, sorrel leaves and bundle of stems. Simmer for 20 minutes; discard stem bundle.

[2] In a small bowl, beat the egg yolks; add a small amount of the sorrel mixture, stirring constantly. Return all to the pan. Cook and stir until the soup thickens (do not boil). Cool; chill for several hours. Add the salt and pepper. Garnish with a dollop of sour cream and additional sorrel if desired. **Yield:** 4 servings (1 quart).

elderberry blossom tea

GENEVIEVE CORLEY
AMESBURY, MASSACHUSETTS

Elderberry is a shrub in the honeysuckle family and thrives in moist, sunny areas, usually in open woods or in fields and along streams and roads. To harvest blossoms, shake the stem over a bucket; loose petals will fall off easily. Dry blossoms on a cookie sheet lined with paper towels in an airy space out of direct sunlight, for several days. Store in an airtight container. This tea is an old-fashioned brew that was once used as a cold remedy. Certain varieties of elderberry are not edible. Be sure to check with a county Extension agent if you are unsure.

- 1 to 2 tablespoons dried elderberry blossoms or 2 to 3 tablespoons fresh elderberry blossoms
- 1 cup boiling water

Sugar to taste

Thin lemon slice

In a tea cup or mug, steep the elderberry blossoms in boiling water for 5-10 minutes; strain. Add the sugar and lemon. **Yield:** 1 serving.

calendula paella

- 4 cups chicken broth
- 2½ cups uncooked long grain rice
- 1 cup chopped onion
- 4 garlic cloves, minced, divided
- 1 teaspoon salt
- ½ teaspoon ground turmeric
- ¼ teaspoon pepper
- 1 bay leaf
- 1 large green pepper, julienned
- 3 green onions, sliced
- 1 teaspoon minced parsley
- 1 teaspoon dried thyme
- ¼ teaspoon hot pepper sauce
- 2 tablespoons olive oil
- 1 cup sliced fresh mushrooms
- 2 medium tomatoes, chopped
- 1 package (10 ounces) frozen peas
- ½ pound fresh frozen uncooked shrimp, peeled and deveined
- 2 tablespoons lemon juice
- 1 pound boneless skinless chicken breasts, thinly sliced
- ½ cup calendula petals (about 12 blossoms)

[1] In a saucepan, combine the broth, rice, onion, half of the garlic, salt, turmeric, pepper and bay leaf; bring to a boil. Reduce heat; cover and simmer for 20 minutes or until rice is tender.

[2] Meanwhile, in a skillet, saute green pepper, onions, parsley, thyme, hot pepper sauce and remaining garlic in oil for 2 minutes. Add the mushrooms. Cook until the green pepper is crisp-tender. Add the tomato and peas; heat through. Discard bay leaf; add the rice mixture to vegetable mixture and keep warm over medium-high heat.

[3] In another skillet, cook and stir shrimp in lemon juice for 2 minutes. Add chicken; cook until chicken is no longer pink and shrimp is fully cooked, about 3-5 minutes. Add rice and vegetables with the calendula petals; toss. **Yield:** 10-12 servings.

Editor's Note: Make sure to properly identify flowers before picking. Double-check that they're edible and have not been treated with chemicals.

TASTE OF HOME TEST KITCHEN

Calendulas have bright-yellow petals that lend a sunny cast to food. The flavor of the petals has been described as tangy to slightly bitter.

HUNTING & FISHING COOKBOOK

CALENDULA PAELLA

FLOWER GARDEN SALAD

HUNTING & FISHING COOKBOOK

**MARY KAY DIXSON
CATLIN, ILLINOIS**

The fragrance and flavor of this salad is outstanding. Pick the blossoms early in the morning.

flower garden salad

6 to 8 cups mixed salad greens

1 cup packed rose petals

1 cup nasturtium petals, if available

1 cup marigold blossoms, if available

1 tablespoon snipped fresh lemon thyme

DRESSING:

$1/3$ cup raspberry-flavored vinegar

$3/4$ cup olive oil

1 tablespoon brown sugar

1 teaspoon ground mustard

$1/8$ teaspoon salt

In a large salad bowl, toss the greens, flowers and thyme. In a jar with tight-fitting lid, combine the dressing ingredients and shake well. Drizzle over salad; serve immediately. **Yield:** 6-8 servings.

Editor's Note: Make sure to properly identify flowers before picking. Double-check that they're edible and have not been treated with chemicals.

huckleberry cheese pie

**DIANNE DOEDE
TROUT LAKE, WASHINGTON**

Huckleberries sprout up in sandy and rocky places and in oak woods and bogs, clearings and burned-over areas in the Pacific Northwest and the eastern and southern United States. They are similar to blueberries but are black and have 10 hard little seeds. This pie is one of my family's favorites—with a cookie-like crust, a fluffy cream filling and a layer of luscious huckleberries on top, it always brings smiles!

$1 1/4$ cups all-purpose flour

5 teaspoons confectioners' sugar

$1/2$ cup butter, melted

TOPPING:

$3/4$ cup sugar

$1/4$ cup cornstarch

4 cups fresh or frozen huckleberries

$1/3$ cup water

FILLING:

1 package (8 ounces) cream cheese, softened

½ cup confectioners' sugar

1 tablespoon lemon juice

1 teaspoon grated lemon peel

1 teaspoon vanilla extract

1 cup heavy whipping cream, whipped

[1] In a bowl, combine flour and confectioners' sugar. Stir in butter. Press onto the bottom and sides of two greased 9-in. pie pans. Bake at 375° for 8-10 minutes or until golden brown. Cool on a wire rack.

[2] For topping, combine sugar and cornstarch in a saucepan; stir in berries and water. Cook and stir over medium heat until mixture comes to a boil; boil for 2 minutes. Cool.

[3] In a mixing bowl, beat cream cheese, sugar, lemon juice, peel and vanilla until light and fluffy. Fold in whipped cream. Spoon half into each crust. Spoon topping over filling. Chill for 1 hour. **Yield:** 2 pies (12-16 servings).

lamb's-quarter quiche

DOROTHY HOLDERBAUM
ALLEGAN, MICHIGAN

Some of the first fresh foods available in spring are nature's own wild salad greens! This quiche uses lamb's-quarter, a green found along roadsides and in fields throughout the United States and much of Canada. It tastes like mild spinach and can be cooked alone or mixed with other greens.

1 medium onion, chopped

2 tablespoons vegetable oil

4 cups chopped lamb's-quarter (tender new leaves)

3 eggs

1 can (12 ounces) evaporated milk or 1⅔ cups milk

½ teaspoon salt

½ teaspoon pepper

2 cups (8 ounces) shredded cheddar cheese, divided

1 unbaked pie pastry (9 inches)

[1] In a skillet, saute onion in oil until tender. Add lamb's-quarter; cook and stir until wilted. Cover and remove from heat.

[2] In a mixing bowl, beat eggs and milk. Stir in the salt, pepper, 1 cup cheese and lamb's-quarter mixture. Pour into the pie shell. Sprinkle with the remaining cheese.

[3] Bake at 400° for 10 minutes. Reduce heat to 350°; bake 30 minutes more or until a knife inserted near center comes out clean. Let stand 5-10 minutes before cutting. **Yield:** 6-8 servings.

mulled grape cider

SHARON HARMON
ORANGE, MASSACHUSETTS

A fall favorite, Concord grapes are just one of many varieties that grow wild throughout the country. Most grape plants have lobed, heart-shaped leaves with lots of veins on woody vines. I came up with this recipe when I attempted to make grape jelly and ended up with 30 jars of delicious grape syrup instead. I decided to try simmering the syrup with spices to make a beverage, and my friends loved it!

5 pounds Concord grapes

8 cups water, divided

1½ cups sugar

8 whole cloves

4 cinnamon sticks (4 inches)

Dash ground nutmeg

[1] In a large saucepan or Dutch oven, combine grapes and 2 cups water; bring to a boil, stirring constantly. Press through a strainer; reserve juice and discard skins and seeds.

[2] Pour juice through a double layer of cheesecloth into a slow cooker. Add sugar, cloves, cinnamon sticks, nutmeg and remaining water. Heat on low for 3 hours. Discard the cloves and cinnamon sticks before serving. **Yield:** 10-12 servings (2¾ quarts).

morel mushroom soup

GERALDINE DAVENPORT
MADISON, WISCONSIN

The distinctive wild morel mushroom makes a brief appearance every year from late February in the South to May in the North. They have ridged or pitted cone-shaped caps, are generally tan or creamy white and can grow up to 6 inches tall. Morels should never be eaten raw and before cooking, be sure to soak them in salted water. My husband and I have been picking morels each spring for as long as I can remember. Some years we have an abundance, so I came up with this recipe. This rich, flavorful soup is a great way to use these mushrooms.

    1 pound fresh morel or other
      mushrooms, sliced
    2 tablespoons lemon juice
    1 large onion, chopped
    3 tablespoons butter
    2 tablespoons all-purpose flour
    1 quart milk
    3 chicken bouillon cubes
  1/2 teaspoon dried thyme
  1/2 teaspoon salt
  1/8 teaspoon pepper

Sprinkle the mushrooms with lemon juice. In a saucepan, saute the mushrooms and onion in butter until tender. Sprinkle with the flour; stir well. Gradually add the milk, bouillon, thyme, salt and pepper. Bring to a boil; boil and stir for 2 minutes. Reduce heat; simmer the soup for 10-15 minutes. **Yield:** 6 servings.

persimmon rice pudding

OPAL AMIDON
GARDEN GROVE, CALIFORNIA

Experienced persimmon pickers know exactly what to look for when they are seeking out this luscious fruit—ones that are fully ripe, yellowish-orange, red-purple, soft and slightly shriveled with a gooey, orange flesh. Unripe persimmons are very astringent—even the slightest taste can be very unpleasant. A persimmon tastes best when very ripe—so ripe, it almost looks spoiled! I often buy large quantities of persimmons in the grocery store, remove the pulp and freeze it. This way, I can enjoy persimmons—and this rice pudding—all year!

    4 cups cooked long grain rice
    2 cups ripe persimmon pulp
 1 1/4 cups sugar
 1 1/4 cups milk
  1/3 cup all-purpose flour
    1 egg, beaten
    1 teaspoon vanilla extract
  1/4 cup chopped walnuts
  1/4 cup raisins

[1] In a large bowl, combine rice and persimmon pulp; set aside. Combine sugar, milk, flour, egg and vanilla; add to the rice mixture and mix well. Stir in walnuts and raisins.

[2] Pour into a greased 3-qt. baking dish. Bake, uncovered, at 350° for 45 minutes or until pudding is set. Serve warm or cold. **Yield:** 10-12 servings.

wild asparagus salad

KAREN GRASLEY
QUADEVILLE, ONTARIO

Often found growing wild in wooded areas, fields or along roads, wild asparagus is grown from seeds of garden plants scattered by birds. In some areas, it is such a delicacy that it's considered bad manners to ask people where they find it! The crisp-tender asparagus and flavorful dressing make this a wonderful side dish.

  3/4 pound wild asparagus, trimmed
    2 tablespoons chopped stuffed
      olives
    1 hard-cooked egg, chopped
  1/2 cup vegetable oil
    5 tablespoons lemon juice
    3 tablespoons cider vinegar
    3 tablespoons sugar
  1/2 teaspoon salt
  1/2 teaspoon paprika
  1/2 teaspoon ground mustard
Dash cayenne pepper
Cherry tomatoes, halved

[1] Cook asparagus until crisp-tender; drain and rinse in cold water. Place in a shallow dish; top with olives and egg.

[2] In a jar with a tight-fitting lid, combine oil, lemon juice, vinegar, sugar, salt, paprika, mustard and cayenne pepper; shake well. Pour over asparagus. Chill for several hours or overnight. Garnish with tomatoes. **Yield:** 4 servings.

pine nut divinity

3 cups sugar

²/₃ cup water

½ cup light corn syrup

2 egg whites

⅛ teaspoon salt

1 teaspoon vanilla extract

1 cup pine nuts, toasted

[1] In a large saucepan, combine sugar, water and corn syrup; bring to a boil over medium-high heat, stirring constantly. Cook over medium heat without stirring until a candy thermometer reads 260° (hard-ballstage), about 10-15 minutes. Remove from heat.

[2] In a large mixing bowl, beat egg whites and salt until stiff peaks form. Beat on high and gradually pour hot sugar mixture in a thin stream over the egg whites; continue beating for about 3 minutes. Add vanilla; beat just until candy starts to lose its gloss, about 5 minutes. Stir in pine nuts.

[3] Working quickly, drop by tablespoonfuls onto waxed paper; or pour into a buttered 9-in. square pan and cut into serving-size pieces. Store tightly covered. **Yield:** about 3 dozen.

Editor's Note: We recommend that you test your candy thermometer before each use by bringing water to a boil; the thermometer should read 212°. Adjust your recipe temperature up or down based on your test.

**ED HORKEY
AHWATUKEE,
ARIZONA**

The soft, ivory-colored pine nut has a delicate pine flavor that goes well in both sweet and savory dishes. When I grew up in California, we used to pop the nuts out of pinecones using a screwdriver. Pine nuts found today in the grocery store were likely removed by a labor-intensive process, which makes the nut expensive. My mother made this candy, and it was always popular at bake sales. Pine nuts spoil quickly at room temperature. Store them in an airtight container in the refrigerator for up to 3 months, or freeze up to 9 months.

HUNTING & FISHING COOKBOOK

wild asparagus quiche

CRUST:

- 1 cup all-purpose flour
- 1 teaspoon salt
- 1/2 cup shortening
- 1/4 cup cold water

FILLING:

- 1 1/2 cups (12 ounces) 1% cottage cheese
- 4 eggs
- 2 cups 1% milk
- 2 tablespoons all-purpose flour
- 1 teaspoon Dijon mustard

Dash hot pepper sauce

- 2 cups chopped fresh wild asparagus (1/2-inch pieces)
- 2/3 cup shredded Swiss cheese

Paprika

[1] For crust, in a small bowl, combine flour and salt. Cut in shortening until mixture forms fine crumbs. Add water; toss with a fork until the mixture forms a ball.

[2] On a floured surface, roll out the dough to fit 10-in. quiche pan. Transfer the pastry to quiche pan. Tri pastry to 1/2 in. beyond edge of plate; flute edges. Line unpricked pastry shell with a double thickness of heavy-duty foil. Bake at 400° for 5 minutes. Remove foil; bake for 5 minutes.

[3] For filling, in a blender, combine the cottage cheese, eggs, milk, flour, mustard and pepper sauce; cover and process until smooth. Pour into crust.

[4] Arrange asparagus evenly over filling. Sprinkle with Swiss cheese and paprika. Bake at 375° for 25-30 minutes or until a knife inserted near the center comes out clean. **Yield:** 6 servings.

MARY WEAVER GLENWOOD SPRINGS, COLORADO

I enjoy hunting for wild asparagus, and one day I decided to make it into this tasty, lightened-up quiche. This is perfect for a springtime luncheon or brunch.

WILD ASPARAGUS QUICHE

cinnamon blueberry jam

BARBARA BURNS
PHILLIPSBURG, NEW JERSEY

Watching my grandmother can hundreds of jars of tomatoes, peaches and pears inspired me to first try making jams and jellies myself. I can remember, as a girl, marveling at all the jars in her cellar.

- 1 pound fresh or frozen blueberries (about 1 quart)
- 3 1/2 cups sugar
- 1 tablespoon bottled lemon juice
- 1/4 teaspoon ground cinnamon
- 1/8 teaspoon ground cloves
- 1 pouch (3 ounces) liquid fruit pectin

[1] Crush blueberries; measure 2-1/2 cups and place in a large saucepan. Add sugar, lemon juice, cinnamon and cloves; bring to a rolling boil over high heat, stirring constantly. Quickly stir in pectin. Return to a full rolling boil; boil for 1 minute, stirring constantly.

[2] Remove from the heat; skim off foam. Carefully ladle hot mixture into hot half-pint jars, leaving 1/4-in. headspace. Remove air bubbles; wipe rims and adjust lids. Process jam for 10 minutes in a boiling-water canner. **Yield:** 4 half-pints.

Editor's Note: The processing time listed is for altitudes of 1,000 feet or less. Add 1 minute to the processing time for each 1,000 feet of additional altitude.

HUNTING & FISHING COOKBOOK

fresh blackberry pie

GLADYS GIBBS
BRUSH CREEK, TENNESSEE

I grew up on a farm, and we always picked wild blackberries in early summer and used them to make pies.

- 1 cup sugar
- 1/3 cup quick-cooking tapioca
- 1/4 teaspoon salt
- 4 cups fresh blackberries, divided
- 2 tablespoons butter

Pastry for double-crust pie (9 inches)

[1] In a large saucepan, combine sugar, tapioca and salt. Add 1 cup blackberries; toss to coat. Let stand for 15 minutes. Cook and stir over medium heat until the berries burst and mixture comes to a gentle boil. Remove from the heat; gently stir in remaining berries.

[2] Line a 9-in. pie plate with bottom pastry; trim pastry even with edge of plate. Add filling; dot with butter. Roll out remaining pastry to fit top of pie; place over filling. Trim, seal and flute edges. Cut slits in top.

[3] Bake at 400° for 35-40 minutes or until crust is golden brown and filling is bubbly. Cool on a wire rack. **Yield:** 6-8 servings.

asparagus cress soup

TERESA LILLYCROP
PUSLINCH, ONTARIO

Here's a refreshing soup that combines two spring treats: fresh asparagus and peppery watercress.

- 3/4 cup chopped green onions
- 1/4 cup butter, cubed
- 3 tablespoons all-purpose flour
- 2 1/2 cups chicken broth
- 1 1/2 pounds fresh wild asparagus, cut into 1-inch pieces
- 1/2 bunch watercress, stems removed (about 1 cup packed)
- 1 1/2 cups half-and-half cream
- 3/4 teaspoon salt
- 1/4 teaspoon white pepper
- 1/8 teaspoon cayenne pepper

Sour cream

BLUEBERRY BREAKFAST SAUCE

[1] In a large saucepan, saute onion in butter for 3-4 minutes or until soft. Stir in flour to form a smooth paste. Cook for 2 minutes. Gradually stir in broth and bring to a boil. Add asparagus and watercress; cover and simmer for 5-7 minutes or until the vegetables are tender. Cool.

[2] In a blender, process soup in batches until smooth. Return all to pan; stir in the cream. Heat on low until cooked through (do not boil). Season with the salt, white pepper and cayenne. Serve with a dollop of sour cream. **Yield:** 6 servings.

blueberry breakfast sauce

- 1/2 cup sugar
- 1 tablespoon cornstarch
- 1/3 cup water
- 2 cups fresh or frozen blueberries

In a 2-qt. saucepan, combine the sugar and cornstarch; gradually stir in water. Add the blueberries; bring to a boil over medium heat, stirring constantly. Boil for 1 minute, stirring occasionally. Serve warm or cold over French toast or pancakes. **Yield:** about 2 cups.

ELLEN BENNINGER STONEBORO, PENNSYLVANIA

This fresh-tasting sauce, chock-full of berries, tastes great served over pancakes, French toast, waffles or even ice cream. Whether you use fresh or frozen blueberries, the flavor is fantastic... and with only four ingredients, it cooks up in a flash.

Safe Handling & Preparation
OF FISH & GAME MEAT

Keep in mind, that as with any perishable farm-raised meat, poultry or fish, bacteria can be found on raw or undercooked wild game (meat, poultry and fish) as well.

Bacteria multiply rapidly in temperatures between 40° and 140°F. Cross-contamination can occur if raw meat or its juices comes in contact with cooked foods or foods that will be eaten fresh, such as salad. Freezing does not kill bacteria. Only cooking fish to 145°F, game meat to 160°F and game birds to 165°F will kill bacteria.

How game meat is handled in the field is very important. The animal should be eviscerated within an hour of harvest and the meat refrigerated within a few hours. Meat is damaged and can be ruined if not dressed, transported and chilled properly.

At home, refrigerate game immediately at 40°F or lower. Cook or freeze (0°F) game birds and ground game within 1 or 2 days; game animals within 3 to 5 days.

Scale, gut and clean fish as soon as they're caught. Live fish can be kept on stringers or in live wells as long as they have enough water and mobility to breathe. Wrap both whole and cleaned fish in water-tight plastic and store on ice.

Keep 3 to 4 inches of ice on the bottom of the cooler. Alternate layers of fish and ice to ensure the fish stays cold. Store the cooler out of the sun and cover it with a blanket.

Cook freshly caught fish in 1 to 2 days or freeze. For top quality, use frozen fish in 3 to 6 months.

Enhancing Flavor and Tenderness

Because their diet and activity levels are different than that of domestic animals and poultry, the meat of game animals has a different, stronger flavor. The animal's age, diet and the time of harvesting determine the meat's quality. Younger animals are more tender, and the best time to hunt is in the fall, after a plentiful spring and during summer feeding.

In general, wild game is less tender than meat from domestic animals because the wild animals get more exercise and have less fat. Any fat from game generally has a bad taste and should be removed. For maximum tenderness, most game meat should be cooked slowly and not overdone.

Game birds are poultry and considered white meat. Because they are birds of flight, how-

> **The animal's age, diet and the time of harvesting determine the meat's quality.**

ever, the breast meat is darker than domestic chickens and turkeys, which generally do very little, if any, flying.

To reduce gamey flavor in either game birds or mammals, soak the meat overnight in the refrigerator in a solution of either 1 tablespoon of salt per quart of cold water or 1 cup of white vinegar per quart of cold water. Be sure to use enough solution to cover the meat completely.

You can also marinate the game to give it good flavor or to tenderize it. Always marinate it in the refrigerator (1 to 2 days for birds; 3 to 4 days for game animals). Discard used marinade and use a fresh batch of marinade to baste meat while it cooks.

Safe Defrosting

There are three ways to defrost frozen game: in the refrigerator, in cold water and in the microwave. Never defrost on the countertop.

Whole birds or ground meat may take 1 to 2 days or longer to defrost in the refrigerator; roasts may take several days. Once raw poultry defrosts, it will be safe in the refrigerator an additional day or two before cooking. Meat and poultry thawed in the refrigerator may be safely refrozen without cooking it first.

To defrost game in cold water, be sure the meat is in a leakproof plastic bag or airtight packaging. Submerge the product in cold water, changing the water every 30 minutes. A whole game bird (3 or 4 pounds) or package of parts should defrost in 2 to 3 hours; larger amounts of game may take 4 to 6 hours.

When defrosting game in the microwave, plan to cook it immediately after thawing because some areas of the meat may become warm and begin to cook during microwaving. Holding partially cooked food is not recommended because any bacteria present would not have been destroyed.

For the best quality, foods that are defrosted should be cooked before refreezing or, ideally, not refrozen at all.

Doneness Tests

Cooked muscle meats can be pink even when the meat has reached a safe internal temperature. If fresh game has reached 160°F throughout, even though it may still be pink in the center, it should be safe to consume. The pink color can be due to the cooking method, smoking or added ingredients, such as marinades. Cook ground meats and other cuts of game meat, such as chops, steaks and roasts, to 160°F to ensure destruction of foodborne bacteria and parasites.

Whole game birds are safe to eat when cooked to a minimum internal temperature of 165°F. Use a food thermometer to check the internal temperature in the innermost part of the thigh and wing and the thickest part of the breast meat.

HUNTING & FISHING COOKBOOK

alphabetical recipe index

HUNTING & FISHING COOKBOOK

HUNTING & FISHING COOKBOOK

HUNTING & FISHING COOKBOOK

HUNTING & FISHING COOKBOOK

HUNTING & FISHING COOKBOOK

HUNTING & FISHING COOKBOOK